SACRED REALM

Plate i. Aerial view of the synagogue at Kefar Baram in Northern Israel.

SACRED REALM

The Emergence of the Synagogue
in the Ancient World

Edited by
STEVEN FINE

Organized by
Yeshiva University Museum

New York   Oxford
OXFORD UNIVERSITY PRESS
YESHIVA UNIVERSITY MUSEUM
1996

Oxford University Press

Oxford   New York
Athens   Auckland   Bangkok   Bombay
Calcutta   Cape Town   Dar es Salaam   Delhi
Florence   Hong Kong   Istanbul   Karachi
Kuala Lumpur   Madras   Madrid   Melbourne
Mexico City   Nairobi   Paris   Singapore
Taipei   Tokyo   Toronto

and associated companies in
Berlin   Ibadan

Published by Oxford University Press, Inc.
198 Madison Avenue, New York, New York 10016

Oxford is a registered trademark of Oxford University Press

Library of Congress Cataloging–in–Publication Data
Sacred realm : the emergence of the synagogue in the ancient world
edited by Steven Fine : organized by Yeshiva University Museum
p.   cm.
Catalog of an exhibition held at the Yeshiva University Museum.
Includes bibliographical references and index.
ISBN 0–19–510224–X (cloth). —ISBN 0–19–510225–8 (pbk.)
1. Synagogues—Palestine—Exhibitions.
2. Synagogue architecture—Palestine—Exhibitions.
3. Palestine—Antiquities—Exhibitions.
I. Fine, Steven.   II. Yeshiva University. Museum.
DS111.7.S27   1996
296.6'5'09010747471—dc20   95–45029

Photographic credits are on page 193.

1 3 5 7 9 8 6 4 2

Printed in the Hong Kong
on acid-free paper

Contents

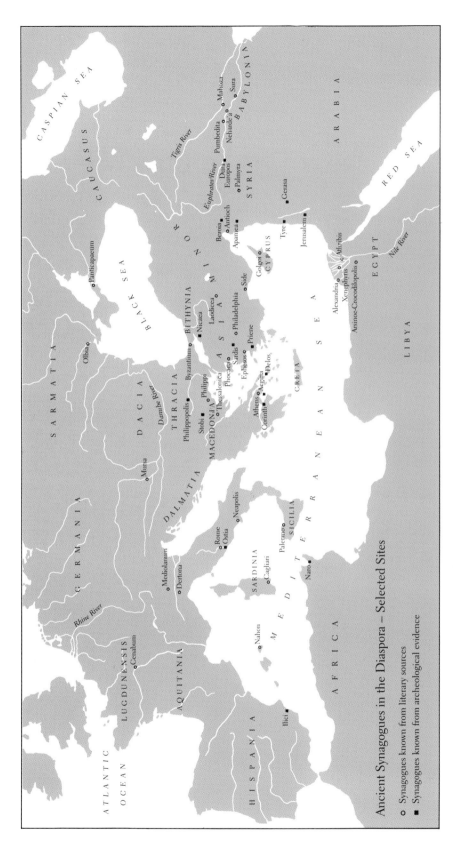

Ancient Synagogues in the Diaspora – Selected Sites

○ Synagogues known from literary sources
■ Synagogues known from archeological evidence

Map 1. Ancient synagogues in the Diaspora, selected sites.

Director's Preface

Twenty-three years ago when Yeshiva University Museum first opened, its inaugural exhibition consisted of ten superbly crafted architectural models of historic synagogues. Among these are Dura Europos (244–45 C.E.), Beth Alpha (c. sixth century C.E.), Touro in Newport, Rhode Island (1763), and the Altneuschul in Prague (c. 1280). The models were accompanied by three audiovisual pieces illustrating the development of the synagogue following the destruction of the Jerusalem Temple in 70 C.E. The concept, research, and construction of the exhibition were overseen by a committee headed by Professor Rachel Wischnitzer, the eminent art historian and expert on synagogue architecture, who was then professor of art history at Yeshiva University's Stern College for Women.

Since then, many diverse exhibitions have occupied our halls and galleries that reflect the sweep of Jewish artistic and cultural expression. Most notable are "Ashkenaz: The German Jewish Heritage" (1986–88), "The Sephardic Journey: 1492–1992" (1990–92), and "Beta Israel: The Jews of Ethiopia" (1993–94). We are delighted that "Sacred Realm" offers us the opportunity to return to our roots, as it were, to revisit the origins of the synagogue and explore its development, this time with the full force of a seasoned professional staff of our own, led by Guest Curator Steven Fine, with whom we have enjoyed a long and happy association.

Under Dr. Fine's expert guidance, the story of the synagogue has taken shape in a way that is especially reflective of the mission of this museum: to preserve, exhibit, and interpret artifacts that represent the cultural, intellectual, and artistic achievements of three thousand years of Jewish experience.

The time period of the exhibition (c. 300 B.C.E. to c. 700 C.E.), a millennium overflowing with great Jewish intellectual and spiritual productivity, is a second highly compelling reason why we were so eager to present "Sacred Realm." For a museum of an academic institution distinguished for its ongoing studies of ancient texts—a place where the Rabbinic literature is of paramount intellectual and spiritual importance—this opportunity was not to be missed. Presenting documentary and visual evidence for the history of Jewish religious life is exactly what this museum is all about.

Dr. Fine's exhaustive study of Rabbinic literature and his synthesis of archaeological and textual material have made possible the interdisciplinary linking of text with artifact, which is the defining feature of this groundbreaking installation. Scholars from throughout the world have joined Dr. Fine in making "Sacred Realm" a project of international scope.

Among the many visitors who tour the museum annually are thousands of elementary, high school, and college students, as well as members of Yeshiva University's academic community who study Talmud and Jewish thought daily. For them the juxtaposition of ancient Jewish literature with contemporaneous archaeological discoveries is acutely relevant.

"Sacred Realm" is a cause for celebration in the scholarly community as well, bringing together artifacts and manuscripts from museums throughout the world for the first time. Whether discovered in the last century or just last year, in Israel or in the lands of the Mediterranean, it is our hope that "Sacred Realm" will provoke new thinking about the history of the synagogue and of religion in general in the ancient world.

As a museum committed to serving New York's culturally and religiously diverse audiences, we have learned to seek out and highlight the universal message within the Jewish matrix. "Sacred Realm" presents many of the architectural and artistic forms that were common to Jewish, Christian, and Muslim houses of worship in antiquity and that have persisted in modern synagogues, churches, and mosques to this day. We hope that the exhibition will heighten awareness of these relationships within the general culture and lead to increased mutual respect.

Finally, this entire project would not have been possible without the support of two public agencies—the National Endowment for the Humanities and the New York State Council on the Arts. The Council's confidence in the museum's capabilities resulted in a planning grant that enabled us to realize fully the proposal for "Sacred Realm." Further redevelopment and refinement of the proposal was aided by the encouragement and counsel of Fred Miller, Program Officer at NEH. The award from NEH, Yeshiva University Museum's largest to date from any federal agency, validated our six years of effort and is an enormous source of pride for me, our board members, and staff. Our board chairperson, Erica Jesselson, led the successful campaign to obtain matching funds, and we thank her and all those individuals, corporations, and foundations that helped us meet the match. On behalf of the museum community, I thank NEH and its chairman, Sheldon Hackney, for giving us this opportunity.

Sylvia Axelrod Herskowitz
Director

Fig. i. Synagogue at Kefar Baram, fourth to fifth century C.E., taken by Kohl and Watzinger, 1905–1907.

Fig. ii. Nineteenth-century engraving of the synagogue at Kefar Baram from *Picturesque Palestine* published in 1889.

Editor's Preface

> . . . There within the village [of Kefar Baram] is the synagogue of
> Rabbi Simeon son of Yohai. It is a most magnificent structure [built
> of] large and well carved stones and large, long columns. I have
> never before seen a more magnificent building!
>
> Anonymous Jewish pilgrim, early fourteenth century C.E.

The ancient synagogue of Kefar Baram in the Upper Galilee was visited and chronicled
repeatedly by medieval Jewish pilgrims to the Land of Israel. Modern interest in ancient
synagogues dates to the nineteenth century when European explorers combed the hills
and valleys of the Holy Land in search of biblical treasures. Since that time the remains of
synagogue life have been discovered in over one hundred sites in the Land of Israel and
numerous others throughout the Greco-Roman world. "Sacred Realm: The Emergence of
the Synagogue in the Ancient World" tells the story of those synagogues and their place in
the history of Judaism and of Western civilization.

"Sacred Realm" is the first comprehensive exhibition ever on the history of the ancient
synagogue. The fact that it has been organized by the Yeshiva University Museum is most
significant. It reflects the commitment of both Yeshiva University and its museum to cre-
atively embrace both modernity and traditional Jewish culture *(Torah im Derekh Eretz)*. It
is through the wisdom of Sylvia Herskowitz, Director of the Yeshiva University Museum,
and the unflinching support of Erica Jesselson, Chair of the Board of Trustees, that this
exhibition has come to fruition. It has been an honor for me to work with both of them,
with the staffs of the museum and of the exhibition, and with the numerous individuals
and institutions that came together to make "Sacred Realm" a success.

This catalogue both documents the exhibition and serves as an introduction to the
state of synagogue studies today. The contributors to this catalogue, scholars from diverse
disciplines who reside in the United States, the Netherlands, and Israel, have each presented his or her distinctive visions of the ancient synagogue.

"Sacred Realm" opens with contributions by two of the leading U.S. scholars of
Judaism during the Greco-Roman period, Professor Lawrence H. Schiffman of New York

University and Professor Eric M. Meyers of Duke University. Schiffman briefly surveys the importance of the synagogue within the broader history of ancient Judaism. Meyers summarizes important discoveries of synagogues in the ancient world and their importance for the history of Judaism.

Schiffman's Foreword and Meyers' Introduction are followed by my own contribution. In my chapter I bring together the various types of evidence for the history of the synagogue in antiquity. Both literary and archaeological, these are derived from the Greco-Roman and Babylonian diasporas and from the Land of Israel. I trace how the synagogue became the most important institution in Jewish life. I demonstrate through these varied sources how the synagogue was transformed from a house of meeting into a Sacred Realm.

The next two chapters explore epigraphic and archaeological sources for the history of Diaspora synagogues. We begin with Professor Louis H. Feldman of Yeshiva University, who surveys inscriptions and papyri from antiquity that shed light upon the history of this institution. In fact, epigraphic sources provide the earliest evidence for the history of the synagogue. They also provide important evidence for the place of women in Diaspora synagogues. Dr. Leonard Victor Rutgers of the University of Utrecht then turns to artistic, architectural, and patristic evidence for synagogues in the Diaspora. He presents the diversity of synagogue discoveries in the Diaspora while stressing that which is common to all the extant buildings.

The final two chapters survey archaeological and literary evidence for the history of synagogues in the Land of Israel. Professor Rachel Hachlili of Haifa University discusses synagogue archaeology and art in the Land of Israel from the first to the eighth century C.E. Hachlili stresses the artistic side of synagogues in the Land of Israel, comparing this evidence with non-Jewish archaeological sources. Professor Avigdor Shinan of the Hebrew University of Jerusalem places literary and archaeological evidence of the ancient synagogue within the context of the "Literature of the Ancient Synagogue" in the Land of Israel, the literary record of Jewish religious life in late antique Palestinian synagogues. Shinan also compares the literature of the Palestinian synagogue with the literary sources for the Babylonian synagogue. This literature is our only evidence for the synagogue of ancient Babylonia (modern Iraq), since no archaeological materials are extant.

"Sacred Realm: The Emergence of the Synagogue in the Ancient World," then, provides a window into modern scholarship about the ancient synagogue just as it presents the state of our knowledge of this age-old institution. The voices of the ancient synagogues on view in "Sacred Realm" have long been silent. The legacy of the ancient synagogue to our own time, however, will be apparent to all who enter into this Sacred Realm.

Steven Fine
Curator of "Sacred Realm"
Assistant Professor of
Rabbinic Literature and History
Baltimore Hebrew University

Acknowledgments

Many individuals helped make this exhibition and catalogue possible. Above all, we acknowledge the leadership and scholarship of our Guest Curator, Steven Fine, and his Adjunct Assistant Curator, Rhoda Terry.

We are grateful to the following advisers who, from the beginning, provided encouragement and generously shared their expertise with us: James Charlesworth, George L. Collord Professor of New Testament and Literature, Princeton Theological Seminary; Louis H. Feldman, Abraham Wouk Family Chair in Classics and Literature, Yeshiva University; Joseph Gutmann, Professor Emeritus of Art History, Wayne State University; Rachel Hachlili, Professor of Archaeology, Haifa University; Selma Holo, Adjunct Associate Professor and Director of Museum Studies, University of Southern California; A. Thomas Kraabel, Qualley Professor of Classics, Dean of Luther College; Lee I. Levine, Professor of Jewish History and Archaeology, Hebrew University; Eric M. Meyers, Professor of Religion, Duke University; Leonard Victor Rutgers, Fellow of the Royal Dutch Academy, University of Utrecht; Andrew Seager, Professor of Architecture, Ball State University; and Avigdor Shinan, Professor of Hebrew Literature, Hebrew University. A special note of gratitude must go to Lawrence Schiffman, Professor of Hebrew and Judaic Studies, New York University, for his enthusiastic and unqualified assistance at all times.

A host of curators, archivists, and researchers were exceedingly helpful in bringing this project to fruition. We would like to thank the following: the Israel Antiquities Authority: Ruth Peled, Curator, Chava Katz, Acting Chief Curator, and Rivka Berger, Research Associate; Gila Hurwitz, Curator, Institute of Archaeology of the Hebrew University; Avigail Sheffer, formerly of the Institute of Archaeology of the Hebrew University; Joachim Marzahn, Curator, Deutsches Orient-Gesellschaft; Father Leonard Boyle, Director of the Biblioteca Apostolica Vaticana; Anna Gallina Zevi, Director of the Soprintendenza Archeologica di Ostia; Archaeological Exploration of Sardis, Harvard University: Crawford Greenewalt, Director, Laura Gadbery,

Associate Director, Jane Scott, Research Curator, and Michael O'Grady, Editorial Assistant; John H. Kroll, Professor of Classics, University of Texas, Austin; Metropolitan Museum of Art: Timothy Husband, Curator of Medieval Art, Constance Harper, Editorial Budget Advisor, Sian Wetherill, Assistant to the Curator of Exhibitions, Lisa Pilosi, Conservator, Stefano Carboni, Curator of Islamic Art, Doralynn Pines, Chief Librarian, and Robert Kaufmann, Assistant Librarian of the Watson Library; Jewish Theological Seminary: Mayer Rabinowitz, Chief Librarian, Rabbi Jerry Schwarzbard, Librarian for Special Collections, and Seth Jerchower, Assistant Librarian for Special Collections; Susan Matheson, Curator of Ancient Art, Yale University Art Gallery; Robert Babcock, Rare Book and Manuscript Librarian, Beinecke Library; Gerdy Trachtman and Glenda Friend, Research Associates, Baltimore Hebrew University; Sidney Babcock, Curator, Jonathan P. Rosen Collection.

Special appreciation is extended to Robert O. Freedman, Acting President, and Barry M. Gittlen, Acting Dean, Peggy Meyerhoff Pearlstone School of Graduate Studies, Baltimore Hebrew University.

As always, we were fortunate in being able to draw on the talents and resources of our colleagues at Yeshiva University. We are indebted to Dean Pearl Berger and the staff of the Pollack and Gottesman libraries, especially, Leah Adler, Chief Librarian of the Gottesman Library; John Moryl, Chief Librarian of the Pollack Library; Tzvi Erenyi, Zalman Alpert, Rabbi Berish Mandelbaum, Marie Center, Haya Gordin, Rabbi Theodor Lasdun, Rebecca Malamud, and Marlene Schiffman.

Other University departments that were helpful include Photographic Services: Norman Goldberg, Gary Mann, and Roman Royzengurt; Risk Management: Paul Goldschmidt; Graphic Arts: Judy Tucker; Public Relations: Barbara Goldner; Facilities Management: Jeffrey Rosengarten.

For the inspired design of the exhibition we are indebted to the superb talent of Ted Cohen, our exhibition designer, for creating an environment whose ambience reflects the themes of *Sacred Realm*. We also acknowledge the heroic efforts of exhibit installers Jeff Serwatien and Don Groscost. We thank Albina De Meio for her distinguished efforts as exhibition coordinator, and mount-makers Barbara Suhr and Elizabeth McKean for their beautiful work. The importation and handling of the international loans was masterfully coordinated by Racine Berkow and her associates. Ariel Braun coordinated the loans in Israel.

The following individuals helped us locate and obtain photographs: Steven Fine, Andrew Seager, Leonard V. Rutgers, Eric M. Meyers, Vivian Mann, Barbara Treitel, and Hershel Shanks. The maps of Israel and the Diaspora were created especially for us by Wilhelmina Reyinga-Amrhein.

From the earliest planning of the exhibition through its entire run, the work of the Museum staff was indispensable. We acknowledge their efforts and extend our profound thanks to: Randi Glickberg, Deputy Director; Gabriel M. Goldstein, Curator; Bonni-Dara Michaels, Curator/Registrar; Rachelle Bradt, Curator of Education; Elizabeth Diament, Associate Curator of Education; Eleanor Chiger, Office Manager; Yitzhak Zahavy, Curatorial Intern, and Brenda DeJesus and Andy Peña, Museum Aides.

And, of course, we express our great appreciation to Oxford University Press, publishers of this catalogue. In particular we acknowledge the expertise of Joyce Berry, editor, and Scott Epstein, editorial assistant. At G&H SOHO we thank Jim Harris, president, Françoise Bartlett, managing editor, and Jeanne Borczuk, layout designer.

Sylvia Axelrod Herskowitz
Director of the Exhibition

Donors

Sacred Realm received major funding from the National Endowment for the Humanities with additional support from the Institute of Museum Services, the New York State Council for the Humanities, the New York State Council on the Arts, the New York City Department of Cultural Affairs, the Lucius N. Littauer Foundation, the Forchheimer Foundation, and private donors.

Numerous individuals and foundations provided the funds to match the National Endowment for the Humanities grant. We are pleased to acknowledge them.

Mr. and Mrs. Robert Arnow
Mr. and Mrs. Louis Barnett
Mr. and Mrs. Sanford Batkin
Mr. and Mrs. Stanley Batkin
Mr. and Mrs. Harry Bauer
Mr. and Mrs. Bob Becker
Mr. and Mrs. Paul Becker
Mr. Peter Becker
Mr. and Mrs. Harvey Beker
Mrs. Diane Belfer
Mrs. Abby Belkin
Mr. Philip Belz
Mr. and Mrs. Charles Bendheim
Mr. and Mrs. Jack C. Bendheim

Mr. Henri Bengualid
Mr. Robert Beren
Mr. and Mrs. Hal Beretz
Mr. Meyer Berman
Berman Associates
Mr. and Mrs. Norbert Blechner
Botwinick-Wolfenson
Mr. and Mrs. Ludwig Bravmann
Dr. and Mrs. Egon Brenner
Mr. and Mrs. Joseph Ciechanover
Mr. and Mrs. Marshall Cogan
Mr. Peter Cohen
Mr. and Mrs. Milton Cooper
Rabbi and Mrs. Maurice Corson

Mr. and Mrs. Haron Dahan
Mr. and Mrs. Morton Davis
Mrs. Beatrice Diener
Mr. and Mrs. Charles Diker
Mr. and Mrs. Charles Dimston
Mr. Elliot Eisenberg
Mrs. Helen Elbaum
Mr. Harold Feld
Mr. and Mrs. Joel Finkle
Mr. and Mrs. David Fishman
Forchheimer Foundation
Harry Freund and Jay Goldsmith
Dr. Beatrice Friedland
Mr. and Mrs. Felix Glaubach
Mr. and Mrs. Eugen Gluck
Mr. and Mrs. Moritz Goldfier
Mr. David S. Gottesman
Mr. and Mrs. Milton Gralla
Mr. and Mrs. Morris L. Green
Mr. Alan C. Greenberg
Mr. and Mrs. Claude Gros
Mr. Peter Gruenberger
Mr. and Mrs. Donald Hamburg
The Hebrew Home for the Aged at
    Riverdale
Mr. Benjamin Gottesfeld Heller
Mrs. Fanya Gottesfeld Heller
Dr. and Mrs. Philip Herschenfeld
Mr. and Mrs. Elliot Hershberg
Rabbi and Mrs. William Herskowitz
Mr. and Mrs. Eugene Isenberg
Mrs. Bradley Jacobs
Mr. George Jaffin
Mr. Jerome R. Jakubovitz
Mr. and Mrs. Danny Jesselson
Mrs. Erica Jesselson
Mr. and Mrs. Michael Jesselson
Mr. and Mrs. Gary Joseph
Mrs. Rita Kaufman
Mr. and Mrs. Ilan Kauftal
Mr. Charles Kibel
Mr. and Mrs. Alex Klein
Mr. George Klein
Mr. Harvey Krueger
Dr. and Mrs. Ira Kukin
Mr. and Mrs. David Kupperman
Mrs. Lucy Lang

Dr. and Mrs. Martin Lieb
Dr. and Mrs. Joseph Lieberman
Mr. and Mrs. Marcel Lindenbaum
Ms. Barbara Livenstein
Mr. and Mrs. P. Machnikoff
Mrs. Ruth Mack
Mr. and Mrs. Morton Mandel
Mr. and Mrs. Michael Marton
Mr. and Mrs. Robert Meister
Mr. and Mrs. Hermann Merkin
Mr. and Mrs. Ted Mirvis
Dr. and Mrs. Alfred Moldovan
Mr. David Morewitz
Mr. and Mrs. Simon Naparstek
Mr. Jack Nash
Mr. and Mrs. Melvin Neumark
Mr. and Mrs. Abe Oster
Dr. and Mrs. Michael Papo
Mr. and Mrs. Robert Payne
Mrs. Cecille Platovsky
Mrs. Zita Plaut
Mr. and Mrs. Isaac Pollak
Mr. and Mrs. Otto Pretsfelder
Ms. Gabriella Propp
Mr. and Mrs. Egon Rausnitz
Mr. Raphael Recanati
Mr. and Mrs. Ira Rennert
Mr. and Mrs. Burton Resnick
Mrs. Pearl Resnick
Mr. and Mrs. Ira Riklis
Mr. Yale Roe
Mr. and Mrs. Martin Romerovski
Mr. and Mrs. Howard Rosen
Mr. and Mrs. Philip Rosen
Mr. and Mrs. Aryeh Rosenbaum
Cantor and Mrs. Jacob Rosenbaum
Mr. Irving Rosenbaum
Mr. and Mrs. Marcus Rosenberg
Mr. and Mrs. Ernesto Rosenfeld
Mr. and Mrs. Milton Rosenthal
Mr. and Mrs. Henry Rothschild
Mr. and Mrs. Irving Rubinstein
Mr. and Mrs. Laurence Rubinstein
Mr. Sheldon Rudoff
Mrs. Miriam Saks
Mr. and Mrs. Herman Sandler
Sapirstein-Stone-Weiss Foundation

Mr. and Mrs. Herbert H. Schiff
Mr. Jay Schottenstein
Mr. and Mrs. Robert Schwalbe
Mr. and Mrs. Romie Shapiro
Mr. Marty Silverman
Dr. Ruth Skydell
Mr. and Mrs. John Slade
Mr. Bruce Slovin
Ms. Miri Small
Mr. Sheldon H. Solow
Mr. Ronald Stanton
Mr. and Mrs. Edward Steinberg
Mr. and Mrs. Meyer Steinberg
Ms. Jane Stern Lebell
Erna Stiebel Fund
Mr. and Mrs. Walter Strauss
Mrs. Rosa Strygler

Commissioner Livia Sylva
Mr. and Mrs. Sy Syms
Mr. and Mrs. Morris Talansky
Mr. and Mrs. Ronald Tauber
Mr. and Mrs. David Tropper
Ms. Lucy Ullman
Mr. and Mrs. Martin Vegh
Ms. Lillian Vernon
Mr. and Mrs. Henry Verstandig
Ms. Lisa Walborsky
Ms. Lee Weinbach
Mr. and Mrs. David Weisz
Mr. and Mrs. Joseph Wilf
Wilf Family Foundation
Mr. and Mrs. Ernst Wimpfheimer
Mr. Motl Zelmanowicz
Mr. and Mrs. Benjamin Zucker

Lenders to the Exhibition

American Numismatic Society, New York

Andover Newton Theological School, Newton Center, Massachusetts

Archaeological Exploration of Sardis, Harvard University, Cambridge, Massachusetts

Bible Lands Museum, Jerusalem, Israel

Bibliotheca Apostolica, Vatican City, Italy

The Brooklyn Museum, Brooklyn, New York

Burke Library, Union Theological Seminary, New York

Columbia University Rare Book and Manuscript Library, New York

Hebrew University Institute of Archaeology, Jerusalem, Israel

Israel Antiquities Authority, Jerusalem, Israel

David Jeselsohn Collection, Zurich, Switzerland

The Library of The Jewish Theological Seminary of America, New York

Mendel Gottesman Library, Yeshiva University, New York

The Metropolitan Museum of Art, New York

Musée du Louvre, Paris, France

Musée Royal de Mariemont, Belgium

Museo Archeologico Nazionale, Naples, Italy

Museo Nazionale delle Terme, Rome, Italy

Museum für Spätantike und Byzantinische Kunst, Berlin, Germany
Collection of Mr. and Mrs. Jonathan P. Rosen, New York
Royal Ontario Museum, Toronto, Canada
Simon Wiesenthal Center, Los Angeles, California
Soprintendenza Archaeologica di Ostia, Italy
Yale University Art Gallery, New Haven, Connecticut

Historical Chronology

586 B.C.E.	Destruction of Jerusalem and the First Temple; mass deportation to Babylonia
520–15	Jerusalem Temple rebuilt
332	Alexander the Great conquers the Land of Israel
301	Ptolemy I captures the Land of Israel
219–17	Antiochus III conquers most of the Land of Israel
168–64	Maccabean Revolt
63	Roman conquest of Palestine by Pompeii
37	Herod captures Jerusalem
20–19	Rebuilding of the Jerusalem Temple by Herod begins
c. 30 C.E.	Jesus of Nazareth crucified
c. 40	Philo writes in Alexandria
66–74	First Jewish Revolt against Rome
70	Destruction of the Jerusalem Temple
74	Fall of Masada
c. 75–79	Josephus completes *The Jewish War*
c. 80	Rabbinic Sages assemble at Yavneh
132–35	Bar Kokhba Revolt
c. 200	Redaction of the Mishnah
c. 235	"Sanhedrin" in Tiberias
244–45	Dura Europos synagogue refurbished

259	Babylonian Rabbinic Academy of Nehardea moves to Pumbedita
324	Christianity becomes official religion of the Roman Empire
362	Julian the Apostate attempts to rebuild the Jerusalem Temple
c. 400	Jerusalem Talmud completed
425	Abolition of the Patriarchate
c. 500	Babylonian Talmud completed
c. 600	Qallir writes *piyyutim* (liturgical poetry)
616	Sardis synagogue destroyed
632	Death of Muhammed
638	Arab conquest of Palestine

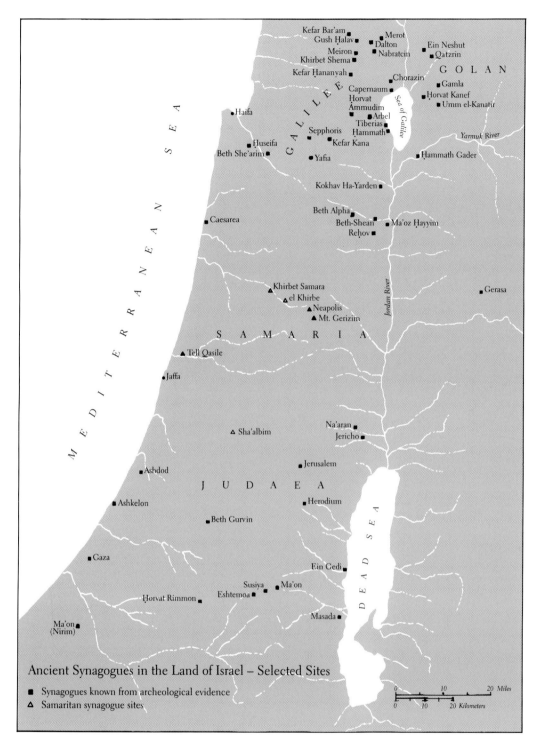

Map 2. Ancient synagogues of the Land of Israel, selected sites.

Ancient Synagogues in the Land of Israel – Selected Sites

- ■ Synagogues known from archeological evidence
- △ Samaritan synagogue sites

Kefar Bar'am
Gush Ḥalav
Merot
Dalton
Meiron
Nabratein
Khirbet Shema
Ein Neshut
Qatzrin
GOLAN
Kefar Ḥananyah
Chorazin
Gamla
Capernaum
Horvat Kanef
Horvat
Ammudim
Umm el-Kanatir
GALILEE
Sea of Galilee
Haifa
Arbel
Tiberias
Sepphoris
Hammath
Huseifa
Kefar Kana
Yarmuk River
Beth She'arim
Yafia
Hammath Gader
Kokhav Ha-Yarden
MEDITERRANEAN SEA
Caesarea
Beth Alpha
Beth-Shean
Ma'oz Ḥayyim
Reḥov
Khirbet Samara
Gerasa
el Khirbe
Neapolis
Mt. Gerizim
SAMARIA
Jordan River
Tell Qasile
Jaffa
Na'aran
Sha'albim
Jericho
Ashdod
Jerusalem
JUDAEA
Ashkelon
Herodium
Beth Gurvin
DEAD SEA
Gaza
Ein Gedi
Susiya
Ma'on
Eshtemoa
Horvat Rimmon
Masada
Ma'on
(Nirim)

0   10   20 Miles
0   10   20 Kilometers

Foreword

The Ancient Synagogue
and the History of Judaism

LAWRENCE H. SCHIFFMAN
New York University

If there is any institution that is closely associated with the development of postbiblical Judaism throughout the ages it is the synagogue. The term "synagogue," derived from the Greek, meaning an "assembly," has come to designate the Jewish house of worship, the "temple in miniature," as the Talmudic Sages called it. The Hebrew term *beit ha-knesset* designates a "building for assembly."

Indeed, the synagogue has been much more than a house of worship. It served the Jewish people as a place of learning, a community center, and often as the seat of the organs of Jewish self-government. This institution came into being in late antiquity—in the age between the arrival in the Near East of Alexander the Great and the destruction of the Temple (Plate ii) in 70 C.E. Many scholars theorize that the synagogue had its origins in the Babylonian Exile when the Jews first had to adapt to the lack of a Temple and to animal sacrifice. Yet there is no evidence, literary or archaeological, for this theory. On the other hand, the history of postbiblical prayer shows that the "service of the heart" was always part of Jewish practice.

It was the synagogue that made possible the adaptation of Judaism to the new reality created by the destruction of the Second Temple in the unsuccessful Great Revolt against Rome in 66 to 73 C.E. The revolt created for the Jewish people a new religious world—one in which the Temple no longer stood, the priests no longer offered the sacrifices, and the Levites had ceased to chant the Psalms. In Temple times, the Jerusalem Temple was understood to be a place in which the Divine Presence could always be approached. In other words, it was the locus of God's abiding in Israel, in fulfillment of the biblical statement "I will dwell among them" (Exod. 25:8). The sudden disappearance of this avenue of com-

Plate ii. Model of the
Second Temple, Holyland
Hotel, Jerusalem, Israel.

muning with God was a tragedy of awesome dimensions. Yet even before the destruction of
the Temple the synagogue served as the environment for the daily prayers, which after the
destruction came to replace the sacrificial ritual. Perhaps as important, the synagogue was
the dominant institution for Jewish life in the Diaspora as early as in Hellenistic times.

That prayer had become increasingly important before the turn of the era is clear from
manifold sources. The growing role of prayer in Jewish life was part of a trend fostered by
the Pharisees, the forerunners of the Mishnaic Rabbis, as well as by diverse groups, such as
the Dead Sea sect. Throughout the Second Temple period, increasing emphasis was
placed on the requirement of daily prayer for all Jews. For many Jews it was the emerging
synagogue that served as the locus of their prayers. Dramatic evidence of the role of prayer
in Jewish life comes from the very fortresses of the rebels against Rome—from Masada,
Gamla, and probably Herodion—where buildings that were used as first-century–C.E. synagogues have been excavated.

The synagogue, then, did not come into being as a reaction to the destruction. Yet in
many ways its development was part of a process whereby Judaism had already created the
mechanisms for the continuation of the synagogue in the era of destruction and exile—
even before the Roman legions had set foot in the Land of Israel. As the Jewish population
moved north to the Galilee and the Golan in the years following the fall of Masada in 73
C.E., it established a large number of synagogues and houses of study. On these same sites
later generations built the Late Roman and Byzantine period synagogues, the remains of
which literally dot the archaeological landscape.

But the synagogue was much more than just a house of worship. Its architecture, furnishings, and decoration were a sign of how Jews in late antiquity perceived their role in God's
world and sought to establish a sanctified place to serve as a center for their religious and spiritual quest. It was there that the Jews sought to approximate the sanctity of the Temple and to
ensure the continuation of Jewish practice in a new and increasingly hostile environment.

The study of the ancient synagogue began in some senses with the rise of the modern
historical study of Judaism in the nineteenth century, but it has been spurred on by the
development of Jewish archaeology, which began as the Land of Israel started to be colo-

nized anew by Jews in modern times. Further, the discovery of the Cairo Genizah (Fig. iii), the great treasure trove of medieval manuscripts from the storehouse of the synagogue of Fostat in Old Cairo, made available important literary sources for the history of the synagogue in late antiquity and the early Middle Ages. With the establishment of the State of Israel and its academic institutions, and with the rise of academic Judaic studies in North America, this process has made great progress. Today, scholars are recovering and re-creating the world of the Judaism of the Second Temple and Talmudic periods, and the central place of the synagogue in that world continues to be recognized.

Indeed, the "Sacred Realm" exhibit and the studies in this volume are a sign of the great accomplishments already achieved in this field of study. More than that, they are a testimony to the partnership of archaeology and text, which underlies historical research on the synagogue. Further, this exhibit highlights the close partnership of Israeli institutions and scholars with their American counterparts in excavation and textual research and in exhibiting the rich cultural treasures of the land, people, and State of Israel to the wider international public.

In the exhibit and in the catalogue that follows, we will enter the world of the Jews of late antiquity—those of the Land of Israel and the Diaspora—and share with them the joys and sorrows that were associated with the life of the synagogue. We will get a glimpse of the daily life of Talmudic period Jews and learn of their prayers and their hopes. By tracing the art and architecture of the synagogue, we learn about the cultural influences on these Jews, what they shared with their neighbors, and how they differed from them. Most of all, we will see how the synagogue then—as now—brought Jews together for the common goals of study and prayer, and how these activities transported them from the "real" world in which they lived and worked into the realms of sanctity and holiness.

Fig. iii. Solomon Schechter in the Cairo Genizah collection at Cambridge University shortly after its purchase in 1896.

SACRED REALM

Ancient Synagogues

An Archaeological Introduction

ERIC M. MEYERS
Duke University

An archaeological introduction to ancient synagogues could not begin without taking note of the unique contribution of a single individual to the subject, one whose work goes back more than seventy years. This figure is Eleazar Lipa Sukenik (Fig. 1.1), pioneer archaeologist who singlehandedly developed the field known as synagogue archaeology. Not surprisingly, Sukenik's inspiration for scientific fieldwork came from the American giant in biblical archaeology, William Foxwell Albright, director of the American School in Jerusalem in 1920–29 and 1933–36.[1] Albright's programmatic work at Tel Beit Mirsim in the northern Negev established the framework for stratigraphic excavation as well as laid out the fundamentals of ceramic typology, work soon to become the key to all dating in archaeology.[2] In fact, Sukenik spent the academic year 1923–24 studying with Albright in Jerusalem.[3] There he also worked with another of Albright's students, William Carroll of Yale University, at the archaeological site of Beitar, where the Jewish rebel and messianic pretender Bar Kokhba made his last stand in 135 C.E. Sukenik also explored the southern Ghor region in Transjordan with Albright and his team, which culminated in the discovery of Bab edh-Dhra, a site associated with the cities of the plain in Genesis 14.[4]

The year 1923–24 was critical in Sukenik's training as an archaeologist, but unlike his Protestant colleagues at the American School, who were preoccupied with the realia of the biblical world in hopes of authenticating the Bible, he envisioned archaeology as a mechanism for authenticating Jewish ties to the Land of Israel. In the archaeology of ancient Jewish synagogues, on which he first came to focus, he discovered a vehicle for facilitating the rebirth of the Zionist state, and in 1925–26 at Dropsie College, Philadelphia, Sukenik wrote his doctoral dissertation on the current state of knowledge of ancient synagogues.[5] On

Fig. 1.1. Eleazar L. Sukenik (center) and volunteer workers at the Beth Alpha synagogue excavation in 1929.

Fig. 1.2. Nahum Slouschz (center) and workers pose with the stone menorah discovered during the excavations at Hammath Tiberias in 1921.

returning to Palestine he was appointed archaeologist at Hebrew University, taking as his assistant the young Nachman Avigad. Avigad, who died only recently (1991),[6] is perhaps best known for his subsequent excavations of the Jewish Quarter in Jerusalem.[7] The first Jewish resident of Palestine to conduct an archaeological excavation, however, was Nahum Slouschz, who in 1921 had already uncovered one of the synagogues (Fig. 1.2) at Ḥammath Tiberias on the southwestern shore of the Sea of Galilee. Some 500 meters southeast of this site M. Dothan uncovered in 1961 another synagogue with a magnificent mosaic.[8]

It was the chance discovery of an ancient synagogue with a zodiac mosaic at Beth Alpha in 1928 and Sukenik's excavations there in 1929 that brought him into the limelight and so influenced his son Yigael, then ten years old. Located in the eastern Jezreel Valley, Beth Alpha was also a kibbutz. On December 30, 1928, a young member of the settlement reported to Sukenik, who was then in Jerusalem, that some settlers had come upon a colorful mosaic while preparing an irrigation ditch. Sukenik realized immediately that they had come upon the floor of an ancient synagogue, and within a week he left with Avigad to excavate the site of the discovery. To everyone's delight and surprise, the mosaic was complete, with a zodiac at its center, framed in the corners by representations of the four seasons.[9] On the southern, Jerusalem-oriented wall, in front of an apse, the mosaic featured a depiction of a Torah Shrine with a menorah on either side, together with other ritual objects. On the northern end of the mosaic carpet was a scene depicting the Binding of Isaac. Sukenik hurried back to Jerusalem for a photographer (Fig. 1.3) and returned bringing Yigael as well.

The impact of the discovery on the settlers was enormous. In the remains of the ancient synagogue they saw not only a mixing of a lively Jewish and pagan art but the remnants of Jewish settlement from a forgotten era, justification for their present settlement, and an expression of pride in Jewish tradition. Sukenik himself became an international celebrity overnight; even *The New York Times* (Fig. 1.4) ran a headline on April 29, 1929: "Old Mosaics Trace Origin of the Jews."[10] His hopes for establishing a discipline of Jewish archaeology had far exceeded his expectations. What perhaps only his son Yigael (who later took the surname Yadin) could best understand and implement one day, however, was the role such a discipline would have in the molding of a national Jewish state. Beth Alpha

OLD MOSAICS TRACE ORIGIN OF THE JEWS

Dr. Sukenik Excavates a Synagogue in Palestine Which Makes New History in Judaism.

DATES BACK TO JUSTINIAN

Discoverer Declares Find Is the Connecting Link of Road Between Jerusalem and Rome.

By WYTHE WILLIAMS.

Wireless to THE NEW YORK TIMES.

BERLIN, April 28.—Discoveries have recently been made in Palestine which may prove to be as important as the recent excavations in Egypt at King Tut-ankh-Amen's tomb. They were reported here during the present congress that commemorates the centennial of the Berlin Archaeological Institute.

Dr. Sukenik, Professor of Archaeology at the University of Jerusalem, who has been directing excavations at Beth Alpha, a small community in a glen in the Gilboa foothills, believes the origin of the Jewish race may eventually be traced as a result of epigraphs in mosaics taken from a synagogue which has just been uncovered and which dates from the reign of the Emperor Justinian.

Dr. Sukenik maintains that this mosaic is one of the most important archaeological discoveries in the study of Palestinian Judaism since the destruction of Jerusalem by Hadrian and that from now on it may, from a comparison at the Beth Alpha synagogue, be possible to state the age of all antiquities.

Accidental Discovery.

The professor believes that Beth Alpha may become the mark of distinction between the periods of Hadrian and Herakles.

Only a few weeks ago word was received at the University of Jerusalem that the inhabitants of Beth Alpha, while digging in a courtyard for water, found a mosaic pavement. Dr. Sukenik immediately had the pavement removed and found, in the middle of a place inhabited for years and visited by dozens of scientists annually, the walls of a synagogue that was scarcely a hand's-breadth under the surface of the earth.

The area now excavated measures 28x14 meters and the building faces Jerusalem. The walls are of rough limestone, from the Gilboa hills, and they show traces of plaster and paint. The forecourt and courtyard were paved with white and black limestone mosaic formed of large stone squares placed in simple lineal ornamentation. But in the prayer hall, which was divided into three naves by pillars of black basalt, rises a mosaic of bright and beautiful colors. The stones measure only half a centimeter and they are of natural colors set in twenty-two different shades. The colors of the jewelry worn by the angels and by Virgo of the zodiac—emeralds, topaz and amethysts—are shown by crystal squares. The inscription is in both Hebrew and Greek, and all is in a remarkable state of preservation.

Concerning the pictures portrayed in the mosaic, Professor Sukenik says:

"In the history of art we have found at Beth Alpha the connecting link of the road from Jerusalem to Rome."

Drawings Are Primitive.

The drawings in the Beth Alpha mosaics are of such a primitive and obviously original style that, according to their discovery, it is out of the question to believe that they have any connection with the higher and late-Greek art.

One portion shows a sun chariot drawn by four horses, distinctly pictured as living animals. The feet have no proportion to the heads. This, says Dr. Sukenik, is an expression of symbolization.

Such symbolization is shown in other pictures. The twelve figures of the zodiac are portrayed and among them Virgo is shown sitting on a throne, which is distinctly a forerunner of the Holy Virgin in the early Byzantine mosaics.

Also in the portrayal of Abraham sacrificing Isaac, with an altar and a tree to which a ram is tied, all is as primitive in style as is the art of Abyssinia.

In a perfectly naturalistic drawing of the scorpion, God's hand replaces God's voice while Isaac is being sacrificed. It is the same spirit of symbolism that created from Ixthus (the Greek word for fish) the symbol of Christ's name among the early Christians.

God's voice becomes God's outstretched hand, and so the Jew in the village at Beth Alpha drew the hand in the same manner as the Christian drew the fish in the catacombs of Rome.

Dr. Sukenik plans to return to Palestine in June and continue the work already begun near the third wall of Jerusalem and in the City of David, where he has already found traces of the Jewish nation which, even after the insurrection of Bar Kochba in the year 153 A. D., was not quite so impoverished or suppressed.

Fig. 1.3. Photographing the Beth Alpha mosaic synagogue, 1929.

Fig. 1.4. A *New York Times* article reporting the discovery of the Beth Alpha mosaic, April 29, 1929.

Plate I. Model of the Beth Alpha synagogue (Cat. 64).

(Plate I) was only the beginning, but it gave to the study of the ancient synagogue in the Land of Israel a momentum and a sense of purpose greater than it was to have in other places. But in the more than seventy years since the first excavation of Jewish sites in Palestine, much has changed in the archaeological enterprise. Today, no professional archaeologist would place nationalistic or political concerns on a par with scientific concerns. The excitement of ancient synagogue studies transcends the religious and national identities of contemporary scholars.

Archaeological methods have indeed changed through these seven decades; while as recently as twenty-five years ago chronology still played a central role, today it is only part of a much larger concern for the processes that influence individual site selection, construction techniques, building style and decoration, and how these factors relate to corresponding factors at other sites. When I began my first excavation of an ancient synagogue at Khirbet Shema in Galilee (Plate II, Fig. 1.5)[11] some twenty-five years ago, the common pottery of Roman and Byzantine Palestine was little known and poorly published. Thus, though the team I had organized as the Meiron Excavation Project wanted to pursue the archaeology of the synagogue in the context of a larger, regional focus, we could not

Plate II. Khirbet Shema synagogue, view to the southwest.

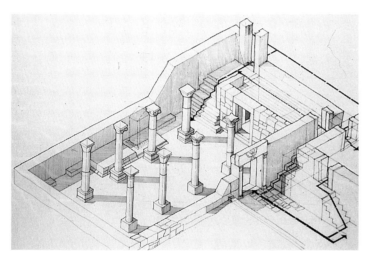

Fig. 1.5. Isometric drawing of Khirbet Shema broadhouse synagogue.

ignore the fact that the ceramic typology of the region—and of the late antique period in general—had not yet been established. Developments in field techniques have also changed enormously over the years. Contemporary archaeologists place greater emphasis on recording procedures, especially on the field notebook, with photos, plans, daily log, and narrative. None of these items was used in the early days of excavation in Palestine the way it is today. The results of recent excavations reflect an increased sophistication in recording techniques. Today, it is almost unthinkable to excavate a site without using computers for data processing and even for recording data from field books, organizing finds, and sorting all types of information by date, type, find spot, and so on. It is clear that archaeologists are in a new era from the point of view of methodology and interpretive strategies and are trying to refine even further the way they dig and retrieve data.

In addition to focusing on synagogues in their regional context, the Meiron Excavation Project emphasized the site context of the synagogue as much as was possible.[12] It is the site context of the structure that enables us to understand it better and the regional context that enables us to understand better its demographics, interrelationships with other sites, and overall settlement patterns.

Another concern of the new archaeology is to place much greater attention on faunal as well as botanical remains at a site. Even though analysis of such data may not always produce striking or dramatic results, making them available to scholars will allow future generations to interpret the context of a site. Examination of faunal remains has recently become very important in regard to understanding ethnic identity. Thus the presence or absence of pig remains, for example, is usually seen to indicate Jewish presence, though in more urban areas of mixed Jewish and Christian populations such as Tiberias, the presence of pig is to be expected. The Mishnah mentions pigs in public markets frequented by Jews (Mishnah Uktzin 3:3). In fact, a good deal of swine remains are extant from the Galilee. Swine, forbidden as food in the Bible (Lev. 11:7), is rarely found in either earlier Israelite or later Jewish sites.

Given the many advances in archaeological method and interpretive strategies, a reconsideration of the ancient synagogue in all its manifestations is warranted. Because so much of the material associated with many of the excavations has not yet been published or has been only partially published—much of the work having been done in survey, haste, or salvage—it is hoped that this exhibition will encourage younger scholars to collect and publish this material. Some of it is quite substantial: architectural members both decorated and undecorated, inscriptions, pottery, and other artifacts.

SOURCES AND METHODS

Plate III. Aerial view of the synagogue at Gamla, a city in the Golan Heights.

More than one hundred ancient synagogues have been discovered in the Land of Israel during this century, among them at least three structures from the end of the Second Temple period (Masada, Gamla [Plate III], and Herodium) and at least one from the second century (Nabratein). Most, however, date from the third to the eighth century C.E. (from the Middle Roman period to the Byzantine period). This picture of a thriving third-century Jewish community is surprising—and flies in the face of a long-held scholarly assumption that Judaism in the Land of Israel declined following the two revolts against Rome (66–74, 132–35 C.E.) and with the rise of Christianity in the East and its anti-Jewish legislation (which commenced in the fourth century). Archaeology of the ancient synagogue, however, has demonstrated conclusively that despite such developments, despite the eclipse of the office of Patriarch in 425 C.E., despite the challenge of the Babylonian community for religious hegemony (200–500 C.E.), late antique Jewry in Palestine flourished from the Middle Roman period well beyond the Islamic conquest (third to eighth centuries). This picture is also borne out by numerous documents within the Rabbinic canon as well as in recently uncovered documents from the Cairo Genizah (an old synagogue in Cairo where a trove of Jewish documents was discovered at the end of the nineteenth century) depicting a level of cultural and religious achievement hitherto thought unimaginable.[13]

Just as the plethora of ancient synagogues in the

Fig. 1.6. Theodotos inscription from a latter Second Temple period synagogue in Jerusalem (Cat. 37).

Roman–Byzantine period points to an anomaly between popularly held views about Jews and the ancient literature, so the dearth of archaeological evidence regarding early synagogues proves important when compared with early literary references. The writings of Philo of Alexandria, Josephus, the New Testament, and early Rabbinic literature suggest that synagogues were common in first-century Palestine. A late source in the Palestinian Talmud (Megillah 3:1, 738) and parallels mention 480 synagogues in Jerusalem in the time of Vespasian in the first century, although this large number was derived in a homiletical manner rather than from historical memory. Only three synagogues and the following first-century inscription (Fig. 1.6) date roughly to this period:

> Theodotos, son of Vettenos the priest and synagogue leader [archisynagogos], son of a synagogue leader and grandson of a synagogue leader, built the synagogue for the reading of the Torah and studying the commandments, and as a hostel with chambers and water installations for the accommodation of those who, coming from abroad, have need of it, which [that is, the synagogue] his fathers, the elders and Simonides founded.[14]

In this instance the archaeological evidence clearly substantiates the literary record, but in many other instances archaeological reality and literary evidence may not agree. The correlation of literary and archaeological sources presents the most compelling rationale for bringing the study of textual remains into direct dialogue with the study of material culture, for only when they intersect can we hope to develop a keener perspective on the social and historical reality that lies behind the evidence.

It is a common assertion of students of both Hebrew Scripture and Jewish history that while the precise setting for the origin of the synagogue is not known, the idea for it originated in the Exile, after the destruction of the Temple in Jerusalem in 587–86 B.C.E.[15] By the waters of Babylon, where the exiled Judeans "wept and remembered" Zion (Psalm 137:1), they were forced to face the urgent issues of how to maintain their identity; how to address their God, who in the eyes of many had forsaken them or judged them too harshly; and how to worship without a holy sanctuary that was linked to a holy space, Jerusalem. The prophet Ezekiel may have played a special role in this regard when he spoke of the *miqdash me'at* ("little temple," Ezek. 11:16), or the prophet Jeremiah, when he referred to the *beit am*, house of the people (Jer. 39:8). Together with their immediate concerns of collecting and editing their sacred documents, through which they would ensure the portability of their national history and corpus of law and lore,[16] coping with the trauma of the Exile by developing a new worship system without a temple left an indelible imprint on the collective memory of the Jewish people. With the existence of cultic centers outside Jerusalem before and after the Exile, it is fair to assume that by the sixth century B.C.E. the notion of worship beyond Jerusalem in some sort of communal setting had taken root in the Land of Israel. That we find a cult center at Elephantine in Egypt in the fifth century B.C.E. and at Leontopolis in the Hellenistic period, and synagogue inscriptions in the Fayyum in the third century B.C.E., should not be surprising.[17]

DIASPORA SYNAGOGUES

Very little is known of the earliest Diaspora synagogues, designated "prayer houses" (*proseuchei*) in the literature and epigraphy, though no doubt they drew from contemporary Egyptian models for inspiration. But by the first century the historian Josephus (*Ag. Ap.* 2.175) tells us about several features of the Alexandria synagogue, and Philo cites other details (*Embassy to Gaius* 156, *On Dreams* 2.156, *Life of Moses* 2.216). Among these is the importance of the reading of the Law within synagogues. Philo consistently refers to the synagogue in first-century Alexandria as a *proseuche*. This special use of the term, meaning "prayer house," may reflect a more limited role for the Egyptian or early Diaspora synagogue than the later, generally multipurpose *beit ha-knesset*, or "house of assembly," which we know primarily from Palestine.

The earliest extant example from the Diaspora comes from the Greek island of Delos (Fig. 1.7), birthplace of Apollo, and dates from the first century B.C.E.. Apparently the island, a free port since the second century, attracted a number of Samaritans, who have left epigraphic remains elsewhere.[18] Four ex-voto inscriptions containing the term *theos*

Fig. 1.7. The "synagogue" on the island of Delos in the Aegean Sea.

Plate IV. The synagogue at Sardis, in Asia Minor.

hypsistos (highest god) have been found in the main rectangular hall (16.9 × 14.4 meters). Along the western wall are benches with a marble seat or throne, which some have identified with the "seat of Moses" (Matt. 23:2).

Another important synagogue in the Greek world is known from Priene and probably dates to the fourth or fifth century, but possibly as early as the third century.[19] It was adapted from a private dwelling, and two plaques inscribed with Jewish symbols (menorah, shofar, lulav, and etrog) were discovered on its floor. The building was rectangular, measuring 19 × 14 meters.

The largest Diaspora synagogue excavated thus far is in Turkey at Sardis (Plate IV), capital of ancient Lydia. Originally built in the third century, later remodeled several times, and completely refurbished in the fourth century, the complex has an atrium forecourt with three entrances and a large rectangular hall with a stepped apse (54 × 18 meters). The hall contained two aediculae, one of which was a Torah Shrine, but some scholars assume there were two Torah Shrines.[20] A raised bema was situated in the center of the sanctuary, and a large table decorated with an eagle and flanked by lions stood near the apse. A Greek inscription found in the hall refers to "the place that protects the law [i.e., Torah]."[21] Another Greek inscription records the donation of a seven-branched menorah.

The most outstanding synagogue found in the Diaspora is in Dura Europos (Fig. 1.8) in Syria, located on a caravan route along the Euphrates. Originally converted into a

Fig. 1.8. Model of the Dura Europos synagogue (Cat. 27).

sacred space from a private dwelling, it is preserved in second- and third-century phases. Its final phase (244/5–56 C.E.), destroyed during the Sassanian invasion, consists of a forecourt and rectangular main hall (14 × 8.7 meters) with magnificent frescoed wall panels. A small Torah Shrine or aedicula for displaying the scroll stands on the west wall. Each of the four walls is decorated with scenes from the biblical narratives. This corpus of art represents the largest and most important collection of Jewish art to survive from antiquity; its interpretation, which continues, is controversial and stimulating.[22] The synagogue is broadhouse in plan, that is, with focus of worship on the long wall.

Another major synagogue to survive intact from antiquity is the synagogue at Ostia, the port of Rome. While an earlier, possibly first-century, stage was found under the preserved floor of a later building, the main phase of use is a fourth-century building (24.9 × 12.5 meters). A Torah Shrine is the central feature of the main hall, located in the southeast corner, while a bema is situated opposite the main entrance.[23]

Other notable examples of synagogues from the Diaspora include Stobi in Macedonia (formerly Yugoslavia), Aegina in Greece, Apamea in Syria, Gerasa in Jordan, Ḥamman-Lif in Tunisia, Philippolis in Bulgaria, Misis in Asia Minor (ancient Mopsuestia), Eleche in Spain, and in Reggio Calabria in southern Italy. No doubt others will be found, such as that recently proposed in the Athenian Agora and dating to the late Roman period.[24]

Several generalizations about these buildings can be made. First, their style and plans reflect local conditions and architectural planning. Several were converted from private dwellings to public sanctuaries (e.g., Dura Europos, Priene, and Delos), and others were converted to churches (Apamea and Gerasa). Second, the orientation of the synagogue was toward Jerusalem, wherever it was located, and focused on the Torah Shrine, associated with an apse, an aedicula, or a niche.[25] Such an intentional arrangement emphasized the importance of Scripture in the synagogue liturgy. Third, the Diaspora synagogues share a common vocabulary of Jewish symbols, such as menorahs and other temple-related or Jewish festival-related objects (e.g., shofar, lulav, and etrog). All of these features point to a common Judaism that undergirded these Diaspora communities and united them with the larger Jewish community that included Eretz Israel. Many of the artifacts featured in this exhibition, in fact, illustrate the strong ties that united these diverse communities irrespective of the divergent approaches to Jewish belief and practice that no doubt were a part of them.

SYNAGOGUES IN THE LAND OF ISRAEL

One of the most surprising results of recent research on ancient synagogues in Israel is an apparent dramatic increase in the numbers of synagogues from about the middle of the third century C.E.[26] As noted, in the third century paganism appears to have begun a decline; but it was also a rather chaotic period in Eretz Israel as in much of the Roman world, with famine, plague, and inflation eating away at the economy and general political instability contributing to an uncertain atmosphere.[27] As Lee Levine has recently pointed out, scholars have not yet been able to correlate these two seemingly contradictory developments. Possibly the downturn in the local economy in the third century has been exaggerated somewhat.[28] In addition, just as Yitzhak Magen has suggested that the decline of paganism contributed to the expansion of Samaritanism, so too did it enable Judaism to fill some of the vacuum that Christianity was soon to fill.

In any event, a fairly long time elapsed between the construction of the three first-century synagogues of Masada, Gamla, and Herodium; the dozens built in the third century; and the scores built even later. The one synagogue that clearly fits into the second century is the first-phase, broadhouse synagogue from Nabratein (Fig. 1.9) in Upper Galilee. It is a tiny building (11.2 × 9.35 meters), with space for four columns, though there is no definitive evidence for them. Although it has no fixed Torah Shrine, two small platforms flank the southern, Jerusalem-oriented wall. An imprint on the floor in the center of the hall suggests that a table or small stand had been placed there, possibly for reading or translating Scripture. The problem of the beginning date for the appearance of a fixed Torah Shrine (Plate V, Fig. 1.10; Plate VI, Fig. 1.11) in the Palestinian synagogue is resolved in the next phase (third century) of the building when it had six columns and the shrine was attached to the Jerusalem wall and situated on a platform or bema.[29]

Fig. 1.9. Plan of the mid-third–century synagogue and village at Nabratein.

(a)

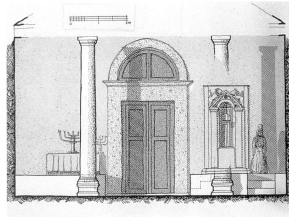

(b)

Fig. 1.10. (a) Reconstructed drawing of the pediment at Nabratein; (b) reconstructed drawing of the Torah Shrine.

Plate V. Torah Shrine pediment from the synagogue at Nabratein.

The careful and systematic excavation and survey work of the past decades have, therefore, led to a complete undoing of the older typologically based views about the architectural development of the synagogue in Eretz Israel, from an "early" Galilean basilica, with the focus of worship on the short wall and consisting of a central aisle and two side aisles; to a transitional broadhouse (fourth century) with bema and Torah Shrine, focusing worship on the long wall; to a Byzantine apsidal building, focusing worship on the apse in the short wall. This view emerged only after the resolution of the question regarding the matter of sacred orientation toward Jerusalem in an architecturally and liturgically acceptable and meaningful way.[30] The Tosefta (Megillah 3:21–23) presents instructions for its liturgical solution, suggesting that the elders sat facing the congregation, with their backs to Jerusalem, and that the chest bearing the Torah scrolls was positioned similarly. The same text requires doors opening to the east.[31]

In a Galilean basilica, the short wall faces south or is oriented toward Jerusalem. Since most basilicas in Galilee are entered from the facade wall via the portico and main entrances, in order to comply with the generally accepted custom, which is based on various biblical texts that support the idea of praying toward Jerusalem (1 Kings 8:44 = 2 Chron. 6:34; 1 Kings 8:48 = 2 Chron. 6:38; Dan. 6:11), one would have to perform the so-called awkward about-face. The principle of sacred orientation toward Jerusalem, attested

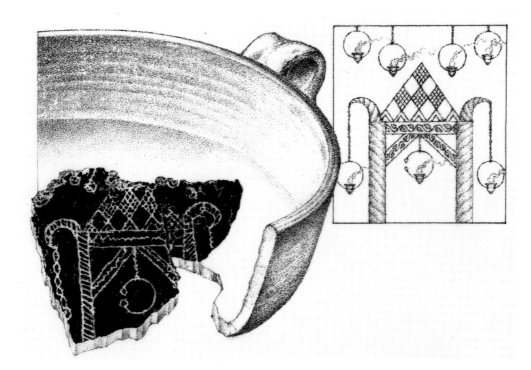

Fig. 1.11. Reconstructed drawing of Nabratein sherds as they would appear on the bottom of a ceramic vessel (left) with depiction of the Torah Shrine (insert, right).

Plate VI. Sherds with image of a Torah Shrine from Nabratein (Cat. 52).

in the Jewish Diaspora and reflected in Samaritan synagogues, albeit orienting worship toward the site of the Samaritan temple on Mount Gerizim rather than toward Jerusalem, was also operative in the first-century buildings at Masada and Herodium.[32] But even in the four Upper Galilean synagogues I have excavated, in all their multiple phases (two are broadhouses: Khirbet Shema and Nabratein, first phase; and the others, different sorts of

Plate VII. The synagogue at Gush Ḥalav, view to the northwest.

(b)

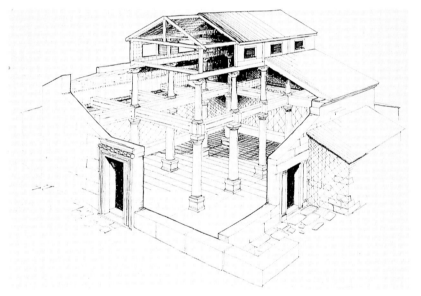

(a)

Fig. 1.12. (a) Cutaway drawing of Gush Ḥalav synagogue, view to the north. (b) One of the seven hanging lamps discovered at the synagogue of Gush Ḥalav (Cat. 46).

basilicas: Meiron and Gush Ḥalav [Plate VII, Fig. 1.12], 4 kilometers northeast of Meiron), the principle of sacred orientation is resolved in numerous creative ways. Only at Meiron, which has been poorly preserved since antiquity, is there no trace of a bema or an architectural feature that may be reliably identified with a Torah Shrine.

Indeed, various sites and different synagogues suggest different solutions for sacred orientation, depending on the state of preservation of the building and its architectural members. The series of broadhouse structures at Khirbet Shema, the first of which dates to the third century, for example, presents the possibility of a bema without a fixed Torah Shrine and subsequently one with a fixed shrine. It is quite possible that the small storage facility under the balcony on the east side was first used as a repository for the scrolls and later converted to another use.[33]

At Khirbet Shema the Torah Shrine and bema, as at other broadhouses, are located on the long, Jerusalem-oriented wall (cf. Susiya or Eshtemoa near Hebron, southeast of Jerusalem). The older, typologically based views understood the addition of a fixed Torah Shrine with bema to be associated with the ascendancy of the Jewish Scripture in the worship setting in response to Christianization of the country, which began in earnest after Constantine's conversion in 312 C.E. But again both the theological notion of the importance of Scripture and the principle of sacred orientation had been central features of the synagogue since the end of the Second Temple period. It is likely that the ark was portable in some synagogues, an idea that harks back to the biblical Ark of the Covenant. By the Byzantine period the ark is fixed in most examples and is often located in an apse (Naaran near Jericho and Beth Alpha). Taken over from the church at this late date, too, is the chancel screen, which separated the area of the Torah Shrine in the apse from the congregation.

During the Byzantine period greater emphasis was placed on interior decoration, especially colorful mosaics. Even at this time there was still great diversity among synagogue buildings. Some exhibited virtually no representational images of animals or humans (Meiron, Jericho, Reḥov), while others were lavishly decorated, even with the pagan zodiac motif (Plate VIII) (Sepphoris,

Plate VIII. Mosaic pavement from a synagogue in Sepphoris. (a) Zodiac wheel and (b) zodiac figure of the Jewish month of *Marheshvan*, Scorpio; (c) a woman symbolizing the season of autumn *(Tishrei)*.

(a)

(b)

(c)

Naaran, Ḥammath Tiberias, Beth Alpha). In general, the more liberal attitudes toward representational art may be found in synagogues bordering pagan areas or located on major trade routes or Roman roads, though the conservative view reflected in the mosaic at Ein Gedi, where the zodiac is depicted only in a list of the signs, is found along the Rift Valley, a major roadway. Similarly, a predominance of Greek inscriptions over Hebrew or Aramaic may be predicted by their location in relation to the Greek-speaking cities (i.e., the coastal port cities and in the Decapolis) or areas along major trade routes (Tiberias, Sepphoris, etc.).[34]

Aside from these general patterns, which make some diversity in synagogues predictable, interregional diversity, such as in the Meiron or Beth Shean areas, indicates that various congregations or their leaders or patrons held some concepts more dearly than others—especially the second commandment. But surely in spite of this diversity we must emphasize the common elements in all these synagogue buildings and their settlements: their shared focus on Scripture, their historic attachment to Jerusalem, and their commitment to make their "house of assembly" a gathering place for all sorts of activities. This would explain some of the variety and the considerable resources that might be spent on a public building to accommodate the special interests of donors and community leaders as well as such matters as topography and local resources.

There is still no consensus on the origin of the synagogue plan—understandable in view of the fact that there is such a variety of plans. But no one would disavow that, despite some forms and plans that relate to Near Eastern temple prototypes, the overwhelming influence was Greco-Roman or Hellenistic. Some of the early Galilean basilicas may be indebted to Roman public buildings for their plan or inspiration; the apsidal basilica is no doubt influenced by the emergence of the Christian church, which had a central nave, side aisles, apse, narthex, and atrium.[35] But none of this adoption or adaptation should surprise us about the late antique world, one that was brimming with multicultural options and diversity, all of which were facilitated by the Hellenistic milieu of the Levant.

In all of the ancient synagogues discovered, there is no evidence for the separation of women into a designated area or balcony. Surely a medieval development, the segregation of women is not borne out by the archaeological data. Nonetheless, modern literature on the ancient synagogue is replete with mention of "the women's gallery."[36] However, the tremendous architectural unity of the synagogue in both ancient Palestine and the Diaspora should not lead us to assume that the status and role of women were the same in every community.

As successor to the Jerusalem Temple, the synagogue became the vehicle that enabled Judaism to become movable, and hence to survive. While the Rabbinic Sages ultimately attached to it the sanctity it was to achieve, this came later, a fact that emerges clearly from the chapters in this volume. As its liturgical function gained dominance over its communal function, the synagogue achieved greater sanctity and the Jewish people became increasingly confident—despite negative pressures from the world about them, which first became more Christian, then more Islamic. As these religions observed their fellow brothers and sisters of the Book, they no doubt were impressed and influenced by the synagogue, which inspired both church and mosque. In both traditions it is almost unthinkable to read Sacred Writ from the floor level, and the bema, or raised ambol, became standard. But it was the Jewish tradition alone that preserved its sacred Scripture in rolled, scroll form, another significant way in which Jews made their house of worship imitate the Temple of old (the scrolls are depicted in the gilt glass piece from the Metropolitan Museum of Art [Cat. 14] featured in the exhibition and possibly in some of the numerous Bar Kokhba coins [Cat. 39]).[37]

left: Fig. 1.13. Mosaic pavement from the Samaritan synagogue at Shalabim depicting two menorahs with Greek and Samaritan inscriptions (Cat. 77).

right: Fig. 1.14. Samaritan oil lamp from Netanya depicting a Torah Shrine and ritual implements (Cat. 72).

SAMARITAN SYNAGOGUES

I have already alluded to the probability of a Samaritan Diaspora and the fact that the synagogue at Delos may have belonged to that community.[38] Three synagogues previously known from Palestine (but outside of Samaria) have been tentatively identified as Samaritan: those at Beth Shean, Shalabim, and Tel Aviv, the last until only recently identified as a church. Only Shalabim (Fig. 1.13) is oriented toward Mount Gerizim; the identity of the others is a matter of current debate.[39] These synagogues contain important parallels to Jewish synagogues in the Land of Israel.

Each of these synagogues has inscriptions written in the distinctive Samaritan script. More recent surveys and excavations in the region of Samaria proper have produced dramatic new evidence of the high artistic achievement (Fig. 1.14) and architectural sophistication of the Samaritan synagogue. Synagogues have been discovered at Khirbet Samara (Fig. 1.15), El-Khirbe near Sebaste, Mount Gerizim, the Azzan Yacaqov at Ur-Natan (Khirbet Majdal), and Kefar Fama. Each of these structures has been associated with Baba Rabah, who is reported to have built eight synagogues in the fourth century.[40]

The most distinguishing aspect of the newly discovered Samaritan synagogues is their common orientation toward Mount Gerizim and the apparent practice of worshipping facing the holy mountain. Somewhat surprising, ignoring for a moment the possibility that the building on Delos might be Samaritan, is that none of these buildings dates earlier than the fourth century C.E. Where the Samaritans prayed before that time is a mystery. Moreover, to date all the

Fig. 1.15. Mosaic depicting a Torah Shrine from the Samaritan synagogue at Khirbet Samara.

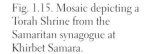

Samaritan synagogues of ancient Palestine have been located at the edge of or outside a settlement[41]—very unusual in respect to the location of Jewish Palestinian synagogues, but similar to those of the Diaspora, often found outside the town. The excavator of these buildings, Y. Magen, has suggested that some of the Samaritan synagogues were modified in the Byzantine period after the fashion of churches, especially those in which apses were added. He also believes this adjustment coincided with the switch from Greek to Samaritan script.[42] Unlike their Jewish counterparts, the sponsors of Samaritan mosaics, those responsible for their decoration, and those who commissioned architectural fragments and lamps observed scrupulously the Pentateuchal ban against making graven images, human or animal. Magen points out that there are no exceptions to the rule, which is in keeping with the Samaritans' strict reading and interpretation of the Pentateuch.[43] Finally, the artistic repertoire of the Samaritans includes the Torah Shrine, menorahs, images of the biblical showbread table, the tongs, and the trumpet instead of the shofar. Their images closely resemble those of Jewish mosaics. In fact, the mosaic pavement of the Beth Shean synagogue bears striking resemblance to Jewish mosaics from nearby Beth Alpha, Hammath Tiberias B, Jericho, and Naaran. The same father-son team of artisans responsible for the mosaic pavement at Beth Alpha was responsible for this mosaic. Were it not for some rather small inscriptions in Samaritan script discovered at Beth Shean, no one would have ever thought to identify the building as Samaritan. This reflects the close connections between Jews and Samaritans during this period.

The strength and vigor of the Samaritan community in the fourth and fifth centuries C.E., apparently under the impetus of their leader Baba Rabah, coincided with the decline of paganism in Eretz Israel. This cluster of settlements in the center of Samaria was doubtless a major factor inhibiting the spread of Christianity into the Samaritan heartland. Only in the mid-sixth century, when Zenon erected a church on Mount Gerizim, did the Samaritans revolt and begin to abandon the sacred area above modern Nablus. They returned only later, in the Middle Ages.[44]

CONCLUSION

I began this chapter with reference to the discovery of the Beth Alpha synagogue and what it meant to the kibbutzniks of that settlement and to the early Zionist immigrants to Palestine in the late 1920s. Surely the remains and artifacts of so many houses of worship from antiquity from both Eretz Israel and the Diaspora mean a great deal to the people who visit them, attend this exhibition, or read this book. What precisely this precious legacy will mean for those who come to know and appreciate it is a key test for those men and women who are so deeply embedded in today's secular world. The ancient synagogue is a reminder that any space anywhere can be imbued with sacred meaning, for after all, when men and women of good intent gather together to acknowledge God, to revere the words attributed to God as recorded in Scripture, the space they inhabit becomes holy. Hence, early tradition in Rabbinic law required that if a synagogue was destroyed or converted to other purposes, that place was to be revered.

"Sacred Realm: The Emergence of the Synagogue in the Ancient World" constitutes a precious legacy to be remembered and not forgotten, to be seen and to be reexperienced, and to be appreciated for the unique role the synagogue has played in the Jewish experience. Though the synagogue harks back to the Jerusalem Temple, it also creates new sacred space, which enables humans to sanctify time and to be in touch with eternity—and who does not want to experience an echo of eternity?

From Meeting House to Sacred Realm

Holiness and the Ancient Synagogue

STEVEN FINE

Baltimore Hebrew University

The synagogue is among the most influential religious institutions in the history of Western civilization. In this place of "coming together" (Greek *synagoge*, Hebrew *beit ha-knesset*), Judaism created a communal religious experience that previously was almost unknown.[1] Within the ancient synagogue believers assembled to read the Sacred Scripture, to pray, and to form community with their God. This "democratic" notion of religious experience is in stark contrast with the great and small temples of the ancient world, including the Jerusalem Temple, where professional priests performed religious acts on behalf of a community that stood by piously. The synagogue was an important model for the early church. In fact, it was within synagogues that the message of Christianity was first preached. Centuries later the synagogue and the church were the models Mohammed and his followers used for their new "place of prayer" and scriptural reading, the mosque. This chapter traces the ideological development of the synagogue from the earliest evidence of its existence through the rise of Islam. What are the origins of the synagogue, and how did it become a Sacred Realm?

A "PLACE OF MEETING": THE SECOND TEMPLE PERIOD

No one knows when and where the synagogue first developed. Some trace its origins to the Babylonian captivity (586–16 B.C.E.), during which time Judeans distant from their homeland are said to have assembled to "sing the Lord's song in a strange land." Others see its beginnings in a series of third-century Greek inscriptions from Egypt that describe Jewish "prayer places." Some first-century Jews traced its origins to Moses himself. Yet the origins of the synagogue may never be known—it was not an institution that developed in a revolutionary way, breaking away from an established religious institution, as did Luther at Wittenberg Cathedral. Rather, the synagogue seems to have begun as a "still, small voice," as a simple place where Jews came together to read Scripture. Joining in synagogue life in no way dampened Jewish allegiance and dedication to the great "house of God," the Temple of Jerusalem. In fact, by the first century C.E. numerous synagogues existed in Jerusalem itself, including gatherings of Jews from lands as distant as Cyrene and Alexandria in North Africa and the provinces of Cilicia and Asia in Asia Minor.[2] An inscription found within the shadow of the Temple Mount in Jerusalem portrays the religious life of a first-century synagogue. Called the Theodotos inscription (see Fig. 1.6), it tells us that the synagogue was endowed by three generations of the family of an individual called Theodotos. There the Torah was read and the commandments were studied. Pilgrims stayed there when they visited Jerusalem and perhaps purified themselves in ritual baths for their ascent to the Temple. Philo, the philosopher and communal leader of Alexandrian Jewry during the first century C.E., describes synagogues, often elegantly decorated, as being common in Roman Alexandria. There, he wrote,

> The Jews every seventh day occupy themselves with their ancestral philosophy, dedicating that time to acquiring knowledge and the study of the truths of nature. For what are our prayer places throughout the cities but schools of prudence and bravery and control and justice, as well as of piety and holiness and virtue as a whole, by which one comes to recognize and perform what is due to men and God? (*The Life of Moses*, 2. 216)

Missing from this description and from many others that we might cite is the one element of synagogue service that may be taken for granted: prayer. This is particularly odd, since

Fig. 2.1. The synagogue at Masada.

the name recorded in literary and epigraphic sources for most Diaspora synagogues (and one Palestinian synagogue) is *proseuche*, which means "prayer place." Possibly these sources stress that element of Jewish liturgy which is uniquely Jewish, taking for granted the aspect that was shared with other religious groups, communal prayer. Yet the overwhelming impression gained from extant sources is that early synagogues were places of communal Scripture reading and instruction. Besides the Theodotos inscription, two synagogue buildings have been discovered in Israel: one on Masada, the other at Gamla in the Golan Heights.[3] The Masada synagogue (Fig. 2.1) was built at the time of the first Jewish Revolt against Rome (66–74 C.E.) during the rebels' defiant and ill-fated occupation of this crag in the desert. The room that has been identified as a synagogue is 11.5 × 10.5 meters, with a small room measuring 3.6 × 5.5 meters at its northwestern corner. The hall was lined with benches. Fragments of the books of Ezekiel (Fig. 2.2) and Deuteronomy were uncovered. Other religious texts were found scattered on Masada, many within a short distance from the synagogue. The meeting hall on Masada seems to have been a place of public Scripture reading, by definition a synagogue. Philo uses the word "synagogue" to describe the religious gathering places of the Essenes earlier in the century:

> For that day has been set apart to be kept holy and on it they abstain from all other work and proceed to sacred places [*hierous . . . topous*] which they call synagogues [*sunagogai*]. There, arranged in rows according to their ages, the younger below the elder, they sit decorously as befits the occasion with attentive ears. Then one takes the books [*biblous*] and reads aloud and another of especial proficiency comes forward and expounds what is not understood. . . . (*Every Good Man Is Free*, 81–82).

Fig. 2.2. Ezekiel fragment from Masada.

Particularly important for us is the term Philo used to describe these synagogues: "sacred places" (*hierous . . . topous*). His is the first text to explicitly call these places sacred. What is the source of this holiness? It is apparently the "Sacred Scripture" (a term used in contemporary literature) that was studied within the synagogue.

Evidence of communal prayer in places of religious meeting before 70 C.E. is found in one source, the so-called Damascus Document. First discovered in the Cairo Genizah and then among the Qumran scrolls,[4] the document states:

> And all who enter the house of prostration, let him not come in a state of uncleanliness requiring washing. . . .

Prostration, most likely prayer in general, in a specific place seems to have been essential to the ritual life of this community. Just as purity was required for entry to the Temple of Jerusalem, it was required for participation in this sectarian "house of prostration." This attitude was the result of the Qumran sect's perception that the Temple had been profaned by the authorities in Jerusalem. The sect thus went into the desert and behaved as if the Temple had been destroyed, applying Temple imagery to themselves, praying together, and rejecting the "profaned" Temple. This response to the loss of the Temple foreshadows the program of the Rabbinic Sages after 70 C.E., a period when the Temple was, in fact, lost.

70 C.E.–C. 220 C.E.: SANCTITY WITHOUT THE TEMPLE

From these modest beginnings synagogues, after the destruction of the Temple in 70 C.E., developed as the single most important institution in Jewish life, a position they have held ever since. As the institution grew, its importance was expressed through an ever-increasing attribution of sanctity. The earliest evidence for this appears in the writings of the Sages of the Mishnah, the Tannaim. After the destruction of the Temple the Tannaitic Sages took it upon themselves to reformulate Judaism for an age in which the Temple could no longer be the focal point of religious experience. While waiting for the messianic reconstruction of the Temple, the Sages reconstructed religious practice to emphasize the elements of Judaism that had survived the destruction. At the center of this development stood the Holy Scriptures. While the Temple was gone and the Jewish hold on the Land of Israel was increasingly tenuous, the Torah and its study were left intact by the great national tragedy. The place where Scripture had been studied and community wrought for genera-tions before 70 C.E., the synagogue, became the institutional focal point for the Rabbinic reconstruction of Judaism.

As before 70 C.E., the importance of Scripture in synagogues was stressed by the Sages, who ascribed a certain amount of holiness to the synagogue because of this relationship. This is stated in terms of case law in the Mishnah, the most important corpus of early Rabbinic tradition. The text sets forth the conditions under which the people of a town might sell their communal religious properties:

> The people of a town who sold their town square:
> they must buy a synagogue with its proceeds;
> If they sell a synagogue, they must acquire a [scroll] chest.
> If they sell a [scroll] chest, they must acquire cloths [to wrap sacred scrolls].
> If they sell cloths, they must acquire books [of the Prophets and Writings]
> If they sell books, they must acquire a Torah [scroll].
> But, if they sell a Torah [scroll], they may not acquire books.
> And if they sell books, they may not acquire cloths.
> And if they sell cloths, they may not acquire a chest,
> And if they sell a chest, they may not acquire a synagogue.
> And if they sell a synagogue, they may not acquire a town square.
> So too, with the left-over [money].
> They may not sell public property to an individual, because they are lowering its holiness, so Rabbi Meir.
> They [the Sages] said to him: If so, then they cannot sell from a larger town to a smaller town. (Mishnah Megillah 3:1)

The source of holiness in this text is the Torah scroll. Places or objects physically closest to or resembling the Torah scroll are considered to be more holy. Thus the town square, where Scripture was read publicly but infrequently, has a small amount of holiness. Scrolls of the Prophets and Writings that look like Torah scrolls are just one step less holy than the Torah scroll. In a world in which the Temple did not exist, the Torah came to be seen as the supreme source of holiness, the embodiment of the Divine Presence. Other sources suggest that the entire congregation was gathered before the Torah chest[5] and that various items, including lamps, bore dedicatory inscriptions.[6] In some synagogues the Torah cabinet (*teva*) had an arched lid and stood upon a stand or was placed on a carpet.[7] The scrolls were wrapped in fine, colored cloths (*metzuyarot*) adorned with bells and placed upon a specially designated table (Fig. 2.3).[8] Communities taxed themselves in order to build synagogues and to procure Torah scrolls.[9]

While most synagogues in second-century Palestine were probably not very impressive buildings and may even have been converted houses,[10] the Tannaitic Sages projected their vision of a grand synagogue on a synagogue in the rich Diaspora community of first-century Alexandria:

> Said Rabbi Judah: Whosoever never saw the (double stoa) of Alexandria of Egypt[11] never saw the great honor of Israel his entire life.
>
> It was a kind of large basilica, a portico within a portico. Sometimes there were there twice as many people as those who went out of Egypt.
>
> There were seventy-one thrones within it, equal (in number) to the seventy-one elders, each one made of twenty-five myriad. A wooden platform [*bema*] was in the center.
>
> The *hazan ha-knesset* [leader] stood at the horn [of the altar], with the flags in his hand. When one began to read, the other would wave the flags and all the people would answer "amen" for each and every blessing. Then the other waved the flags and all of the people answered "amen."
>
> They did not sit in a jumble, but the goldsmiths sat by themselves, the silversmiths by themselves, the blacksmiths by themselves, the common weavers by themselves, and the fine weavers by themselves.
>
> So that when a traveler would come he would be taken care of by his [fellow] craftsmen, and from that [interchange] a living could be procured. (Tosefta Sukkah 4:6).

In describing the synagogue in such intense and extravagant hues, this text illustrates the "great glory of Israel." It is brighter than life. What is to be

(a)

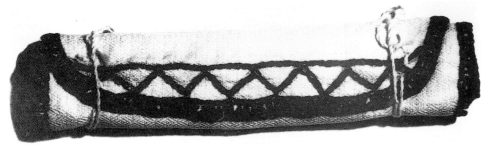

(b)

Fig. 2.3. Cloth wrapper for documents found on Masada: (a) original, (b) facsimile (Cat. 38).

noted here, however, is the importance of reading the Torah to this synagogue. As in the Second Temple period literature, synagogue prayer is not to be seen.

A second notable feature of this text is the terminology used to describe the architecture, furnishings, and liturgy of the synagogue. All are drawn from Tannaitic descriptions of the Temple: the Temple Mount is said to have been built as "a portico within a portico"; the members of the Sanhedrin sit in seventy-one chairs; the daily sacrifice is orchestrated by a *hazzan ha-knesset*; and prayer is offered accompanied by the waving of flags. The Alexandria synagogue, in all its glory, was to be something like the Temple.

The attribution of Temple motifs to synagogues was an important way in which their sanctity was expressed. Thus we see in Mishnah Megillah 3:3:

> Additionally, Rabbi Judah said:
> A synagogue that was destroyed:
> eulogies are not said in it,
> ropes are not twisted in it,
> nets are not stretched in it,
> fruit is not spread on its roof [to dry].
> It is not used as a shortcut, for it is written:
> "I will destroy your sanctuaries" (Lev. 26:31)—
> they are sacred even when they are destroyed.
> Grasses grow within them:
> They must not be picked [so as to provoke] sadness.

In this text the source of sanctity differs from that seen in Megillah 3:1. Synagogues are holy because they share in the sanctity of the Temple. This tradition suggests that a synagogue that has been destroyed through no fault of its community is still to be treated as holy—expressed graphically in prohibition against using a synagogue ruin as a shortcut. In Mishnah Berakhot 9:5 the use of the Temple Mount for this purpose is also forbidden. Both destroyed religious centers are to be treated, according to the Mishnah, with residual sanctity. Through creative exegesis of Leviticus 26:31 some of the sanctity of the Jerusalem Temple is ascribed to synagogues.[12]

Other Tannaitic texts apply Temple motifs in more direct ways. Tosefta Megillah 3:23–25 focuses on the internal arrangement of the synagogue community toward the Holy City of Jerusalem, suggesting that synagogue doors should open toward the east, like those in the Temple. The text further asserts that the ideal synagogue should be built on the acropolis of a town like a (or, the) temple. Other texts hint that synagogues were furnished with seven-branched menorahs, reminiscent of the Temple. Such large lamp stands would have more than ideological significance. They provided lighting necessary for the public reading of Scripture.

The period after the destruction of the Temple saw an explosion in the types of religious activities carried out in synagogues. The most important were liturgical. For the first time, prayer became an important feature of synagogue life. The Mishnah ascribes the beginning of this development to the single most influential Sage of the years immediately after 70 C.E., Rabbi Johanan son of Zakkai (Fig. 2.4):

> At first the *lulav* [palm frond, willow and myrtle] was taken up in the Temple seven [days] and in the countryside [*medinah*] one. When the Temple was destroyed, Rabbi Johanan son of Zakkai decreed that the *lulav* be taken up in the countryside seven [days] in memory of the Temple. (Mishnah Sukkah 3:12)

The taking up of a palm frond, tied together with twigs of willow and myrtle and held with a citron, in the "countryside," that is, the synagogues, was intended to preserve the "memory of the Temple."

Other examples of Temple rites the Sages introduced to synagogues are shofar blowing,[13] the priestly blessing,[14] prayer offered at the same times as it had been in the Temple,[15] and the recitation of blessings at the reading of the Torah.[16] All became synagogue functions under the influence of the Tannaitic Sages. Prayer modeled on Temple liturgy was an essential factor in the sanctification of the synagogue from the late first to the early third century C.E. This phenomenon is well expressed in a tradition that appears in a late Tannaitic collection, the *Mekhilta of Rabbi Ishmael*:

> In every place [where I cause My name to be remembered I will come to you and I will bless you] (Exod. 20:21). Where I reveal Myself to you, in the Temple. From here they said: The Tetragrammaton may not be pronounced in the outlying areas [*ba-gevulin*].

> Rabbi Eliezer son of Jacob says: If you will come to my house I will come to yours. To the place which my heart loves my feet will lead me.

> From here they said: Whenever ten people congregate in the synagogue the divine presence is with them, for it is written, "God [*Elohim*] stands in the congregation of God [*El*]" (Ps. 82:1). . . .[17]

Fig. 2.4. Bar Kokhba coin depicting a lulav bundle (Cat. 39).

Just as the Temple is a place where the Divine can be found, God is present when a quorum assembles for prayer in the synagogue. The synagogue becomes a place where, through prayer, the believer can come into communion with the Divine. The *Mekhilta* is the first text to describe the synagogue as something more than a temple-like study hall. It has become a place of theophany through prayer.

For the early Rabbinic Sages, synagogues were the institutional focal point for the reconstruction of Judaism. In their hands the meeting house in which Scripture was studied before 70 C.E. became an institution infused with Temple qualities. It became the sacred place of the time when the Temple did not exist. During the first centuries of the Common Era the basic contours of this institution were drawn. Synagogues became places in which the Divine could be encountered through communal acts of Torah study and prayer.

SYNAGOGUES IN THE LAND OF ISRAEL, C. 220–700 C.E.

During the late Roman and Byzantine periods the synagogue blossomed. Archaeological evidence suggests that synagogues could be found throughout Jewish areas of the Land of Israel during late antiquity. In fact, an easy way to distinguish a Jewish district from a Christian area during the Byzantine period is to chart the locations of the more than one hundred synagogue ruins in Israel and to compare this map with known discoveries of churches. Jews were concentrated in the eastern Galilee (particularly the Upper Galilee), the Golan, and areas of Judea surrounding Jerusalem. Christians were most numerous in the western Galilee, the coastal plain, and Judea.

Palestinian Jews saw the synagogue as the essential institution of the Jewish community during late antiquity. Jewish communal self-identity was clearly invested in their synagogues, as expressed in the ever grander synagogues found throughout the Land of Israel. This new significance is expressed in the development of homiletical literature, the *midrashim*, much of which was based upon homilies delivered in synagogues and study houses. The liturgy of the synagogue became more complex during the Byzantine period. Intricate liturgical compositions, called *piyyutim*, were recited by celebrated authors. These *piyyutim* (Fig. 2.5) also followed the weekly and festival scriptural and liturgical cycles. Finally, building upon a tradition that can be traced to the Second Temple period, homiletical renditions of Scripture into Aramaic (*targumim*) were composed for the benefit of Aramaic-speaking Jews. Most Jews in the Land of Israel spoke Aramaic and Greek in their daily lives. Hebrew, the language of Scripture and hence of most liturgy, came to be restricted to the synagogue context. In *targumim* and in an Aramaic *piyyut* the synagogue was called the "language of the holy house," the "holy house" being the synagogue. In archaeological remains as well we find synagogues called "holy places" in numerous inscriptions. Based upon models first seen in Tannaitic literature, synagogues became for the Sages the Jewish "holy places" of late antique Palestine. The sanctity of the synagogue became so great that the institution was projected into sacred time. It would continue to be important, they thought, even in messianic time when the Temple would be in full operation.

We will begin our survey with the successors of the Tannaim, the Amoraim in the Land of Israel and those generally anonymous scholars who followed them. By the third century the Sages were widely accepted as the intellectual and religious elite of Palestinian Jewry. Under the able leadership of Rabbi Judah the Prince, the status of the Sages was accepted by both Jews and the Roman authorities. The developing Rabbinic elite attempted to exert broad influence within Jewish society while claiming special status for itself.

A text representative of Rabbinic attention to synagogues is preserved in the Jerusalem Talmud (Fig. 2.6). This tradition strongly advocates synagogue attendance, presenting this institution in the most vivid tones:

A.   Huna said: He who prays behind the synagogue is called evil, for it is said: "The evil will go around [when baseness is exalted among the children of men]" (Ps. 12:9).

B.   Rav Huna said: Anyone who does not enter a synagogue in this world will not enter a synagogue in the world to come.
What is the [scriptural] basis?
"The evil will go around [when baseness is exalted among the children of men]" (Ps. 12:9).

C.   Rabbi Johanan said: He who prays at home it is as if he is surrounded by a wall of iron. . . .

D.   Rabbi Phineas in the name of Rabbi Hoshaya: He who prays in the synagogue is like one who sacrifices a pure meal offering [*minḥah*].
What is the [scriptural] basis?
"God [*Elohim*] stands in the congregation of God [*El*]" (Ps. 82:1).

E.   Rabbi Jeremiah in the name of Rabbi Abbahu: "Seek out the Lord where He may be found" (Isa. 55:6).
Where may He be found?
In the synagogues and study houses.
"Call upon Him when He is near" (ibid.).
Where is He near?
[In the synagogues and study houses].

above left: Fig. 2.5. *Piyyut* by the synagogue poet Yannai from the Cairo Genizah.

above: Fig. 2.6. Jerusalem Talmud, first edition, Venice, 1523.

F.   Said Rabbi Isaac son of Rabbi Eleazar: Not only that, but their God stands behind them. What is the [scriptural] basis?

"God [*Elohim*] stands in the congregation of God [*El*]" (Ps. 82:1). . . .

G.   It is a firm promise [*berit kerutah*] that he who toils at his study in the synagogue will not quickly forget it [that is, his learning]. . . . (Jerusalem Talmud, Berakhot 5:1, 8d–9a)

Each of these traditions is intended to strengthen the position of the synagogue within Jewish communal life. Taken together, this medley of Rabbinic sayings constitutes an extremely powerful statement. Let us analyze each section to see what is new in this document.

Section F is reminiscent of the text *Mekhilta of Rabbi Ishmael* and thus follows upon that Tannaitic precedent. Similar sentiments are often represented in Amoraic literature. We find it, for example, in a homiletical comment on Song of Songs 2:9 preserved in a sixth–seventh-century collection, the *Pesiqte de Rav Kahane*:

"My beloved is like a gazelle or a young hart" (Song of Songs 2:9). Said Rabbi Isaac: As a gazelle leaps and skips from tree to tree, from thicket to thicket, and from grove to grove, so the Holy One leaps from synagogue to synagogue, from study house to study house. Why?
In order to bless Israel. . . .[18]

The playful image of God as a "young hart" deals with the problem of how God can be in more than one holy place at a time. Similarly, we find in a tradition in the Jerusalem

Talmud that synagogues were seen as places where individuals could commune with God. Having described the vast distances separating the earth from each of the seven heavens and the vast size of the hoofs of the beasts of heaven, the mystery of Divine Immanence is asserted in this text:

> See how high above His world He is! Yet a person can go into a synagogue and stand behind a column and pray in a whisper, and the Holy One, Blessed be He, listens to his prayer.
> For it is said: "Hannah was speaking in her heart; only her lips moved, and her voice was not heard" (1 Sam. 1:13).
> Yet the Holy One, Blessed be He, heard her prayer. (Jerusalem Talmud, Berakhot 9:1, 13a)

Here the synagogue is a place where the prayer of a single individual can traverse the expanses of the heavens, and God himself will receive it. The model of Hannah is important because "speaking in her heart" became the model for the recitation of Rabbinic prayer, and the synagogue is subtly equated with the Tabernacle at Shilo where she prayed to God for her son Samuel.

Sections A and C go so far as to decry those who avoid synagogue worship. They are "evil," says Rav Huna, because they sneak around, avoiding the synagogue at prayer time. Even more threatening is Rabbi Johanan's statement warning the person who does not pray in community that his prayers will not be heard by God. We know, for example, of two scholars of the generation following Rabbi Johanan—Rabbi Ami and Rabbi Assi—who chose not to attend any of the "thirteen" synagogues in Tiberias, "praying between the pillars [of the study house] where they were studying."[19] A practical inducement is promised by this text for those who choose to study in synagogues. In section G Rabbi Johanan promises that their studies within synagogues will be retained longer. This appears to be a clear attempt to lure the Sages and their followers away from their study houses and into the synagogues for prayer.

Section D makes explicit a trend nascent in Tannaitic sources. While the Tannaim established the thrice daily prayer services at the times when sacrifices took place in the Jerusalem Temple, the Amoraim made this phenomenon explicit. While the Temple lay in ruin, synagogue prayer is a temporary replacement for the Temple service.

The application of Temple motifs to synagogues and to synagogue prayer was expanded greatly by the Amoraim, without concern that synagogues could ever really take the place of the Temple. As we will see, they were actually read into the cosmic order, effectively neutralizing any possibility of supercession. Synagogues came to be called "small temples," based upon an interpretation of Ezekiel 11:16:

> Rabbi Samuel b. Isaac: "I will be unto them a small sanctuary [*miqdash me'at*]" (Ez. 11:16):
> These are synagogues and study houses.[20] (Babylonian Talmud, Megillah 29a)

In later literature this theme is developed further, where specific rituals derived from the Temple were transferred to synagogues. Synagogue poetry focuses on such Temple rites as the service of the high priest in the service on the Day of Atonement and the priestly courses described in 1 Chronicles 24:7–18. A late midrash discovered in the Cairo Genizah asserts this phenomenon explicitly:

> As long as the Temple existed, perpetual sacrifices and offerings would atone for the sins of Israel.
> Now synagogues are to Israel in the place of the Temple. As long as Israel prays in them, their prayers are in place of the perpetual sacrifices and offerings.
> [By reciting] prayers at their proper time and directing their hearts, they merit and will see the

rebuilding of the Temple and [the reestablishment of] the perpetual sacrifices and offerings, as it is said: "And I will bring them to my holy mountain and I will rejoice in my house of Prayer" (Isa. 56:7) their sacrifices and offerings will be received well on my altar, "for my house shall be called a house of prayer for all of the nations."[21] (Babylonian Talmud, Megillah 29a)

The "templization" of prayer was instrumental to the "templization" of synagogues.

In section B Rav Huna suggests a status for synagogues that is unknown in Tannaitic literature. The synagogue is projected into "the world to come." It is unclear whether the world to come refers to a postmortem reward or to the eschatological future. What we can know, however, is that synagogues will be there to serve the needs of the pious. This notion is expressed in a select number of Rabbinic sources. It is stated explicitly in a later collection of *midrashim*, Deuteronomy Rabba:

> Anyone who enters synagogues and study houses in this world merits to enter synagogues and study houses in the world to come.
> Whence this?
> For it is said: "Happy are those who dwell in your house, they will again praise you, selah" (Ps. 84:6).[22]

The promise of heavenly synagogue and study houses attendance is here based on the exegesis of Psalm 84:6: "Those who dwell in your house . . . will again praise you." When will this "again" happen? In the world to come. Other sources project synagogues into the biblical past. King Solomon, for example, not only built the Temple, he built synagogues in Jerusalem![23] The meeting house of earlier generations has become a part of Jewish sacred time. Another point worthy of attention is the mention of the study house. Rabbinic study houses came into their own during the third century, taking on many attributes of synagogues. Some Sages, in fact, considered the study house to be holier than the synagogue.

The Rabbinic Sages provide a detailed description of the interior of a third-century synagogue. As in Mishnah Megillah 3:1, closer proximity to the biblical scrolls occasions greater holiness:

> All of the furnishings of the synagogue are like [in holiness to] the synagogue.
> All of the furnishings of the synagogue are like [in holiness to] its bench [*safsal*] and its couch [*qaltara*].
> The curtain [*kila*] on the ark [*arona*] is like [in holiness] to the ark [which was seen as more sacred than the synagogue building because the biblical scrolls were stored in it]. Rabbi Abbahu put a cloak [*golta*] under the curtain [*bilan*] [of the ark].
> Rav Judah in the name of Samuel: the bema and planks [*levahin*] do not have the sanctity of the ark, and do have the sanctity of the synagogue.
> The reading table [*ingalin*] does not have the sanctity of the ark, and does have the sanctity of the synagogue. (Jerusalem Talmud, Megillah 3:1–3, 73d–74a)[24]

Those synagogue fixtures that have the sanctity of the synagogue but not the greater sanctity of the ark are the benches, the sofa, the bema, the planks, and the reading table. Only those furnishings that are in constant, close proximity to the ark—the curtain and the cloak—have the sanctity of the ark. For the ancient reader of this text the identification of the various appurtenances of the synagogue was self-evident. A third-century Jew, we may assume, knew exactly what a *qaltara* looked like and just what a *bilan* was. For us, however, it is hard to know what each of the terms denotes. Scholars since the Middle Ages have struggled with them, and I have provided what appears to me to be reasonable identifications. The identity of the *ingalin* as a reading table is clear from parallels in contemporaneous non-Jewish literature in Greek. It becomes even clearer when we know that the table upon which the Gospel book is placed in modern Greek Orthodox churches is called an *analogein*. Here we see that another of the surviving forms of late antique religion preserves the denotation of this term in Talmudic literature.

The traditional term to describe the Torah Shrine, the *arona*, is particularly important for understanding the ideological development of the synagogue. In Amoraic literature this term generally replaces the Tannaitic *teva* (chest). *Arona* bears biblical resonances referring not just to a big cabinet but to the biblical Ark of the Covenant. This relationship is made clear in a tradition attributed to Rabbi Huna the Great of Sepphoris, a major city in the Lower Galilee recently excavated by American and Israeli archaeologists. Rabbi Huna the Great of Sepphoris is said to have lamented on the occasion of a public fast that

> Our fathers covered it [the Ark of the Covenant] with gold, and we cover it [the Torah ark] with ashes. (Jerusalem Talmud, Ta'anit 2:1, 65a)

The Torah Shrine was covered with ashes as a sign of mourning. The ark is here cast as the Ark of the Covenant, which stood in the Holy of Holies of the Tabernacle and the Solomonic Temple. The curtain before the ark is called the *parokhta* in another tradition, reminiscent of the Temple *parokhet* (curtain).[25] The ark and the *parokhet* thus join the menorah as synagogue vessels bearing the names of Temple appurtenances.

The relation between synagogues and the Temple became so basic to Jewish conceptions that sources go as far as to treat the biblical Tabernacle as a kind of big synagogue and the Ark of the Covenant as a Torah Shrine:

(a)

Fig. 2.7. (a) Bronze amulet found in the apse of the synagogue at Maon (Nirim) (Cat. 80). (b) Drawing of amulet.

(b)

When Moses told Bezalel to make the Tabernacle
Bezalel said: "What is the purpose of the Tabernacle?"
He said to him: "To cause the Divine Presence to dwell there and to teach Israel Torah."
Said Bezalel: "Where is the Torah put?"
He said to him: "When we make the Tabernacle, we will make an ark. . . ."[26]

The intimate relationship between the Torah scroll and its ark expressed in this text is transferred metaphorically in the Jerusalem Talmud to a Sage who has lost his knowledge of Torah:

> Rabbi Jacob son of Abaye in the name of Rabbi Aha: An elder [*zaken*] who forgets his learning through no fault of his own is treated with the sanctity of the ark. (Moed Qatan 3:1, 81d)

The body of the Sage is to be treated as an ark for the knowledge of Jewish tradition, the "oral Torah," which this scholar has stored in it.

The Torah Shrine was considered by some to be a place of considerable power. This is expressed in an amulet discovered in the Genizah which instructs that it be buried "under the ark of the synagogue."[27] In fact, nineteen bronze amulets (Fig. 2.7), wrapped in cloth and inscribed in Aramaic and Hebrew, were discovered among remains of the Torah Shrine and other appurtenances in the apse of the sixth-century synagogue at Maon (Nirim), near Gaza.[28] Scholars hypothesize that "some of the amulets were suspended from the wall near or behind the Ark of the Law, or even from the ark itself."[29]

Why were the amulets kept near the Torah Shrine? Their contents provide part of the answer. The opened examples appeal for healing and divine protection[30] and contain formulae that are reminiscent of both liturgical texts and synagogue inscriptions. It is apparent that the power of these amulets derived both from their literary similarity to Scripture and liturgy and from their proximity to the Torah Shrine. Like synagogue inscriptions today, the terminology used in extant amulets often draws on biblical and liturgical formulations. For example, *Amen, Amen Selah*, a phrase similar to biblical formulae, appears both in amulets[31] and in synagogue inscriptions.[32] The formulae of these amulets (Fig. 2.8) closely parallel other amulets discovered in the Cairo Genizah.[33]

Liturgically, the end of this period saw the development of complex rituals for the reading of Torah that clearly express that the scroll was the manifestation of godliness within its community. Thus we find the lifting of the scroll by the leader with the proclamation:

Fig. 2.8. (a) Inscribed pot sherds from the synagogue at Horvat Rimmon (Cat. 75). (b) Reconstructed drawing of inscribed pot sherds.

(a)

(b)

(a)

(b)

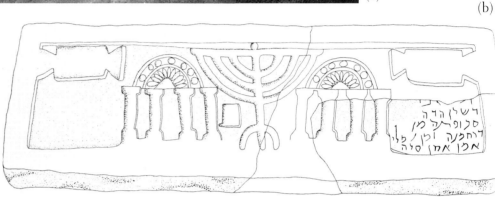

Fig. 2.9. (a) Lintel with a menorah and two aediculae from a synagogue at Belvoir (Cat. 65). (b) Reconstructed drawing of the Belvoir lintel. (c) Column fragment with dedicatory inscription from a synagogue at Beth Guvrin (Cat. 78).

(c)

"One is our God, Great is our Master, holy and awesome eternally."
He begins pleasantly and says: "The Lord is God" (1 Kings 18:39), the Lord is His name.
The people respond after him as he says it twice, and they respond after him two times.
Immediately he unrolls the Torah scroll a space of three columns, elevates it and shows the surface of its script to the people standing to his right and left.
Then he turns it [the raised scroll] in front and behind him, for it is a precept for all men and women to see the script, to bow (or prostrate themselves) and exclaim: "This is the Torah which Moses set before the Children of Israel" (Deut. 4:4).
He further exclaims: "The Torah of the Lord is perfect, restoring the soul. . . ."[34]

Literary sources from the third to the seventh century and beyond treat the synagogue as a place of Torah par excellence. It has become a place of prayer as well, one that is projected into both the messianic future and the biblical past. The synagogue has become so essential to Rabbinic conceptions of Judaism that it awaits the pious in the "world to come." Contemporaneous archaeological sources parallel literary sources in many ways. Synagogues of various architectural forms developed throughout the Land of Israel, based on regional types. North of the Sea of Galilee the "Galilean type" was most popular, while in the Jordan Rift Valley the apsidal basilica became the norm. The architecture of these buildings is discussed by R. Hachlili in Chapter 5. Synagogues throughout the Holy Land were called "holy places" in their Aramaic and Greek dedicatory inscriptions—in Kefar Ḥananyah in the Western Galilee; at Ḥammath Tiberias, Beth Shean, and Naaran in the Jordan Rift Valley; in

(a)

(b)

Fig. 2.10. (a) Pilaster capital with dedicatory inscription from Tiberias (Cat. 53). (b) Dedicatory inscription with a menorah from Binyamina (Cat.71).

Geresa in modern Jordan; and in Gaza and Ashkelon on the coastal plain. We will discuss just a few examples of the Jewish holy places that have been recovered by archaeologists.

The idea of placing dedicatory inscriptions (Figs. 2.9 and 2.10) within public contexts was by no means unique to Jews. This form of public benefaction was central to Greek, Roman, and Byzantine social contexts, as it is within the churches and synagogues of the modern followers of eastern forms of Christianity and Judaism. Tannaitic and Amoraic[35] sources mention synagogue dedicatory inscriptions, though the earliest extant inscriptions from the post-destruction era date to the fourth century. As among Christians, each synagogue donor contributed a portion of the synagogue and its decoration, with no individual donating the entire building. Through this type of benefaction the donor received prestige within the community, and presumably in the eyes of God as well. While the phrase "holy place" is quite rare in Christian inscriptions, other attributions of sanctity—"holy monastery," "holy church," and the like—are common.

The term "holy place" (*atra qedisha* in Aramaic, *hagios topos* in Greek) appears for the first time in two inscriptions from the fourth-century mosaic pavement of Hammath Tiberias B.[36] The inscriptions, in Aramaic and Greek, are quite similar. The Aramaic text reads:

> May peace be unto all those who gave charity in this holy place, and who in the future will give charity. May he have His blessing[37] Amen, Amen, Selah, it is fitting,[38] Amen.[39]

And the Greek text (Fig. 2.11) :

> Remembered for good and for blessing Profuturos the elder who made this stoa of the holy place. Blessing upon him, Amen, Shalom.[40]

Fig. 2.11. Mosaic inscription in Greek from Hammath Tiberias B. This inscription marks the benefaction of Profutros to the "holy place."

How did the congregation at Ḥammath Tiberias decorate its "holy place"? Located on a bluff overlooking the Sea of Galilee, the building was constructed as a basilica on a north-south axis with a broad side aisle in which the Aramaic inscription was laid. The ornate floor is reminiscent of high-quality mosaic pavements from Antioch on the Orontes, to the north in Syria. While only the floor and a few architectural features are extant, the excavator has suggested a plausible reconstruction of this basilica (see Fig. 5.3). The central nave was laid with a panel containing a dedicatory inscription flanked by rampant lions on its northern end. In the center of the room is a zodiac wheel. Opposite the platform upon which the Torah Shrine undoubtedly stood is the image of a shrine flanked by two menorahs and some smaller ritual objects.

According to the excavator's reconstruction, the Shrine stood on the southern, Jerusalem-facing, side of the building and looked much like that illustrated in the mosaic. Christians, too, made images of the sacred precinct of the church on church pavements (Plate IX). Excavation has shown that orientation of Torah Shrines on the Jerusalem wall of

Plate IX. Mosaic pavement with image of a Shrine from a church in the eastern Mediterranean (Cat. 76).

synagogues was virtually the rule in the Land of Israel. This factor, together with the presence of the menorahs, clearly reflects an attempt to associate the synagogue with the Temple. Images of Torah Shrines appear on mosaics and in other media at a number of sites. The upper part of a stone aedicula uncovered at Nabratein in the Upper Galilee bears a close resemblance to the image of a Torah Shrine (see Plate XXXII) in the Beth Alpha mosaic. Large seven-branched menorahs (see Plate XXV) were uncovered in another synagogue in Ḥammath Tiberias, at Maon (Fig. 2.12) in Judea, and elsewhere. Flanking menorahs within the former were reminiscent of the Temple and served to illuminate the synagogue hall. Christian altars were also lighted with many lamps that, as in the synagogue, focused attention on the bema. In an image of a menorah from Naaran (sixth century, near Jericho) the desire to provide additional light is even clearer. An additional lamp is shown hanging from each side of each of the two menorahs.

Fig. 2.12. Reconstructed menorah from the synagogue at Maon (Judea).

The zodiac wheel at Ḥammath Tiberias B is reminiscent of the months of the Jewish year, which begin with each new moon. This relationship was made in a recently discovered synagogue mosaic from Sepphoris, where both the names of the months and the zodiac signs are listed in each segment of the wheel (Plate VIII). The image of the sun god Helios at the center of the composition is harder to explain. It appears, however, that Jews and Christians alike used this image to symbolize the sun. The image of this pagan god (no matter how neutered or "reinterpreted") would certainly have been disliked by the Rabbis. This dislike might account for the pillar, rather than Helios, that sits in the chariot in the synagogue mosaic from Sepphoris.

Ḥammath Tiberias seems not to have been controlled by the Sages. Twice in the dedicatory inscriptions we hear of "Severos, student of the illustrious patriarch," who apparently had considerable power. The relationship between Severos and the patriarch is particularly illuminating. During the first two centuries after the destruction of the Temple a Rabbinic family that traced its lineage to the first-century Sage Hillel became the leaders of the Tannaitic community. By the late second century the leader of this dynasty, Rabbi Judah the Prince (c. 140–225), combined religious authority with political prestige acquired from the Roman authorities that was unmatched among late antique Jews. One well-known adage has it that "from the days of Moses until Rabbi [Judah] we have not found Torah and [worldly] prominence in one place (that is, in one person)."[41] By the fourth century the Rabbis differed greatly with the patriarchate, upon whom they were dependent both economically and for their social position. The patriarchate aligned itself increasingly with the wealthy urban aristocracy rather than with the Rabbinic community. Ḥammath Tiberias was a synagogue of this urban aristocracy.[42] While not "Rabbinic" in the sense that the Rabbis might have preferred, the community there articulated its "holy place" as a ritual space where Torah and Torah reading were central, where prayer was recited, and where Temple motifs were used in the decoration. Within its walls one could strive and hope, as the inscription says, for "His blessing, amen, amen selah. . . ." Prayer in synagogue inscriptions appears to have been extremely important in Palestinian synagogues. Such biblical phrases as "Amen, Selah" and "Peace unto Israel" appear in Aramaic and in Greek inscriptions at numerous sites and in extant liturgy.

Fig. 2.13. Mosaic dedicatory inscription to the "holy place" in Aramaic from the synagogue at Naaran.

The importance of the Torah within synagogues is reflected in a number of ways. Apses containing the Shrine, often enclosed by chancel screens, developed during the fifth and sixth centuries. The function of these screens is unclear, although they clearly served to demarcate the bema and the ark as a realm of Torah. At Naaran (Fig. 2.13), near Jericho, the sixth-century synagogue is called "holy place" in four inscriptions. The most expansive of these reads:

> Remembered for good everyone who donates and contributes, or will [in the future][43] give in this holy place, whether gold, silver or anything else. Amen. Their portion is in this holy place. Amen.

Three of the inscriptions at Naaran were laid near the Torah Shrine and the fourth inside the main entrance, in line with the Shrine. Located as they were, these inscriptions were most likely to be seen by the community. The cramped accumulation of inscriptions in the ark panel of the mosaic may suggest a pious desire to be near the ark, and possibly near the image of Daniel, who appears in a prayer position before the ark. Daniel's position in prayer, with hands lifted up to heaven, was common in the ancient world. He appears in this "orans" position in an image from En Samsam in the Golan, and perhaps in the Susiya synagogue mosaic in Judea. The fact that the biblical ancestor is illustrated praying in the synagogue before the ark on the Jerusalem side of the building is significant, emphasizing the importance of prayer there. His position is also important, since we have no images of late antique Jews per se praying. It is quite likely that the image of Daniel parallels a prayer stance that was taken up by Jews in late antique Palestine within their synagogues.

The image of Daniel is but one biblical scene that appears in synagogue art from the Land of Israel. The Binding of Isaac appears at Beth Alpha, Noah's Ark at Gerasa, and David Playing His Harp at Gaza. Each of these images parallels themes common to Jewish liturgical poetry from late antiquity. These scenes are also well known in contemporary Christian art.

Most of the archaeological sources for synagogues in the Land of Israel are either floor pavements or large architectural members. Few liturgical appurtenances are extant. One of the most important of these is a lamp found near Kefar Maḥer, a village 5 kilometers east of Acre. (It is now in the Musée de Mariemont in Belgium. This is the first time the piece has been exhibited outside Belgium.) This fifth–sixth-century bronze polycandelon (Fig. 2.14) bears a long dedicatory inscription in Aramaic to the "holy place" of Kefar Ḥananyah:

> This polycandelon [*kelilah*] . . . to the holy place of Kefar Ḥananyah. . . . May they be remembered for good. Ame[n] selah, shalom, ptp t.[44]

Kefar Ḥananyah is a village on the border of the Upper and Lower Galilee. Dedicatory inscriptions on church lamps such as this were common.[45] "Amen, selah, shalom" is reminiscent of floor inscriptions, liturgical texts, and amulet formulae. The two menorahs that appear on the lamp, each flanked by a *lulav* and a shofar, are also common in ancient Jewish art. Jews used the menorah as a symbol for their minority group, much as Christians used the sign of the cross during this period. It was a reminder of the Temple and of actual synagogue furnishings. An unusual feature of the inscription is the formula "ptp t."[46]

Fig. 2.14. Polycandelon from the synagogue at Kefar Ḥananyah (Cat. 51).

Joseph Naveh suggests that it has a parallel in an amulet from the Cairo Genizah that also says "ptp t." If he is right, the lamp (or perhaps the synagogue) seems to be imbued with magic, or perhaps to need protection from it.

Archaeological and literary sources, read together, present a clear portrait of synagogues in the Land of Israel during the late Roman and Byzantine periods. These community centers were ascribed by Jewish communities throughout the Land of Israel with sanctity. The Torah scroll and Temple imagery are ultimately the sources of this sanctity. The sanctity of the synagogue, the Sacred Realm, is an expression of the centrality of this institution in Jewish life during this period.

DIASPORA SYNAGOGUES, c. 200–700 c.e.

A Palestinian traveler arriving at one of the Diaspora communities of the Mediterranean basin or perhaps of Babylonia was likely to find numerous powerful and often wealthy communities. Synagogues speckled the landscape, each building reflecting both the uniqueness of the community and those elements that bound all Jews together. Archaeological and literary sources suggest that synagogues served local communities from Spain in the west to North Africa, Bulgaria, and the lands of the Fertile Crescent to the east. Synagogues took various architectural forms during this period, ranging from large basilicas to remodeled houses. The evidence is amazingly uniform in its portrayal of synagogues as places of scriptural study. Temple motifs were very important in the articulation of these ritual spaces, which served as the focal points for often wealthy and acculturated Diaspora communities.

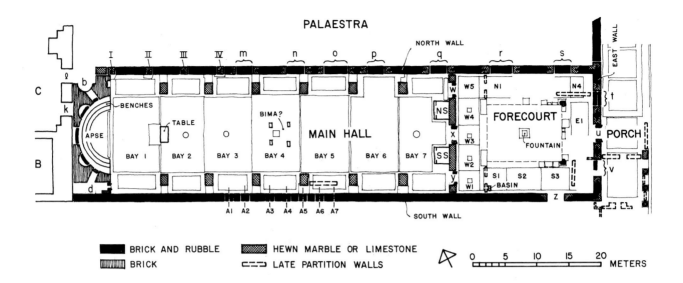

Fig. 2.15. Plan of the
synagogue at Sardis.

Synagogues often reflected the power of a local community. The synagogues of Philo's
Alexandria during the first century are one example. The massive fourth-sixth-century
synagogue of Sardis (Fig. 2.15) in Turkey (Asia Minor) is another. This was no doubt the
case in Antioch on the Orontes as well, where Jews had been a powerful minority since
Seleucid times. In fact, the synagogue was so powerful in fourth-century Antioch that it
drew the vitriolic attention of a major leader of the Christian community, John
Chrysostom, who apparently perceived the Jews as a danger to the spiritual well-being of
his flock. In a series of eight sermons, this Church Father attempted to dissuade his followers from attending the synagogue during the Jewish New Year (Rosh ha-Shanah), the
Day of Atonement (Yom Kippur), and the Festival of Tabernacles (Sukkot) and from par-
ticipating in other Jewish religious rituals.

John polemicized against those who considered synagogues "holy places" (*topon
hagion*).[47] His diatribe is particularly enlightening since it reflects accurately what we know
of synagogues both from the Rabbinic Sages and from archaeological evidence from the
Diaspora. His congregation thought the synagogue to be holy for two reasons: because the
sacred scrolls that were kept and stored there and because synagogues bore the sanctity of
the Jerusalem Temple. So we read:

> But since there are some of you who consider the synagogue to be a holy place, we must say
> a few things to them as well.
> Why do you revere this place when you should disdain it, despise it and avoid it?
> "The Law and the books of the Prophets can be found there," you say.
> What of it?
> You say, "Is it not the case that the books make the place holy?"
> Certainly not! This is the reason I especially hate the synagogue and avoid it, that they have
> the prophets but do not believe in them, that they read these books but do not accept their
> testimonies. . . .[48]

In fact, synagogue inscriptions from throughout the Mediterranean basin call the syna-
gogue a "holy place." The earliest, in Greek, which dates to 280–81 C.E., was erected in
Stobi in Macedonia. Others have been discovered in Philadelphia and Side in Asia Minor.
In Philadelphia in Lydia we hear of the "most holy synagogue of the Hebrews," and in

Side in Pamphylia the synagogue is called "the most holy first synagogue." A synagogue at Naro (Ḥamman Lif) in Tunisia is called a "holy synagogue" in a Latin inscription.

The presence of biblical scrolls within the Jewish holy place was, as John knew, an important feature of the synagogue. Torah Shrines were important elements of Diaspora synagogue architecture from at least the third century. The Torah Shrine of the synagogue at Dura Europos, dated 244–45 C.E., is the keystone of this synagogue, with its beautifully preserved wall paintings that retell Jewish sacred history visually. No doubt similar programmatic painting existed in other synagogues elsewhere in the ancient world. Images of Torah Shrines often appear in Jewish funerary art in ancient Rome, where the doors of the Shrine are often open to reveal the sacred scrolls. A Torah Shrine that originally must have looked much like these images has been excavated in the synagogue of Ostia, the port of Rome.

Particularly important for interpreting John's remarks is the ancient synagogue of Sardis, northwest of Antioch (Asia Minor). During the second half of the third century a monumental building in the gymnasium complex at Sardis had been handed over to the Jewish community to serve as a synagogue—the largest synagogue to be preserved from antiquity. A model of the structure as it might have looked during the fourth century was made especially for this exhibition by the Sardis Expedition team (see Fig. 3.15). The present interior plan of the building dates to the fourth century,[49] when Jewish renovators installed two shrines on the eastern (Jerusalem) end of the building. An inscription found

Fig. 2.16. Ashlar with menorah from Nicaea, modern Iznik.

within the hall refers to the *nomophylakion*, "the place that protects the Torah." A second inscription demands pious behavior toward the Scriptures: "Find, open, read, observe."[50] One scholar argues that this inscription was originally attached to the Torah Shrine.

In fact, the image of a Torah Shrine with its doors open, showing scrolls within, was also uncovered at Sardis. A reproduction of this piece is exhibited in "Sacred Realm" (Cat. 23). A mosaic inscription laid next to a large bema in the center of the hall[51] mentions "a priest [*heuron*] and *sophodidaskalos*" (teacher of wisdom, or wise teacher).[52] This synagogue was a place where the teaching of wisdom, undoubtedly Scripture, took place.

Suprisingly, only one biblical verse appears in an inscription stemming from a Diaspora synagogue. Psalm 136:25 is inscribed on a large ashlar discovered in Iznik in ancient Nicaea in Asia Minor (Fig. 2.16). The verse "He who gives bread to all flesh, for his mercy endures forever" was an important element of the liturgy among the Rabbis in Palestine and Babylonia. It is possible that its appearance here is also liturgical. If so, it is the only archaeological confirmation of John's claim that Jews pronounced a liturgy in Diaspora synagogues at this time.[53]

The associations his parishioners made between synagogues and the Jerusalem Temple were particularly upsetting to John. New Testament texts reflect great respect for and interaction with the Jerusalem Temple by Jesus and his early followers. Christians, beginning with the third-cen-

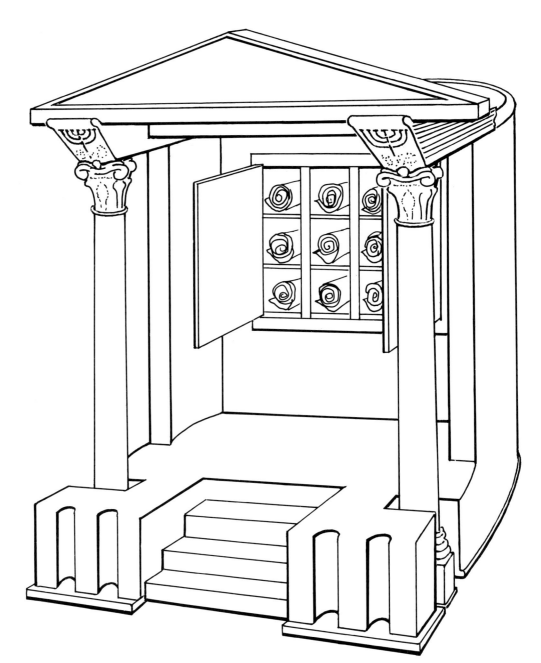

Fig. 2.17. Drawing of the fourth-century Ostia synagogue Torah Shrine, reconstruction.

tury father Eusebius of Caesarea in Palestine, had expressed the sanctity of church buildings through resort to Jerusalem Temple imagery.[54] Unlike pagan temples, which were easily disdained, the Jerusalem Temple was an integral part of Christian tradition. Some within John's congregation transferred this attachment to the Temple to synagogues, and John polemicized against their error, asking:

> What sort of ark [*kibotos*] is it that the Jews now have, where we find no propitiatory, no tablets of the law, no Holy of Holies, no veil, no high priests, no incense, no holocaust, no sacrifice, none of the things that made the ark of old holy and august?

The relationship that John attacks between the synagogue Torah Shrine and the Ark of the Covenant might have been readily understood by Palestinian Jews, who themselves used Temple imagery without fully equating the Torah ark and the Temple ark. Diaspora Jews might have "pleaded guilty" to this notion as well. A third-century Torah Shrine (Fig. 2.17) in the synagogue of Ostia was called a *kiebotos* in its dedicatory inscription (Fig. 2.18)—the same term John used. At Dura the Torah Shrine is called a *beit arona* (literally, house of the ark) in one of its dedicatory inscriptions. As in the Land of Israel, *arona* (ark) here hearkens to the biblical Ark of the Covenant. This relationship is reinforced through the image of the Temple on the upper facade of the shrine and through images of the Ark of the Covenant throughout the wall paintings that look like Torah Shrines. Further substantiating John's testimony is the title of "the priest [*heuron*] and teacher of wisdom" from Sardis. A priest named Samuel was instrumental in refurbishing the Dura synagogue in 244–45 C.E.. While there were, as John suggests, "no high priests" in ancient synagogues, Jews who traced their lineage back to the Temple priesthood did frequent synagogues.

Fig. 2.18. Dedicatory inscription of the earlier Torah Shrine from the synagogue at Ostia (Cat. 15).

A relationship between synagogues and the Temple that John does not mention is the presence of seven-branched lamps, reminiscent of the Temple menorah. Inscriptions mark the donation of a seven-branched menorah (*heptamyxion* in Greek) at both Side and Sardis. In fact, a large fragment of a menorah (Plate X) that was once a meter in breadth was discovered in the Sardis synagogue. Other images of menorahs (Fig. 2.19) from throughout the empire suggest that synagogues were often illuminated and decorated with seven-branched lamp stands.

John considered synagogues to be places of magic. He noted with disdain how sick Christians turned to Jews to be healed by "charms, incantations and amulets." In truth, the accusation of magic is a kind of name calling, part of John's "rhetoric of abuse."[56] Nevertheless, Jews during late antiquity were known for their magical prowess. Terminology drawn from Jewish contexts even became part of the repetoire of interna-

Plate X. Inscribed marble menorah from the synagogue at Sardis; (a) obverse, (b) reverse.

(a)

(b)

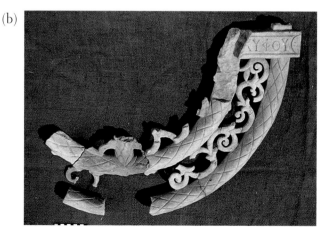

(a)

(b)

(c)

Fig. 2.19. (a) Menorah plaque from Priene (Cat. 25). (b) Plaque with a menorah from the synagogue at Sardis (Cat. 24). (c) Plaque with aedicula with a menorah from Asia Minor (Cat. 26).

tional magical lore. We have seen that amulets were known within Palestinian synagogues during late antiquity. This was true in the Diaspora as well, at least in one synagogue. Two plaques (Fig. 2.20) showing magical eyes decorated the synagogue's ceiling. E.R. Goodenough describes the iconography of one of these tiles:

> [The eye is] being attacked by snakes and three daggers, above which du Mesnil was certain that he could make out the letters IAO. A beetle or scorpion advances to attack the eye from below, while lines down from the eye apparently indicate two streams of tears.[57]

Goodenough suggests that "labeled *Iao*, it certainly is not itself the 'evil eye,' but a good eye, suffering and hence potent against the evil eye." The synagogue at Dura Europos seems to have been a place of magical power.

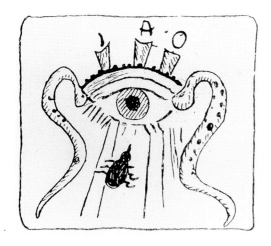

Fig. 2.20. Drawings of inscribed "evil eye" tiles from the synagogue at Dura Europos, c. 244–45 C.E.

More startling are remains of human "finger" bones that were deposited under the door sill of the synagogue's main door and its right door—its only entrances.[58] Such foundation deposits were also discovered in pagan structures at the site. The synagogue was treated by its community as a kind of Jewish temple. This discovery, which has generally been ignored or downplayed by scholars, is striking in light of biblical purity prohibitions against contact with the dead. According to these laws, which were scrupulously observed by the ancient Rabbis in Palestine and Babylonia, barred priests like Samuel the synagogue leader would have been forbidden from entering the building! Clearly, a notion of sanctity that would have been foreign to the ancient Rabbis is at play here. Though there is a great similarity between the Dura synagogue's wall paintings and Rabbinic tradition, the Jews of Dura lived a religious lifestyle that was not synonymous with that of the Rabbis.

To conclude, the image of synagogues portrayed in the polemics of John Chrysostom accurately reflects the nature of the institution during his time. Synagogues in the Greek- and Latin-speaking Diaspora were often "holy places" where Scripture was read and Temple imagery employed. At least some were places of prayer where magic was carried out. The bones discovered at Dura remind us, however, how little is known about these synagogues and their communities. While the remains and the polemics bear striking similarities, the particulars of each community, and its distinctive religious approach, are virtually unknown to us.

THE SANCTITY OF BABYLONIAN SYNAGOGUES

The largest and most powerful Diaspora community during late antiquity resided between the Tigris and Euphrates rivers in a land Jews called Babylonia and we today call Iraq. The origins of this community are traceable to the destruction of the Jerusalem Temple by Nebuchadnezer in 586 B.C.E., when Judeans were taken into the Babylonian Captivity. With the ending of this forced exile by Cyrus in 538 B.C.E., a small number of stalwarts returned to their homeland and rebuilt the Temple. Most, however, remained to build a Jewry that continued to thrive until the 1950s. No archaeological evidence for the history of the synagogue has yet been unearthed in Iraq, and our knowledge of synagogues in Babylonia, which begins during the third century C.E., is dependent almost entirely upon sources preserved in the Babylonia Talmud. Late antique Babylonian synagogues are represented in this exhibition by early manuscript and printed editions of the Babylonian Talmud and are our only link to this ancient and important Jewish community.

During the third to fifth century most Babylonian synagogues seem to have been very much like those that existed in the Land of Israel. They were places where Jews came together to study Scripture and to pray. Some synagogues, for example, Hutsal and Shaf ve-Yativ in Nehardea, seem to have had a more central position in the religious lives of Babylonian Jews than did any of their Palestinian counterparts.[59] It was said that the Divine Presence could be encountered in these synagogues with greater intensity than anywhere else in the world.

These synagogues are presented in the Babylonian Talmud, Megillah 28a–29a, a text with a polemical intention. It is part of a continuing rivalry between the Palestinian and Babylonian Rabbis for hegemony within the Jewish world during late antiquity. The first shot in this discussion is made by a Palestinian Sage, Rabbi Assi, who claims that the sanctity of "synagogues in Babylonia is contingent" upon their continued use.[60] This is in contradistinction to Palestinian synagogues that are destroyed against the will of their community, whose "sanctity stands" even when destroyed (Mishnah Megillah 3:3). The Babylonian retort opens with a claim that the divine presence is no longer in the Land of Israel at all. It has gone to Babylonia:

> It has been taught: Rabbi Simeon son of Yoḥai said:
> "Come and see how beloved are Israel in the sight of God; in that in every place to which they were exiled the *Shekhinah* (Divine Presence) went with them. They were exiled to Egypt, the *Shekhinah* went with them, as it says: Did I reveal myself to the house of your father in Egypt (1 Sam. 2:27).
> They were exiled to Babylonia, the *Shekhinah* went with them, as it says: For your sake I was sent to Babylon (Isa. 43:14)."
> It does not say "He will cause to return," but "He will return."
> This teaches that the Holy One, Blessed be He, will return from the exile.

The anonymous voice of the Talmud then asks: In Babylonia, where is the Divine Presence?

> In Babylon where is it?
> Rav said: In the synagogue of Hutsal.
> Samuel said: In the synagogue of Shaf ve-Yativ in Nehardea. . . .

Having some difficulty with the idea of a movable Divine Presence, the anonymous voice explains "[Both] here and there? Rather, it is sometimes in one, and sometimes in the other."[61] The text continues with stories of Rabbinic holy men and their experiences within the Divine at Shaf ve-Yativ:

> The father of Samuel and Levi were sitting in the synagogue of Shaf ve-Yativ in Nehardea.
> The *Shekhinah* came, they heard the tumult and they rose and left.
> Rav Sheshet [who was blind] was once sitting in the synagogue of Shaf ve-Yativ and the *Shekhinah* came.
> He did not leave, and the ministering angels came and threatened him.
> He turned to Him and said: Sovereign of the Universe, if one is afflicted and one is not afflicted, who gives way to whom? God thereupon said to them: leave him.[62]

The pericope continues with a medley of traditions on the significance of synagogues in Babylonia:

> "I have been to them a small sanctuary" (Ez. 11:16).
> Rabbi Samuel son of Isaac said: This refers to the synagogues and study houses [which are in Babylonia]. . . .

> Rava expounded: "Why is it written: 'Lord you were a habitation [*ma'on*] for us' (Ps. 90:1)?
> Rava said: At first I would study at home and pray in the synagogue. Once I heard this which David said: "Lord, I love the habitation [*ma'on*] of your house" (Ps. 26:8). I have studied only in the synagogue.
> Rabbi Eleazar son of Qappar said: In the [messianic] future the synagogues in Babylonia will be set in place in the Land of Israel. . . .

With this, the Babylonian Talmud has trounced to its own satisfaction Rabbi Assi's claim of Palestinian superiority. Synagogues in Babylonia are not less holy than their Palestinian counterparts, and two synagogues are places of special contact with the Divine. In fact, one who wants to come close to God must come to Babylonia. He is no longer "housed" in Palestine.

This special status of Shaf ve-Yativ within Babylonian Jewry during the eighth and ninth centuries is expressed in a tradition preserved in the Epistle of Rav Sherira Gaon (d. 998) that reflects upon the origins of Babylonian Jewry during the Babylonian Captivity:

> Know that at first, when Israel was exiled in the exile of Jehoiakim and the "craftsmen and the smiths (2 Kings 24:16)" and a few prophets among them, they came to Nehardea. Jehoiakim the king of Judea and his company built the synagogue and built its foundations with stones and dust that they brought with them from the Temple to fulfill that which is said (in Psalms 102:15): "For your servants hold her stones dear, and cherish her very dust." They called that synagogue "Shaf ve-Yativ in Nehardea." That is to say that the Temple traveled [from Jerusalem] and rested here.

Babylonian Jews came to see this synagogue as the connecting thread between their lives in Babylonia and the ancient Temple. A different sort of synagogue than any we have seen in this study, it is literally built of materials brought from the Temple and in some symbolic way has become the Temple. This mythological depiction reflects a very nonmythological reality. The synagogue of Shaf ve-Yativ is an incarnation of the power and confidence of the Babylonian Diaspora as it left antiquity behind and entered the Middle Ages.

CONCLUSION

With the close of antiquity the synagogue was the undisputed Sacred Realm for Jews throughout the Greco-Roman world. Its democratic focus upon community as the locus of holiness had helped Judaism not only to weather the destruction of the Temple but to flourish. The focus within the synagogue was the sacred scroll, and the application of Temple metaphors to synagogues was of central importance in their sacralization. Through the recitation of elaborate prayers the worshipper could transcend this world and, for a moment, stand in communion with the Divine. We have interwoven the various threads representing geographically and chronologically distant Jewish communities during antiquity to create a picture of the development of this institution. These threads came together in a fine tapestry of numerous colors and textures as antiquity came to a close. S.D. Goitein, the great scholar of the Cairo Genizah, describes popular attitudes toward the synagogue and Scripture in early medieval (Fatamid) Egypt. In his description we can sense the success of the ancient synagogue and its legacy to later generations:

> For the popular religion . . . the synagogue was a house of meeting both with God and with one's fellowmen. When the holy ark was opened and the Torah scrolls were exposed to the eyes of the worshipper, he felt himself transported to the presence of God. . . .[63]

Diaspora Synagogues

New Light from Inscriptions and Papyri

LOUIS H. FELDMAN
Yeshiva University

If an account of the religious life of Diaspora Jews of approximately two thousand years ago had been written two centuries or even one century ago, it would have been extremely brief, since so little was known. We would have had many questions: When and where did synagogues first arise? Were there synagogues even at the time when the Temple in Jerusalem was standing? What names were given to synagogues? What did synagogues look like? How big were they? Were synagogues primarily for prayer or for other purposes? How were synagogues organized? Where did ancient Jews get their funds for building and maintenance? Did synagogues have rabbis? Did they have officers and boards of directors? What role, if any, did women play in these synagogues?

Even that which was known through, notably, the writings of Philo of Alexandria, would really tell us very little about the religious life of ordinary Jews. Philo was an extremely wealthy aristocrat, and inasmuch as much of his work is apologetic in nature, its objectivity may consequently be challenged. What has changed the picture dramatically is the discovery, most of it within the past century, of many hundreds of inscriptions and documents written on papyrus, often, to be sure, in tantalizingly fragmentary form. In this chapter I shall present some of the more important discoveries, as well as current debates on the nature of the early Diaspora synagogues.

The great scholar of Jewish history Salo Baron was of the opinion that there were between four and eight million Jews outside the Land of Israel in the first century.[1] Were this the case, we should expect evidence of many hundreds and even thousands of synagogues. This is especially so since there is every reason to believe that the great majority of Jews were observant of Judaism and since the average synagogue was very small. An indication of the large number of synagogues in one community may be found in Philo's statement (*Embassy to Gaius* 20.132) in his account of the desecration of synagogues in Alexandria in the year 38 C.E. This great philosopher and communal leader notes that synagogues were numerous in each of the five sections of the city.

Though new discoveries of synagogues are constantly coming to light, more than sixty-six Diaspora prayer groups or synagogues from antiquity are known from epigraphic and other archaeological evidence. These range from the Black Sea region (Sebastopol, Olbia, Gorgippia, Panticapaeum, Phanagoria) to Syria (Aleppo, Daphne, Antioch, Apamea, Emesa, Dmer, Niha, Dura Europos, Tafas), Lebanon (Beirut, Sidon), Asia Minor (Sardis, Hyllarima, Philadelphia, Miletus, Priene, Acmonia, Amastris, Teos, Pergamum, Phocaea, Smyrna, Myndos, Tralles, Nysa, Side, Ephesus), Greece (Aegina, Corinth, Mantineia, Magne, Philippopolis, Thessaloniki, Delos), Crete (Kastelli Kissamou), Cyprus (Golgoi, Lapethos, Constantia-Salamine), former Yugoslavia (Mursa, Stobi), Hungary (Oescus, Intercisa), Italy (Rome, Ostia, Capua, Venosa, Bova Marina), Sicily (Syracuse), Spain (Eleche, Tarraco), Egypt (Alexandria, Schedia, Xenephyris, Nitriai, Athribis, Crocodilopolis-Arsinoe, Alexandrou-Nesos), Libya (Berenice, Leptis Magna), and Tunisia (Ḥamman Lif) dating from the third century B.C.E. (in Egypt) to the year 500, mentioned in inscriptions and papyri, most of which are in Greek. At Sardis, for example, where we have found over seventy inscriptions from the synagogue, there are only two legible inscriptions in Hebrew, one reading "Shalom" and the other reading "Verus," presumably a reference to the Roman Emperor who ruled jointly with Marcus Aurelius from 161 to 169. In addition, there are a few fragments and one graffito from outside the synagogue.[2]

The great value of inscriptions[3] and documents written on papyri as historical documents is that they are usually contemporary with the people and the events to which they refer. They reflect a broader spectrum of the population—ranging from the poorest in the Roman catacomb inscriptions to the wealthiest donors—than is to be found in literary texts, though, as we shall see, those pertaining to the synagogues generally reflect the wealthier class, which could afford to build or improve the structures and who presumably held the offices in them.

A number of difficulties must be stressed in dealing with this evidence, valuable as it is. It is unfortunate that the types of information that can be derived from inscriptions generally include only the names of the synagogue donors and the details of synagogue administration. They give us precious little information about the beliefs and practices of the Jews who frequented the synagogues. In fact, the average inscription referring to a synagogue contains no more than between ten and twenty words. Most are fragmentary, and reconstructions are often uncertain. Errors in the texts abound, since they were often chiseled by the less learned and since they are generally copies of a first draft on wood or papyrus.[4] Seldom is there reference to an actual date, and sometimes the possible range of dates is several centuries. This is especially true when inscriptions are discovered away from their original site. Frequently there is a real question whether the inscription is that of a Jewish or non-Jewish group, whether pagan or Christian. The names of the people involved are not necessarily conclusive, inasmuch as the Jews very often had non-Jewish names. In particular, it is especially hard to tell whether the donor of a synagogue is a Jew or a Gentile. Moreover, the fact that an inscription or a papyrus refers to people who held honorary positions in synagogues does not necessarily imply that there was an organized Jewish community with a building called a synagogue.[5] Finally, the picture is skewed because an unusually high percentage of the inscriptions, more than a third, come from a single location, Rome, which had perhaps 1 percent of the total Jewish population of the Diaspora.

TERMINOLOGY

The term that appears most commonly in Second Temple period sources in reference to synagogue buildings is *proseuche* (Fig. 3.1).[6] Strictly speaking, a distinction should be made between the term *proseuche* (Latin *proseucha*), literally "prayer," which refers to a building associated with a Jewish community, and the term *synagoge*, which refers to a group of Jews who make communal decisions. It appears that Jews chose this rather neutral term over the many other terms for a local temple that were available to them in the Greco-Roman world so as to avoid any suggestion that their local institutions were rivals for the Jerusalem Temple. Indeed, *proseuche* is the standard term for a place of prayer in Philo (who uses it eighteen times in contrast to *synagoge*, which refers to the gathered Jewish community), Josephus (*Life* 54), the New Testament (Acts 16:13 and 16), and the Roman satirist Juvenal (3.296). This distinction is particularly clear in a papyrus (*CPJ* 138.1) from Egypt in the first century B.C.E., which speaks of a synagogue (*synagoge*) session in a *proseuche*: "At the session [*synagoges*] held in the *proseuche*."

The first use of the word *synagoge* in an inscription in the sense of an assembly of people occurs in Egypt in the second century B.C.E. in a non-Jewish reference. Apparently the term *synagoge* began to supersede the term *proseuche* in Palestine in the first century and thereafter spreads to the Diaspora.[7] That the term "synagogue" refers to a group of Jews is also clear from an inscription from Berenice in Cyrenaica dating from the year 56 in which we read that "it appeared" to the synagogue of the Jews in Berenice to inscribe on a

Fig. 3.1. Dedicatory inscription for a *proseuche* (prayer hall) in Egypt (Cat. 1).

stele the names of those who had contributed to the restoration of the synagogue (*synagoge*, here, however, also referring to the building).[8] In an inscription from Phocaea in Asia Minor dating from the third century we are told that the synagogue (*synagoge*) of the Jews, presumably the corporate body, bestowed a golden crown and privileges upon the donor. In Rome we have found references to sixteen synagogues in the more than five hundred inscriptions that have thus far been discovered in the Jewish catacombs, but these sepulchral inscriptions, with a solitary exception, refer to groups of Jews rather than to buildings. Moreover, the term *proseuche* is also sometimes used for pagan prayer groups, and hence we cannot always be sure that we are dealing with a Jewish group.

The *proseuche* itself, to judge from an inscription from Nitriai in Egypt dating from the second century B.C.E., consisted of more than one hall and included several outbuildings, so that we hear, for example, in an inscription (*CIJ* 2.1444) from Atribis in Egypt, dating from the first or second century B.C.E., of a portico built by a certain Hermes, his wife, and children and attached to the *proseuche*:

> In honor of King Ptolemy and Queen Cleopatra and their children, Hermias and his wife Philotera and their children [gave] this place for sitting [portico] for the *proseuche*.

Another word used for a synagogue, to judge from a papyrus dated 113 C.E. from Arsinoe-Crocodilopolis in Egypt, is *eucheion*, that is, a prayer house. This *eucheion* was apparently more informal and smaller than the town's synagogue (*proseuche*), which is mentioned in the same papyrus. When it comes to the payment for water mentioned in the papyrus, it is the rulers of the *proseuche* who are held responsible, though the charge for both buildings is the same.

In an interesting inscription from Acmonia in Asia Minor, dating from the first century, we read of a structure built by a Roman woman and restored by the Jewish dignitaries of the town:

> This building [*oikon*] was erected by Julia Severa; Publius Tyrronius Cladus, the head for life of the synagogue, and Lucius, son of Lucius, head of the synagogue, and Publius Zotikos, *archon*, restored it with their own funds and with money which had been deposited, and they donated the [painted] murals for the walls and the ceiling, and they reinforced the windows and made all the rest of the ornamentation, and the synagogue honored them with a gilded shield on account of their virtuous disposition, goodwill and zeal for the synagogue.

Here, as in Phocaea in Asia Minor, in an inscription dating from perhaps the third century, the word used for the synagogue built by the donor is *oikos*, that is, "house." Similarly, in the case of the Samaritan synagogue on the island of Delos, the original building was apparently an ordinary house built in the second century B.C.E., which was only converted into a synagogue in the first century B.C.E.

BENEFACTORS OF SYNAGOGUES

Like modern-day plaques, so ancient inscriptions indicate the benefactions of donors to synagogues. In most cases, as we would expect, there are a number of benefactors, but the inscriptions from the Diaspora contain two examples from Egypt, one dating from 37 B.C.E. and the other from the first or early second century C.E., where we hear of a *proseuche* constructed by a single individual or by a family; an example from Aegina in Greece dating from the fourth century; and four instances where synagogues were constructed by women donors in Asia Minor. Indeed, of the fifty-three donor inscriptions from Asia Minor no fewer than nineteen, or 36 percent, identify the donors as women.

The remarkable inscription from Aphrodisias in Asia Minor, dating, it is thought, from the third century, lists some 130 donors of what appears to have been a soup kitchen. We cannot detect from the inscription, which is the longest Jewish inscription discovered outside Israel, whether it was in the synagogue or in another communal facility. Fifty-four of the donors are listed as *theosebeis*, that is, "God-fearers," people who adopted one or more Jewish practices without actually converting to Judaism.[9]

At Sardis the donors included three goldsmiths, as well as merchants in glass, paints, and dyes. An inscription mentions a "fountain of the synagogue," perhaps where the priests washed before blessing the congregation. The main hall of the synagogue itself is clearly the largest synagogue that we have thus far found from antiquity and could accommodate over a thousand people. That the building is a synagogue is confirmed by the discovery of fragments of Hebrew inscriptions as well as a marble plaque (Fig. 3.2) picturing a menorah, lulav, shofar, and two spirals, which have been interpreted to be Torah scrolls. A marble table, flanked by pairs of lions (Fig. 3.3) and weighing over two tons, has been found; it presumably was used for the reading of the Torah. A marble menorah bearing the name Socrates (Plate X), together with eighteen other representations of menorahs, have been found. No fewer than nine of the donors are described as members of the city council, and three are members of the Roman provincial administration.[10] Since those holding public office were required to participate in the worship of the city's gods, it is significant that sometime between 198 and 211 two of the emperors, Septimius Severus and Caracalla, explicitly imposed upon Jews only those obligations that would not conflict with their religion. Apparently the Jewish community remained strong, and relations between Jews and Christians were amicable, inasmuch as we find that the building was never converted into the church, as was the case with many other synagogues, but remained in use until it was destroyed by an attack of Persians in the year 616.

In a number of instances the individual who built, repaired, or adorned a synagogue did so in fulfillment of a vow. In fact, this form is very common in Greek inscriptions discovered in the Greek-speaking pagan cities on the Palestinian coast as well. Paintings, mosaics, masonry, pavements, fountains, menorahs, and altars, as well as whole buildings, were donated. Sometimes, as in an inscription from Berenice in Libya, we are given a list

Fig. 3.2. Plaque with a menorah discovered near one of the twin aediculae of the synagogue at Sardis.

of the eighteen donors, with the amount contributed by each. It is interesting that of the eighteen gifts there was one gift of twenty-eight drachmas, two of twenty-five drachmas each, eleven of ten drachmas each, and four of five drachmas each. Of the eleven who gave ten drachmas, it is surely significant that nine are identified as *archons*, or key officials of the synagogue. Of the four who gave five drachmas each, two are women. Four members of one family, that of a certain Dositheos, contributed a total of 35 drachmas of the total of 208 collected. Sometimes, as in an inscription from Aegina in Greece (*CIJ* 1.723), dating from the fourth century, we are told that the expense for improvements, in this case mosaics, has come from the synagogue treasury:

> Theodoros the Younger being curator, the works of mosaic were executed from the revenues of the synagogue.

At other times we are told that the work had been paid for without using the funds in the synagogue treasury. One indication of the status of a Jewish community was the number of people who contributed to the synagogue. By this standard Sardis in Asia Minor was one of the most successful and one of the richest synagogue communities.

Communities seem to have been quite independent of one another, and in only one instance, in an inscription from Apamea in Syria dating from the year 391, we find someone from another community, Antioch, contributing to the building of a synagogue:

> Under the three most honored *archisynagogi*, Eusebios, Nemeos, and Phineas, the gerousiarch Theodoros and the three most honored elders, Isakios, Saulos, and others, Ilasios, the *archisynagogos* of Antioch, made the mosaic of the entrance [of the synagogue], 150 feet; the year 703, the 7th day of Audunaios. Blessing to all.[11]

Sometimes the donors were non-Jews, as in the case of the pagans from Crete who donated money for the Samaritan synagogue on the island of Delos or of the Roman officials who contributed toward the synagogue in Berenice in Libya. One is reminded of the Roman centurion who, according to the New Testament (Luke 7:5), built a synagogue at Capernaum in Palestine. In some cases, we may suggest, these donors were "God-fearers"

Fig. 3.3. Marble table and lions in the main hall of the synagogue at Sardis.

above: Fig. 3.4. Plaque for a menorah dedicated by a "God-fearer" from the synagogue at Sardis (Cat. 22).

above right: Fig. 3.5. Dedicatory inscription mentioning a "God-fearer" from the forecourt of the synagogue at Sardis.

(Figs. 3.4 and 3.5). Indeed, we hear of two donors in third-century Sardis and another in Tralles in Asia Minor who are designated as *theosebeis*, or "God-fearers," who had fulfilled their pledges to the synagogue. Most remarkably, as we have mentioned, at Aphrodisias, we find inscribed the names of no fewer than fifty-four God-fearers, including nine town councillors. The Jewish community thus had the support of the leading administrators in the city. L. Michael White asks why pagans should have been interested in contributing to such a cause, and his persuasive answer is that they were probably engaged in trading activities with Jews or Samaritans.[12] Clearly, these God-fearers added to the wealth of Jewish communities; and we may conjecture that one major reason the Jews so bitterly resented the attraction that Paul exercised on these "sympathizers" was that they feared he would draw their gifts away from their synagogues. Paul's frequent declaration that he had accepted no gifts from his adherents may thus be understood within this context.[13]

It is noteworthy that a number of inscriptions describe the honoring of women benefactors to the synagogue. Thus, in Phocaea in Asia Minor (*CIJ* 2.738) we hear of a woman, Tation, who donated substantially to the synagogue:

> Tation, daughter of Straton, son of Empedon, having erected the assembly hall and the enclosure of the open courtyard with her own funds, gave them as a gift to the Jews. The synagogue of the Jews honored Tation, daughter of Straton, son of Empedon, with a golden crown and the privilege of sitting in the seat of honor.

The honor of a golden crown was frequently bestowed in the pagan world, as was the privilege of sitting in the front of the building, apparently when the members met for nonreligious purposes. Here clearly the term "synagogue" refers not to a building but to a group of Jews. Again, in Acmonia in Asia Minor, as we noted earlier, we have an inscription referring to the gift of a certain Julia Severa of a building to the Jewish community. Since she is known to have been a priestess in the imperial cult, it is clear that she was a non-Jew, though it is possible that she became a God-fearer. As in Aphrodisias, the reasons a non-Jew such as Julia Severa contributed property to a synagogue may have been because of social, economic, and political ties with the Jewish community.

DEDICATIONS OF SYNAGOGUES

No fewer than seven Egyptian inscriptions, dating from the third, second, and first centuries B.C.E., refer to dedications of the synagogue to the king and queen. In some cases their children are also mentioned. Similarly, an inscription found in Mursa in Pannonia in the former Yugoslavia, dating from the end of the second century, is dedicated to the safety of the emperors Lucius Septimius Severus Pertinax and Marcus Aurelius Antoninus, the Augusti, and Julia Augusta, mother of the camps. Ellis Rivkin[14] has explained these dedications as an attempt by Jews to show their loyalty to the sovereigns in view of the charge that the Jews were really loyal to their rulers in the Land of Israel. Rivkin suggests that these markers served as a substitute for the erection of statues of the emperors and for Jewish refusal to worship them as gods. The fact that the whole building was dedicated to the ruler would seem to be, in effect, an offering to the glory of the ruler. Perhaps when the synagogue inscriptions, as is so often the case in Egypt, state that they are dedicated *hyper* King Ptolemy and his Queen, we should translate the word to mean not "in honor of" but rather "in gratitude to."[15] Alternatively, we may suggest that such language may indicate that the synagogue existed by royal license.[16]

LEADERSHIP IN THE SYNAGOGUE

The organization of the synagogue often paralleled that of non-Jewish communities and reminds one of Greco-Roman collegia or guilds. With the decline of the Greek city-state and its replacement by large empires after the death of Alexander the Great in 323 B.C.E., we find smaller local social units in the Greco-Roman world whose focuses were economic (often guildlike organizations of artisans or merchants) or cultural (based on a common philosophy, such as Epicureanism) or, in a smaller number of cases, religious (such as to honor the goddesses Isis or Cybele or to celebrate mysteries).[17] Another salient fact in the inscriptions is the tremendous number of titles that refer to officials of the synagogues.

Perhaps the most striking fact about the leadership of Diaspora synagogues is that as far as we can tell the leaders were not rabbis or priests. Rather, from the outset the synagogues were led by lay people. One possible exception has been found in Sardis (Fig. 3.6), where a member of the

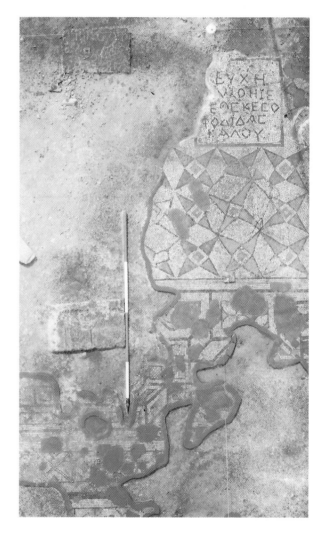

Fig. 3.6. Dedicatory inscription mentioning Samoe, priest and "wise teacher," from the synagogue at Sardis.

community is referred to as a priest and *sophodidaskalos* (literally, wise teacher). A second significant fact is that though the synagogues are scattered over a very wide geographic area, their form of organization was relatively uniform.

The key figure in the governance of the synagogue, to judge from the mention in no fewer than thirty-two inscriptions, was the *archisynagogos*, that is, the head of the synagogue. This title, however, is also found, amazingly enough, among the leaders of pagan religious groups, since meetings of various kinds, and not necessarily of Jews, might have been called in Greek *synagogai*.[18] Such an officer is also mentioned a number of times in the New Testament[19] and was presumably equivalent to the *rosh ha-knesset*, the Temple functionary cited in Tannaitic literature (Mishnah, *Yoma* 7:1, *Sotah* 7:7–8). That the *archisynagogos* was the leading figure in the governance of the synagogue is indicated by the fact that when critics (*Scriptores Historiae Augustae, Alexander Severus* 28.7) sought to satirize the Emperor Alexander Severus in the third century they called him a Syrian *archisynagogos* and a high priest, which they assumed to be the two highest positions in the Jewish scheme of governance. In geographic location the epigraphic references to the *archisynagogos* range throughout the Mediterranean world, and chronologically they cover the period from the first to the sixth century.

We do not know how the *archisynagogos* was chosen, whether through election or appointment. In no case do we find someone who served more than once in the position, and hence it seems unlikely that it was filled by annual elections. This seems to be confirmed by the fact that several were lifetime appointees. We have several instances in which the office was held by father and son and even grandson, but there is no reason to think that the son necessarily inherited the position.

Sources reflect the coexistence of several *archisynagogoi* within the same town. This may be explained by the existence of several synagogues in a given city or by the retention of the title by those who retired from the position.

Bernadette Brooten has called attention to the fact that the inscriptions refer to three women as *archisynagogai*,[20] one from Smyrna in the second or third century, one from Kastelli Kissamou in Crete in the fourth or fifth century, and one from Myndos in Caria in Asia Minor in the fourth or fifth century. The inscription (*CIJ* 2.741) from Smyrna reads:

> Rufina, a Jewess, head of the synagogue, built the tomb for her freed slaves and the slaves raised in her house. No one else has the right to bury anyone [here]. If someone should dare to, he will pay 1,500 denarii to the sacred treasury and 1,000 denarii to the Jewish people. A copy of this inscription has been placed in the [public] archives.

It has been suggested that the women *archisynagogai* received their titles from their husbands, who were *archisynagogoi*, just as there are epitaphs that speak of Jewish priests in the feminine when the meaning clearly is that they were the wives of priests. In the three inscriptions where women *archisynagogai* are mentioned, however, there is no indication of this. Moreover, Paul Trebilco has pointed out that in only three out of twenty-two cases where a husband bore a title did his wife also bear it. In addition, we find eighteen other women with titles in ancient synagogues (Fig. 3.7) throughout the Mediterranean world, notably that of *presbytera* (elder).[21] Brooten concludes from this that women were likely to have served in councils of elders in Hellenistic synagogues, and that such women may have had some share in overseeing synagogue finances and in the reading and study of the Scriptures.[22]

In the case of Rufina from Smyrna, we see that she was a wealthy woman who built a

(a)

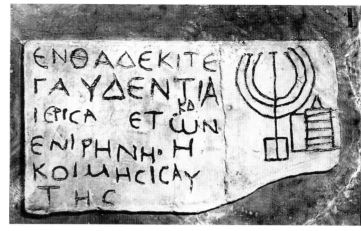

(b)

(c)

Fig. 3.7. (a) Sarcophagus fragment with inscription "Mother of the Synagogue" from the Via Anicia, Rome (Cat. 11). (b) Funerary inscription for a priestess with an image of a menorah and a Torah Shrine from the Monteverde Catacomb, Rome (Cat. 10). (c) Funerary inscription for a woman with an image of a Torah Shrine and two menorahs from the Monteverde Catacomb, Rome (Cat. 7).

tomb for her ex-slaves. The fact that she acted alone and in her own name in building the tomb would indicate administrative ability, and we can guess that she used this ability in managing synagogue affairs as well.[23] In addition, we hear in Rome, Smyrna, Elche (Spain), Samos, and Apamea (Syria) of the male *presbytes* and *presbyteros*, who are perhaps members of a *gerousia* (council) or a *dekania* (group). Women also bear this title in fourth- or fifth-century C.E. inscriptions from Crete, Ciasmus (Greece), Bizye (Thrace), Venosa (Italy, three instances), Rome, Oea (Libya), and Malta.[24]

Other scholars have questioned Brooten's thesis. James Burtchaell, for example, asks how it is likely that women who were legally forbidden to be counted as part of the quorum for prayer and to study Torah, at least according to the Rabbinic tradition, could have served as officers of the community's public affairs.[25] This question assumes, of course, that Rabbinic authority stretched to Diaspora communities.

Others have rejected Brooten's position based upon striking parallels beween the types of honorees mentioned in synagogue inscriptions and the honorees noted in inscriptions in non-Jewish inscriptions. Tessa Rajak and David Noy have pointed to the numerous civic inscriptions of non-Jews in Asia Minor where women and children appear as major donors and as holders of the highest titles on a plane with men and as prominent honorees; as they have pointed out, there is strong evidence for female land ownership in antiquity generally, among both non-Jews and Jews.[26]

It is surely significant that of the forty *archisynagogoi* mentioned in the thirty-two inscriptions, nine are presented as donors, often of substantial gifts. However, in only one of the twenty-three cases in which women are mentioned as donors do we find the woman bearing a title, and even in that case there is no indication that she received the title because of her donation. The fact that we find a boy aged three years referred to as an *archisynagogos* in an inscription from Venosa in Italy dating from the fifth century raises the question whether the attainment of this office by women and children may not have been due merely to the possession of wealth and leads one to suggest that the *archisynagogoi* were benefactors. This may explain why we find overlapping offices in the same synagogue and why the office of *archisynagogos* in some cases was held by several people at the same time.[27] The fact that we also find references to female priests in Leontopolis in Egypt in the first century B.C.E. and in Rome at an undetermined date seems to indicate that such offices were honorary or were held by women by virtue of their being married to men who held these offices. As far as we know, there are no priestesses in Jewish worship, though some scholars argue that we should not necessarily assign to the Diaspora practices that we find in Palestine as mentioned in Rabbinic texts.

The matter of women's participation in Diaspora synagogue life has indeed been hotly disputed by modern scholars, but we must admit that there is no clear evidence that any of the titles of the leaders of the synagogue were honorary; and if, as we may well suppose, there are parallels between the governing structure of synagogues and that of non-Jewish groups, there is significance in the fact that we do not know of any instance in which women were given honorary titles when it came to offices in organizations. And yet, even if we suppose that Brooten is correct in saying that we should not assume a priori that women filled only honorary roles in the synagogue, this cannot necessarily be taken to imply that they filled active roles, let alone that they were real leaders. We may note that in the early church, for example, women who are known to have given considerable amounts of money did not necessarily assume important positions within the church's hierarchy.

As to the function of the *archisynagogoi*, they are depicted in inscriptions from second- or third-century Teos in Asia Minor and from Aegina in Greece as responsible for building synagogues from their foundations. They are represented as the restorers of the synagogue building in Acmonia in Asia Minor in the first century (as we have seen in the inscription of Julia Severa) and as donors of parts of buildings, including mosaic floors in fourth-century Apamea (as we have noted) and of columns in Salamis on Cyprus in an inscription of uncertain date.

Granted that the *archisynagogos* was wealthy, he served, in effect, as a patron of the Jewish community and, with his high standing among both Jews and non-Jews, could act as a mediator for the Jewish community. He was consequently honored by the community, as, for example, in first-century Acmonia, with a golden shield (the equivalent, perhaps, of today's plaques) as a reward for virtuous disposition and good will and zeal toward the community. Indeed, perhaps most amazingly, one did not apparently have to be Jewish to be an *archisynagogos*. In Acmonia, as we have seen, a certain Publius Tyrronius Cladus, who is mentioned in that inscription as an *archisynagogos* for life, had the same tribal name, Tyrronius, as that of prominent pagans in Acmonia. The explanation may be, however, that he was a convert to Judaism or a judaizing Gentile, a God-fearer. In that same inscription we are told that the building was erected by Julia Severa, the high priestess in the imperial cult and, as far as we can tell, had not converted to Judaism.

In addition to the *archisynagogos*, to judge from the inscriptions, some communities had a *gerousia*, a council of elders or senate. To be sure, none of our inscriptions refers to such a *gerousia*, but Philo (*Against Flaccus* 74, 80) mentions such a body in Alexandria. The leader of this council, who is called a *gerousiarches*, was apparently second in importance to the *archisynagogos*. This office is mentioned in no fewer than twenty-four inscriptions, sixteen of them from Rome. The office was apparently held by older men. In three instances we are given their age at death: one was eighty, another sixty-five, and a third fifty-four. The inscriptions give us no clue as to his functions, but Harry Leon has conjectured that he had an important role in the supervision of the property of the congregation, charities, education, care of the sick, burials, and contributions to the Jerusalem Temple and later to the Patriarch in Jerusalem.[28] If so, what is the difference in the functions of the *archisynagogos* and the *gerousiarches*? Perhaps the *archisynagogos* was in charge of the worship service, whereas the *gerousiarches* was, in effect, the president of the synagogue and was in charge of its management. This approach would seem to be contradicted by the inscriptions noted earlier, which describe the *archisynagogos* as building the synagogue or improving its structure. The fact, however, that the position of *gerousiarches* is not mentioned by Philo, Josephus, the papyri, or the Talmud and that we have no statement as to the duties of this officer does raise the possibility that the position may have been merely an honorary one, perhaps like the *Ḥever Ir* mentioned in Rabbinic literature (e.g., Mishnah, *Berakhot* 4:7).

In addition to the *archisynagogos* and the *gerousiarches*, synagogues had officials known as *archontes*, corresponding perhaps to the synagogue board of directors or executive committee today. The fact that in some epitaphs we find Jews who served twice or three times as *archontes* would seem to indicate that they were elected for a term, although some inscriptions identify *archontes* who served for life. The fact, however, that we find *archontes* who had this title while they were still children would indicate that they may have inherited the position or that they were honorary members of the board of directors, so to speak. A few epitaphs (Figs. 3.8 and 3.9) speak of the deceased as the *archon*, and from this some scholars have deduced that at any given time there was only one *archon*, but more likely this implies that the deceased was the ranking member of the board.[29] As to their functions, we have a clue in the fact that in Berenice in Libya public honors were awarded to benefactors upon the vote of the *archontes*. More specifically, we find, in a papyrus (*CPJ* 432.56–57) from Arsinoe in Egypt dating from the year 113, that they paid for the synagogue's water supply.

An important official of the synagogue was the *grammateus*, the scribe or secretary, as we know from the inscriptions of twenty-six scribes. Twenty-five are known from Rome. Six are described as scribes of synagogues. Inasmuch as we do not hear of scribes who served several terms and inasmuch as we rarely hear of a *grammateus* who was chosen for any other position, we may assume that the position was not gained by election. The fact, however, that we hear of scribes aged six, seven, and twelve in Rome would seem to indicate that the office ran in families. Indeed, in one case we find someone designating his own son for the office. That it was a position of some prestige appears to be indicated by the fact that it is often found in epitaphs. The inscriptions tell us nothing about the duties of the *grammateus*, but we may guess that he was in charge of the archives of the synagogue,

left: Fig. 3.8. Funerary inscription for a synagogue leader, *archon*, with an image of a Torah Shrine from the Monteverde Catacomb, Rome (Cat. 4).

right: Fig. 3.9. Burial inscription mentioning a synagogue official, *archon*, from the Vigna Randanini Catacomb, Rome (Cat. 8).

recording its minutes, keeping membership lists up to date, writing letters to the government and other Jewish communities, and, in effect, functioning as a notary.[30]

About another position, that of *exarchon*, mentioned in two inscriptions in Rome, we can only conjecture. The fact that in one of these inscriptions the *exarchon* is said to have died at the age of twenty-eight would seem to indicate that it was not a position of supreme importance, since it seems unlikely that someone could have attained such a truly important position at such a young age. More likely the reference is to a former *archon*.

We know almost nothing about the position of *phrontistes*, mentioned in two inscriptions in Rome, one in Alexandria, and one in Side in Asia Minor. When used in non-Jewish inscriptions the term is the equivalent of the Latin *procurator* and refers to a caretaker or supervisor of some sort, presumably of the synagogue building and perhaps of the cemetery. The fact that one of the inscriptions indicates that the position was held twice by the person who is commemorated would show that it was an elective position. In the two Roman inscriptions (Fig. 3.10) the deceased is reported to have held several positions, the last being that of *phrontistes*. This seems to indicate that it was an important position. We may get a clear indication of the significance of the position from the fact that a certain Theodorus, who held the position of *archisynagogos* in Aegina, is identified as curator or overseer (*phrontiasas*) of the building of the synagogue from its foundations. Here it is clear that he did so partly from his own funds and partly with synagogue funds, as we see from this inscription and from another found nearby. We find that later his son and namesake is spoken of as *phrontistes* and that in that capacity he completed the project begun by his father. Another *phrontistes*, in Side in Asia Minor in an inscription of the fourth century, supplied the marble decoration of the synagogue.

Still another position, that of *hyperetes*, found in one inscription from Rome, would seem to be identified with the *hyperetes* mentioned in the New Testament (Luke 4:20) as the attendant in the synagogue who brought out the scroll of Scripture to be read at the service. He is usually identified with the *hazzan*; the modern equivalent would be the modern *shammash*, or sexton. Harry Leon has, with good reason, conjectured that since the term is found in only one inscription it was probably not a very exalted position.[31]

Another officer, mentioned in a papyrus dating from the year 218 B.C.E., is that of *neokoros*, who there

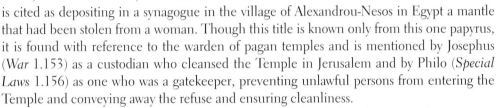

Fig. 3.10. Funerary inscription for a synagogue leader with an image of a Torah Shrine from the Monteverde Catacomb, Rome (Cat. 5).

is cited as depositing in a synagogue in the village of Alexandrou-Nesos in Egypt a mantle that had been stolen from a woman. Though this title is known only from this one papyrus, it is found with reference to the warden of pagan temples and is mentioned by Josephus (*War* 1.153) as a custodian who cleansed the Temple in Jerusalem and by Philo (*Special Laws* 1.156) as one who was a gatekeeper, preventing unlawful persons from entering the Temple and conveying away the refuse and ensuring cleanliness.

Two inscriptions refer to a *prostates*. In non-Jewish inscriptions the term refers to a president or a presiding officer, or it is the Greek equivalent of a *patronus*, a patron or champion of the interests of a group. The latter seems more likely in the Jewish inscriptions, and the reference would be to an ancient forerunner of a *shtadlan*, who represented the Jewish community before the non-Jewish authorities.[32]

Other offices are the *super orans*, mentioned in an inscription from Emerita in Spain dating from the fifth or sixth century C.E. and presumably referring to the chief cantor; and the *spondilla*, mentioned in an inscription from Intercisa in Hungary and perhaps referring to the person who played the flute on certain occasions.[33] There is likewise mention of priests (in Rome, in Corycus in Asia Minor, and in Berenice in Libya), teachers (three instances in Rome), and (strikingly, in view of the number of inscriptions and papyri) only two rabbis (in an inscription from Venosa in Italy dating from the fourth or fifth century).

Another title, found in nine inscriptions from Rome as well as in many other Jewish communities, with no Jewish roots but apparently taken over from pagan Hellenistic and especially Roman sources and particularly from mystery cults, where it denotes an initiate of an advanced degree, is that of *pater synagoges*, father of a synagogue. The corresponding honor of women is that of *mater synagoges*, mother of a synagogue, as we see in the following inscription (*CIJ* 1.523):

> Veturia Paulla F [?], consigned to her eternal home, who lived 86 years, 6 months, a proselyte of 16 years, named Sara, Mother of the Synagogues of Campus and Volumnius. In peace her sleep.

This term is used in the sense of a patron and is an honorary title that is usually assigned to someone who has given a large gift. The title mother of a synagogue, found in inscriptions from Rome, Brescia, and Venosa in Italy, was apparently conferred upon a woman in her own right, presumably because of her wealth and social prominence. The most remarkable of these was Veturia Paulla from Rome, who, as noted earlier, became a proselyte at the age of seventy and died at eighty-six and is referred to as the mother of two synagogues. In one instance, however, we find reference to a woman who is called mother of a synagogue together with her husband, who is referred to as father of a synagogue, where it may well be that the wife held the position because of being married to her husband. Whether the father and the mother of a synagogue had any duties is unknown, but we may guess that they engaged in charitable activities.

FUNCTIONS OF THE SYNAGOGUE

Ancient Diaspora synagogues were not merely houses of prayer; indeed, the most recent student of the subject, Heather McKay,[34] has contended that there is no convincing evidence—whether archaeological, epigraphic, or literary—that synagogues were used for worship services on the Sabbath. Rather, they served more as centers for the Jewish community. Apparently, there were many kinds of synagogues, with various functions, and these differed from place to place and from time to time.[35]

One function of the synagogue was apparently to serve as a meeting place for communal affairs. Thus we find reference in a papyrus dating perhaps from the second half of the first century B.C.E. to a meeting in the *proseuche* of a subgroup of synagogue members, apparently a burial society, very similar to the Jewish burial societies that we find in modern times.[36]

To judge from the synagogue in Stobi in the former Yugoslavia, in addition to the central meeting room, which is described in a fourth-century inscription as a holy place, that is, the sanctuary, we find reference to a *tetrastoon*, which apparently served as a study room and guest house, and a *triklinion*, which was a dining room:

> Claudios Tiberios Polycharmos, also named Achyrios, Father of the Congregation at Stobi, who conducted my whole life according to Judaism, [has], in fulfillment of a vow, [erected] the buildings of the Holy Place and the triklinion, together with the tetrastoon, with my own means, without in the least touching the sacred [funds]. But the right of disposal of all the upper chambers and the proprietorship [thereof] shall be vested in me, Claudios Tiberios Polycharmos, and my heirs for life; and whoever shall seek in any way to alter any of these dispositions of mine shall pay unto the Patriarch two hundred and fifty thousand denarii. For thus have I resolved. But the repair of the tile-roof of the upper chambers shall be carried out by me and my heirs.

Interestingly enough, the rest of the house remained in private use by the family of the donor. Another such case of the conversion of a private home into a synagogue is apparently to be found in Ostia, the seaport of Rome, where we read in an inscription that the property owner gave his rooms for the construction of a synagogue and an ark of the Torah and where we find reference to a dining room and kitchen adjacent to the synagogue. Other examples of synagogues that originally served as private homes are to be found in Priene in Asia Minor, Dura-Europos in Syria, and (probably) the island of Delos off the coast of Greece.

The inscription from Aphrodisias in Asia Minor, whether it was from a synagogue or some other Jewish communal building, seems to allude to a soup kitchen (*patella*) for the relief of suffering in the community.[37] This reference, which would seem to be to food that is given to the poor, would emphasize one of the attractions offered by Jews to non-Jews and would help explain the success of Jews in winning proselytes during this period.[38] This would be particularly significant, inasmuch as, with the exception of Rhodes and perhaps Samos, Greek cities had no permanent arrangements for feeding the poor; at best such distributions occurred at festivals or on special occasions. We may conjecture that one factor that may have led non-Jews to identify with Jews was a commercial one, since of the ten Aphrodisian Jews (admittedly a small sample) whose occupations are given, all are engaged in business, six being involved in the production of food (perhaps because of the necessity of adhering to the dietary laws).

Another purpose of the synagogue was apparently to serve as a house of study. This would also seem to be indicated at Aphrodisias, for example, by the fact that the group of donors (Fig. 3.11) are described as "lovers of learning," though the number of Jews in Diaspora epitaphs who are described as scholars (a compliment that one would expect on tombstones if the deceased was in any sense learned) is not great. The nature of this learning is difficult to discern, especially because contact between these Diaspora communities and the Rabbinic Sages in Palestine was not frequent, let alone intense.

The large group of donors in the inscription from Aphrodisias apparently constituted themselves as a *dekania*, that is, some type of collegial association, under the leadership of a *prostates*. We have noted this term in other inscriptions with reference to a patron. What is noteworthy is that this benevolent association consisted not merely of sixteen born Jews but also of three proselytes and two God-fearers. It is remarkable that the *prostates* was a certain Jael, apparently a woman, though the editors of the first edition of the inscription conclude that since all the other names in the list of donors are masculine this one too must be.[39]

Fig. 3.11. Funerary inscription for a child, "lover of the law," from the Vigna Randanini Catacomb, Rome (Cat. 9).

Another purpose of the synagogue was as a place for dedicating or liberating a slave. Thus, we find in an inscription dating from approximately the year 80 from Panticapaeum on the northern shore of the Black Sea, a description of the manumission of a slave by a widow, in fulfillment of a vow, that took place in a *proseuche*. Both the heirs and the *synagoge*, here an organized Jewish group, agree to act as guarantors of the slave's freedom. In turn, the slave is to show piety toward the *proseuche*, a reference perhaps to a previous conversion to Judaism, since, according to biblical law, a Jew who bought a heathen slave was required to have him circumcised (Gen. 17:12–13). That a *proseuche* also served as the place where the manumission by non-Jews might take place seems likely from an inscription from Gorgippa on the northern shore of the Black Sea, where the new status of the slave (though it is not clear what that status is) is guaranteed by the heirs through the pagan gods Zeus, Ge, and Helios.

RELIGIOUS ASPECTS OF THE SYNAGOGUE

If we look for information about the theology of the Diaspora Jews in their synagogue inscriptions we are grievously disappointed. In several inscriptions, such as in the Crimea and Delos (*CIJ* 1.728), God is referred to as *hypsistos*, that is, highest:

Laodike [here a woman] to God the Highest, saved by His cures, in fulfillment of a vow.

Fig. 3.12. Funerary plaque depicting a Torah Shrine flanked by two menorahs with the word "Blessing" above. From the Monteverde Catacomb, Rome (Cat. 6).

Fig. 3.13. Inscription mentioning a Torah Shrine *(nomophylakion)* from the synagogue at Sardis (Cat. 21).

Hypsistos is the common designation for God in the Septuagint, but it is also used with reference to pagan deities.[40] The fact, however, that the inscriptions refer to *theos hypsistos* rather than to *Zeus hypsistos* would appear to argue that the building is a synagogue after all.[41] Moreover, several inscriptions, dedicated to the well-being of the king and queen of Egypt or to the Roman emperor, look upon God as one who can effect the well-being of rulers who favor them.[42]

Occasionally we find brief prayers: "Blessing" (Fig. 3.12), "Blessing on all," "Blessing on him, Amen," "Blessing on the people," "Help, O God," "May he live," "May he be saved," "Save, O Lord, Amen," "Peace and mercy on all of our holy community," "Peace to the synagogue," "Selah," and "Shalom."[43] In sixteen instances we find the word "salvation," but not with reference to the world to come but to well-being in this life.

The centrality of the Torah is clear from an inscription (Fig. 3.13) found in the hall of the synagogue at Sardis, which refers to the *nomophylakion,* "the place that protects the Torah." Another inscription (Fig. 3.14) from the Sardis synagogue demands that Jews not only read but also observe the laws of the Torah: "Find, open, read, observe." The key word here is *phylaxon,* "observe," which refers to "My commandments" in common Septuagint usage. The *sophodidaskalos,* "teacher of wisdom" or "wise teacher," mentioned in a mosaic inscription in the Sardis synagogue, was surely the key figure in communicating the teaching of the Torah.

One question about which we get almost no information is the relationship of these Diaspora synagogues to the Land of Israel. The lack of reference to Jerusalem and to the hope of rebuilding the Temple, which had been so central in Jewish life, is extremely surprising in view of the fact that apparently funds were collected for the Temple each year from every Jew after the destruction of the Temple. One possible exception to this silence may be found in an undated inscription from Acmonia in Asia Minor, which has a menorah and which is dedicated to all the *patris*, that is, the fatherland, in fulfillment of a vow. Baruch Lifshitz remarks that the term *patris* without doubt refers to the Jewish community,[44] but it is

Fig. 3.14. Inscription reading "Find, open, read, observe" inscribed within a *tabula ansata* from the synagogue at Sardis.

without precedent to refer to the Jewish community as a fatherland. More likely, we may suggest, the reference is to the Land of Israel. The appearance of the menorah upon the inscription would reinforce this interpretation.

Finally, we may refer to *theosebeis*, that is, God-fearers or sympathizers. An inscription at Naucratis in Egypt refers to a Sabbatarian association, thus indicating that these God-fearers were not merely individuals but were organized as a group, as would seem to be indicated by the Aphrodisias inscriptions. There is likewise an inscription from Cilicia in Asia Minor mentioning an association of the Sabbistae that was worshipping a god called Sabbistes. There can be little doubt that the term denotes those who revere the Sabbath, since *sabbatizein* is the usual word in the Septuagint for celebrating the Sabbath. They cannot be Jews, since, as Tcherikover has correctly remarked, Jews would never refer to their God as the God of the Sabbath; and hence they are most likely sympathizers.[45] Moreover, an inscription from Lydia in Asia Minor speaks of a woman named Ammias who offers a prayer to Sabathikos, who presumably is the deity of the Sabbath.

A second-century inscription found in the Roman theater in Miletus, not far from Aphrodisias, speaks of the place of the Jews who are also God-fearers. To speak of God-fearers, that is, non-Jews, who are Jews would seem to be a contradiction in terms.

CONCLUSION

Discoveries of hundreds of inscriptions and papyri, most of them in Greek, despite their tantalizing brevity, have enlarged greatly our knowledge of ancient synagogues (Fig. 3.15). Thus far we have found evidence of more than sixty-six synagogues or prayer groups ranging geographically from the Black Sea region to Egypt and Spain. Such documents are of special value since they reflect a broader spectrum of the Jewish population and since they reflect the contemporary situation with greater accuracy than do literary texts. Confusion arises because the word "synagogue" normally refers not to the synagogue building, which is termed a *proseuche*, but rather to the membership.

Many of the inscriptions, as we would expect, commemorate donors, including Jews who held public office. Some donors were non-Jews, including God-fearers. Some of the

Fig. 3.15. Molding with the image of a menorah and a Torah Shrine from the synagogue at Sardis (Cat. 23).

synagogues were dedicated to the rulers of the land, whether to indicate that they had received a license from the government or to show their loyalty.

What is most striking about the organization of these synagogues is that it so often paralleled that of non-Jewish religious groups. Synagogues were generally led not by rabbis or priests but by lay people. The leading position, that of *archisynagogos*, who served as a patron of the Jewish community, seems to have been held by benefactors, including, most remarkably, several women; but the question of women's participation in the administration of Diaspora synagogues has been hotly disputed. Other officers corresponded to the present-day board of directors, secretary, caretaker, sexton, and patron.

To judge from the inscriptions and the papyri, synagogues served various functions, differing from place to place and from time to time. They were not only places of worship but also meeting places for communal affairs, study halls, guest houses, dining rooms, and places for dedicating or liberating slaves.

Diaspora Synagogues

Synagogue Archaeology in the Greco-Roman World

LEONARD VICTOR RUTGERS
University of Utrecht

If you were strolling in the city center of Sardis, a prosperous town in Asia Minor, during the mid-fourth century you would inevitably happen upon a magnificent synagogue. This synagogue (Fig. 4.1) had been constructed as part of a larger building complex that also housed the city's gymnasium. Visitors to Apamea in Syria would also soon find their way to the synagogue. It was prominently located on the main street, only a few yards from the main intersection of the town. While on their way to the theater, people who walked down the main thoroughfare of Stobi, a major urban center in Macedonia (in the former Yugoslavia), could not fail to notice that one of the imposing facades lining the street belonged to a synagogue of considerable proportions. In Philippopolis (Plovdiv, in present-day Bulgaria) excavations have revealed only part of the town's layout, yet they have revealed enough to show that amid the buildings that have come to light so far, the synagogue was situated off the forum, or central square. In Edessa (southern Turkey), too, a synagogue once existed in the very center of this historic city. Its location explains how this building, in which Edessa's Jewish community must have taken considerable pride, could become an easy prey for zealous Christians, who destroyed it in the early fifth century C.E.

Although Diaspora synagogues were not always located in such prominent positions as those of Sardis, Apamea, Stobi, Plovdiv, and Edessa, it is clear that by the third century C.E. synagogues could be found in every corner of the Greco-Roman world. To date, we know of the existence of at least 150 such synagogues in places that are as far apart as Dura Europos on the Euphrates in Syria, Elche in southeastern Spain, Intercisa in Hungary, and Ḥamman Lif in Roman North Africa. Given the extent of the Jewish

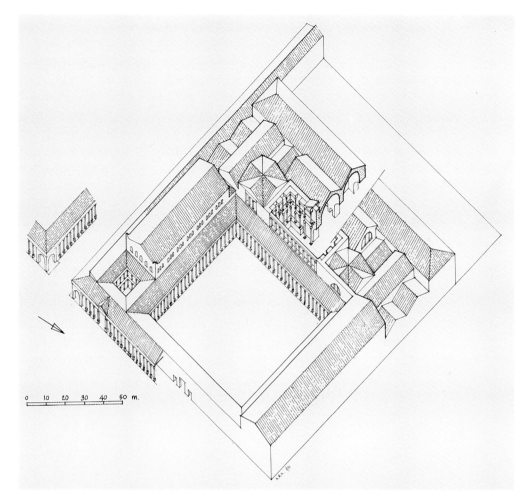

Fig. 4.1. Reconstructed drawing of the Roman urban complex at Sardis. The synagogue is to the left.

Diaspora in antiquity, it hardly needs stressing that during this period many more than 150 synagogues must have existed. Most, if not all, of the Jewish communities outside Palestine had one or more synagogues. Nevertheless, synagogues have not yet been uncovered in many of the cities in which Jews are known to have resided. With the possible exception of Antioch in Syria, the four largest cities of the Roman Empire, including Antioch itself, Rome, Alexandria, and Constantinople, have not yet yielded archaeological remains of synagogue buildings. Literary sources provide ample evidence to suggest that many such buildings existed in these cities and that Jewish communities sometimes used them continuously for centuries.

Only in recent years have scholars begun to study archaeological remains of Diaspora Jewish communities systematically. The unexpected discovery several years ago of a synagogue in Bova Marina in Calabria, on Italy's southernmost shore, shows how the remains of synagogues can suddenly come to light in locations where the presence of such buildings, or even the existence of a Jewish community, was previously unknown.

Keeping in mind the restrictions imposed on the Jewish communities of the Diaspora after the close of antiquity, one may be surprised to note that in the later Roman Empire synagogues were an integral part of the urban landscape. Already in first-century Rome the location of some synagogues was so well known that in his funerary inscription a non-

Jewish fruit seller found it appropriate to describe the site where he sold his produce as "between the old city wall and the synagogue."[1] Yet rather than regarding synagogues merely as useful points of reference in the topography of the ancient city, it was as an institution, community center, and place of worship that the Diaspora synagogue attracted the attention of the ancients. As we shall see in greater detail later, in Asia Minor (today's Turkey) even non-Jews sometimes contributed to the upkeep of synagogues, while at other times, as in a suburb of Antioch in Syria, Christians were fascinated by Jewish religious practices to such an extent that they preferred to attend services in the local synagogues rather than in their own churches.

What did ancient synagogues look like? Diaspora synagogues differed from most contemporary non-Jewish religious architecture in one important aspect. In the Greek world religion had often taken the form of sacrificial worship. Sacrifices were performed outdoors, at an altar that was usually located in front of a temple. The temple itself played only a limited role in Greek religious practice. It was considered "the dwelling of a god" and served primarily to house the cult statue of the god to whom the building was dedicated. Temples also offered space for the deposition of votive gifts.[2] Along similar lines, according Jewish tradition, the Temple in Jerusalem was a place where God's presence in this world rested. Access to the central hall of the Jerusalem Temple was limited to priests. The various festival ceremonies, including the performance of sacrifices, took place in the Temple Court. This was a large area in the open air situated in front of the Temple. It was subdivided into several smaller courts, one of which contained the altar.[3] Before the synagogue came into existence, Jewish and non-Jewish public worship was as much a sacrificial as it was an outdoor affair.

By contrast, on the premises of the Diaspora synagogue there were no altars to be found. The synagogue was not considered "the house of God" in the same sense as the Temple in Jerusalem or Greek temples were, nor did it house cult statues. In antiquity this was common knowledge. The Jewish philosopher Philo and the Jewish historian Josephus report how, on various occasions during the first century C.E., non-Jews purposely insulted Jewish communities in Egypt and the Land of Israel by placing in their synagogues statues portraying, among other people, the Roman emperor. Similarly, in Cagliari on Sardinia, Christians unsuccessfully tried to take over the local synagogue and to forcefully convert the Jewish community in 599 C.E. by erecting in this synagogue a statue of the Virgin Mary, along with a representation of the cross.[4]

It is exactly because worship among Diaspora Jews took forms other than sacrifice that the building in which they congregated looked different from the Temple in Jerusalem or, for that matter, from Greek and Roman temples. Although some Diaspora synagogues, such as the Sardis synagogue (Turkey), certainly looked impressive from the outside, others, such as the one in Dura Europos (Fig. 4.2) (Syria) and the one in Ostia (Plate XI), the port of Rome, indicate that, architecturally, the inside rather than the outside of the building was emphasized. If we are to understand what the Diaspora synagogue really looked like, and if we want to get some sense of what role these synagogues fulfilled, we will have to enter the Diaspora synagogue. It is there, on the inside of the building, that we can find the archaeological and artistic evidence that informs us most directly about the religiosity of the people responsible for the erection of synagogues throughout the ancient Mediterranean.

Before we turn to the interior of the Diaspora synagogue, let us briefly describe the fifteen Diaspora synagogues that have been excavated so far. Traveling clockwise through the

Fig. 4.2. Exterior walls of the synagogue at Dura Europos during excavation.

provinces of the Roman Empire, we will start our journey in North Africa and end it in Jordan, a region then called (Roman) Arabia.

In 1883, French soldiers accidentally discovered a synagogue in Ḥamman Lif (Fig. 4.3), not far from modern-day Tunis (Tunisia). The synagogue contained a splendid mosaic floor dating to the fifth or sixth century C.E. It was cut into pieces soon after it was discovered, and the resulting pieces were sold separately. In 1905, the Brooklyn Museum was able to acquire the most important of these fragments, one of which is shown in this exhibit (Fig. 4.3b).[5] Still another discovery made 1905 an important year for the study of the Diaspora synagogue. In Elche, near Alicante in southeastern Spain, Spanish archaeologists excavated a building they first identified as a church of the fourth century C.E. Only later, after they had analyzed the fragmentary inscriptions set into the mosaic floors, did they realize they had discovered a Jewish synagogue rather than a Christian church.[6]

In Italy, a country that for centuries formed the heartland of the Roman Empire, the discovery of ancient synagogues did not occur until much later. In Ostia, an important synagogue unexpectedly came to light in 1960 during the construction of a highway. This building, which was utilized from the second through the fourth century C.E., may have come into use as a synagogue as early as the second half of the first century C.E.[7] Equally unexpected was the 1985 discovery, in Bova Marina, near Reggio Calabria in southern Italy, of a small but highly interesting synagogue dating to the fourth or fifth century C.E.[8] Continuing our journey into Macedonia (the former Yugoslavia), we encounter the syna-

Plate XI. Exterior wall of the aedicula from the synagogue at Ostia.

(a)

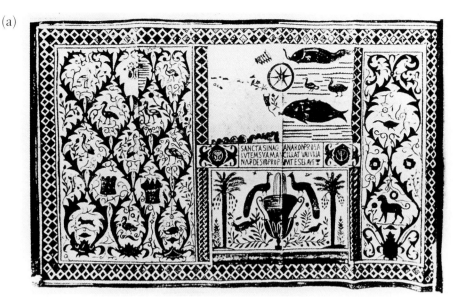

Fig. 4.3. (a) Drawing of the mosaic floor from the synagogue at Ḥamman Lif (Naro), Tunisia. (b) Mosaic lozenge with a menorah from the synagogue at Ḥamman Lif (Naro) (Cat. 3).

(b)

gogue of Stobi. Its existence was evident as early as 1931 when archaeologists deciphered one of the longest Jewish dedicatory inscriptions known from antiquity. This inscription was written in Greek and dates to the third century C.E. It was not until an American-Yugoslav team carried out systematic excavations at the site in the early 1970s, however, that the building described in this inscription could be exposed and studied in detail.[9] More recently, in the mid-1980s, the work of Bulgarian archaeologists has led to yet another surprise discovery in the Balkans, this time in the city of Plovdiv, ancient Philippopolis. While trying to unravel the history of this Roman town they uncovered the extensive remains of a third- or fourth-century synagogue, which was once richly decorated with mosaic floors and various inscriptions.[10] Still farther to the east, in Sebastopol on the Crimea (Black Sea), American-sponsored excavations are bringing to light at this very moment the remains of a synagogue in an area in which several Jewish communities are known to have resided. However, no detailed information on the results of these excavations is as yet available.

When we now turn south to Greece and Roman Turkey and then to Roman Syria, we find the remains of synagogues that testify to both the size and the prosperity of the Jewish communities in these parts of the Roman world. In Greece itself, a fourth-century synagogue, which has received little scholarly attention, came to light in the course of the nineteenth century on Aegina, an island off the coast of Athens.[11] Early in our own century a second synagogue was discovered during the large-scale French-led excavations on the island of Delos, one of the Cycladic islands in the Aegean. Although some scholars continue to disagree, the consensus now is that this building is indeed a synagogue and that it was used as such as early as the first century B.C.E.[12] Likewise at the turn of the century German archaeologists revealed a small fourth-century synagogue in Priene (Plate XII), a once-famous Greek city on the coast of western Turkey. They wrongly identified the building as a church, even though they also discovered, inside the building, two stone reliefs decorated with menorahs. Reproducing the relief shown in this exhibition (Fig. 2.19a) at the very beginning of their excavation report, the excavators never considered that such evidence inevitably documents the existence of a synagogue rather than a church.[13] Farther inland, and more recently, the Harvard–Cornell expedition to Sardis brought to light the remains of the largest and architecturally most impressive of all Diaspora synagogues discovered thus far. It could accommodate an estimated one thousand people, and it seems to have been used unintermittently for at least four centuries before it was destroyed, along with the rest of the city, in 616 C.E.[14]

In Roman Syria Jewish communities were especially widespread. In Apamea, Belgian archaeologists uncovered in 1932 a mosaic floor and several inscriptions belonging to a synagogue dating to the fourth century C.E. Only recently, however, has the architectural history of the building been clarified.[15] Farther to the north, in Aleppo, remains of a synagogue dating to the fifth century C.E. appear to have been incorporated into the Great Mosque. Unfortunately, no systematic study of these earlier remains has ever been made.[16]

Plate XII. Ashlar with an image of a menorah flanked by birds from Priene.

Fig. 4.4. The western wall of
the synagogue at Dura
Europos after restoration.

In Dura Europos, a fairly small Roman garrison town on the Euphrates, excavations carried out under the aegis of Yale University exposed, also in 1932, a synagogue whose discovery was as unexpected as it was significant for our understanding of the Diaspora synagogue. In the course of the third century C.E. the walls of this synagogue had been richly decorated twice with wall paintings (Fig. 4.4). By coincidence, a considerable number of these paintings survived the ravages of time. In an attempt to fortify the city and protect it from the attack of hostile Persian forces, the Roman military had poured sand into the main hall of the synagogue (and into other adjacent buildings) just a few years after the synagogue paintings had been completed. By filling up as much as one quarter of the entire town with sand, the Romans hoped to reinforce the city wall in the direct proximity of which the Dura synagogue was situated. As it turned out, such measures could not stop the Persian armies. But they were crucial for the preservation for posterity of the Dura synagogue and its extraordinary wall paintings.[17]

In 1929, three years before the Dura synagogue was discovered, a joint expedition of Yale University and the British School of Archaeology in Jerusalem excavated a late antique period synagogue in Gerasa (Jordan). Even though much of the building had been destroyed when a Christian church was built on top of it, enough of the mosaic floors remained to show that before the 530s C.E. the Gerasa synagogue was an attractive construction that could not fail to impress those who entered it.[18]

On the basis of the list we have just presented, several preliminary observations concerning the Diaspora synagogue can be made. First, even though few of the Diaspora synagogues that once dotted the Mediterranean landscape have actually been excavated, and even though the synagogues excavated thus far are situated in all parts of the ancient Diaspora, the available evidence is both rich and consistent enough to reconstruct reliably and in detail the architectural and socioreligious history of the Diaspora synagogue. Second, with the exception of the Delos and Ostia synagogues, none of the Diaspora synagogues that have come to light seems to predate the second century C.E. In most Diaspora synagogues, moreover, major construction work appears to have taken place only in the third and fourth centuries C.E. A majority of the extant synagogue inscriptions also date to this period. Such evidence cannot be taken to mean, of course, that prior to the second century C.E. the Jewish communities of the Diaspora did not construct synagogues. The evidence must be taken to mean, however, that only during the second or third century C.E. did an architecture develop that made buildings distinguishable as synagogues. In addition, it appears that in late antiquity the Jews of the Diaspora increasingly had the opportunity to spend money on synagogues, or at least to record publicly such spending in the form of inscriptions. The complicated problem of how precisely the Diaspora synagogue originated will be treated in greater detail later, after the archaeological evidence has been presented.

Most Diaspora synagogues consisted of a complex of rooms and spaces that surrounded a main congregational hall. In Ostia, on Delos, and in Dura Europos, for example, it can still be observed that the walls of the main hall of the synagogue are bonded to the walls of the surrounding rooms. Such archaeological evidence suggests that the main hall and the rooms surrounding it were conceived as architectural units. Put differently, functionally the main hall and the surrounding spaces belong together and were meant to be complementary.

Studying the plans of the fourteen Diaspora synagogues known to us today, one rapidly notices that architecturally or structurally these buildings have much in common. Admittedly, some Diaspora synagogues are larger than others. Despite such differences in size and the great distances that often separated Diaspora synagogues, all these buildings share an architectural language.

What did a visitor see upon entering a Diaspora synagogue? Before entering the synagogue proper, he or she would pass through an entrance area. Sometimes such entrance areas were unpretentious. In Dura Europos (Syria) one first had to walk through a number of rooms before one could enter the synagogue proper. Comparably, in Priene (Turkey) the synagogue was tucked away behind what appears to have been a private house. It was accessible only through a small alley, which in turn gave access to a small vestibule. Conceivably, the vestibule donated by a certain Aurelius Elpidios, an otherwise unknown Jewish communal leader, to a synagogue of Mantineia in Greece was likewise a structure of only modest proportions.

At other times, however, entrance areas were rendered in a more monumental fashion. An impressive 20-meter–long atrium decorated with columns preceded the Sardis synagogue. In Delos and Ostia colonnaded structures once embellished the entrance areas of these synagogues (in Ostia the colonnaded structure was located inside the synagogue). A third-century inscription from Phocaea (Turkey) records how a prominent woman by the name of Tation, who herself was not Jewish, financed the construction of both the main hall of the synagogue and the synagogue's precinct (*peribolos*). Receiving various honors from the local Jewish community in return, Tation spent liberally on what must have been a major construction project.[19]

Independent of whether the entrance area of the synagogues was monumental or not, the entrance areas of many Diaspora synagogues share one feature in particular: the presence of a cistern, water basin, or fountain. The most impressive of these fountains is undoubtedly the one discovered at Sardis. Because it was located in the entrance area to the synagogue (Plate XIII), the excavators believe that the Sardis fountain was accessible to Jews and non-Jews alike. Inasmuch as this area was owned by non-Jews before it was sold to the Jewish community, it is indeed conceivable that the Jews of Sardis did not want to exclude non-Jews from using a fountain on which they had relied for such a long time. Discoveries in the synagogues of Ostia, Delos, Priene, Dura Europos, and Gerasa, as well as inscriptions found in Side in Pamphilia (Turkey), indicate that cisterns and fountains were a regular feature of Diaspora synagogues. An interesting papyrus found in Egypt and

Plate XIII. The forecourt with the fountain of the synagogue at Sardis.

dating to the year 113 C.E. records the amount of money two Jewish synagogues had to pay to be supplied with water. From the sums of money mentioned in this papyrus it follows that in these two particular synagogues water was used in considerable quantities. We would like to know, of course, whether all this water was needed for purposes other than those connected with daily (that is, not strictly religious) needs, but the evidence presently available does not permit us to answer this question satisfactorily. A Greek inscription from Philadelphia in Lydia (Turkey) records the donation to the Jewish community of a *maskaules*, a Greek word that is probably to be viewed as a transcription of the Hebrew *maskel* or the Aramaic *maskilta*. The editor of the inscription translates this word as "basin for ablutions," but then fails to specify the type of purification he has in mind.[20] *Mikvaot*, or ritual baths, do not seem to belong to the standard repertoire of structures associated with the Diaspora synagogue. It has been claimed recently that the synagogue complex at Plovdiv contained such a *mikveh*. Although further research is necessary, the archaeological evidence presently available suggests rather that we are dealing with the remains of yet another fountain instead of a ritual bath.[21]

Passing through the vestibule or atrium, ancient visitors would enter the main hall of the synagogue. From a modern point of view, most Diaspora synagogues are reasonably modest structures. The main hall of the synagogues of Hamman Lif, Elche, Ostia (Fig. 4.5), Bova, Stobi, Plovdiv, Delos (Fig. 1.7), Priene, Apamea, Dura Europos (Fig. 4.6), and Gerasa are either rectangular or square and measure on average 10–25 × 7.5–15 meters. The Sardis synagogue (Fig. 4.7) forms a notable exception to this pattern in that its main hall measures 59 × 18 meters (and the entire complex an impressive 95 × 18 meters). Thus, the main congregational hall of the Diaspora synagogue took up considerably less space than did the typical Greek or Roman temple. As noted earlier, the classical pagan temple and the Jewish synagogue were very different kinds of structures indeed.

The Diaspora synagogue did not impress visitors so much because of its size as because of its often opulent decoration. Although a well-known student of Roman mosaic pave-

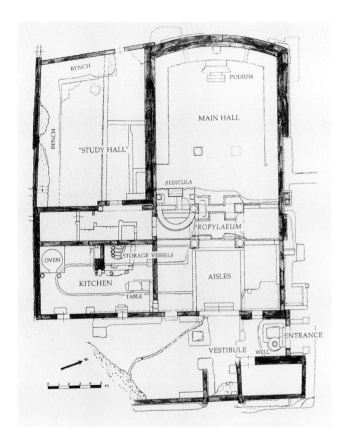

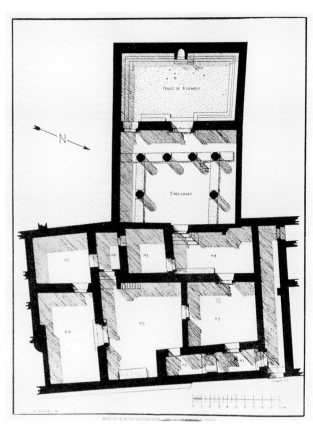

above: Fig. 4.5. The architectural plan of the synagogue at Ostia.

above right: Fig. 4.6. The architectural plan of the synagogue at Dura Europos.

right: Fig. 4.7. The main hall of the synagogue at Sardis.

ments has recently claimed that mosaics did not occur often in Diaspora synagogues, the opposite is true.[22] Remains of mosaic floors have been found in many Diaspora synagogues, including those of Ḥamman Lif, Elche, Ostia, Bova, Stobi, Plovdiv, Aegina (Fig. 4.8a and b), Delos, Sardis, Apamea (Fig. 4.8c and d), and Gerasa. Moreover, in inscriptions relating to the synagogues of Ḥamman Lif, Aegina, Apamea, Emesa (Syria), and

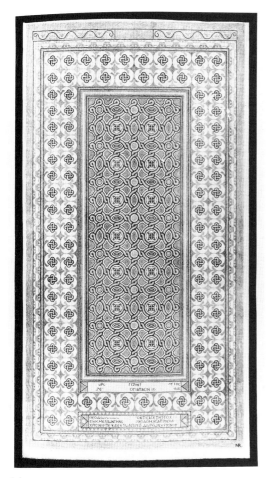

(a)

(b)

(c)

(d)

Fig. 4.8. (a) Drawing of the mosaic floor from the synagogue at Aegina; (b) detail of the mosaic inscription from the synagogue at Aegina; (c) mosaic floor from the synagogue at Apamea; (d) site of the synagogue at Apamea.

Plate XIV. Inlaid marble fragments from the synagogue at Sardis.

Plovdiv, donors proudly proclaim how they themselves were instrumental in having such mosaics installed in the synagogue. The mosaic inscriptions from Apamea, Emesa, and Plovdiv are particularly interesting in this respect because they record exactly the length of mosaic floor donated by the people mentioned in the inscriptions.[23]

Independent of in which Diaspora synagogue they were found, synagogue mosaics from the Diaspora display a general preference for geometric patterns. Figural scenes appear only in exceptional cases. In the synagogue of Ḥamman Lif we find representations of fish, and various types of birds appear in the center of the mosaic pavement. In the synagogue of Gerasa enough of the mosaic floor is left to show that the animals depicted on it were once part of a larger composition representing the story of the Flood. Shem and Japhet were also represented, as Greek inscriptions accompanying these figures indicate. Along with a preference for geometric motifs, however, typically Jewish motifs also enjoyed considerable popularity in mosaic pavements. Sometimes, as at Gerasa and Ḥamman Lif, motifs such as the menorah, shofar, and etrog were fit into the larger geometric framework of decoration. At other times, as at the synagogues of Plovdiv and Bova, a large menorah rendered in detail was the most prominent image in the entire floor. Taking into account that the menorah was the Jewish symbol par excellence in antiquity, we see how the floors of the Plovdiv and Bova synagogues were, in fact, meant to give visual expression to the convictions and self-confidence of the Jews of the Diaspora in the most unequivocal way.

The decoration of the Diaspora synagogue also extended to the walls (Plate XIV) and even to the ceiling. While inscriptions from Sardis and Acmonia (Turkey) record the names of benefactors responsible for the decoration of synagogue walls with paintings, another inscription from Tralles (Turkey) does the same for someone who helped embellish the local synagogue through the donation of revetment plaques.[24] On the walls of the synagogue of Stobi someone painted a few short phrases wishing good luck to Polycharmos, the great benefactor of the Stobi synagogue.[25] Perhaps it was the same person who was also responsible for scratching a large menorah into one of the plastered walls of this synagogue.[26] The painted walls of Dura Europos synagogue, which have been preserved by a fortunate coincidence, give us some sense of the one-time splendor of the wall paintings referred to so summarily in the above-mentioned inscriptions. They also indicate how many ancient wall paintings are now irrevocably lost and how little we really know about the development of wall painting in the Diaspora synagogue.

At Dura Europos (Fig. 4.9) a private house was turned into a synagogue in the course of the second century C.E. The walls of the synagogue were decorated, mostly with geometric designs. Some of this decoration has been preserved under a second program of painting. The second program, which was executed in 244–45 C.E., or eleven years before the building was definitively covered with sand, was exquisitely executed. Narrative scenes now replaced

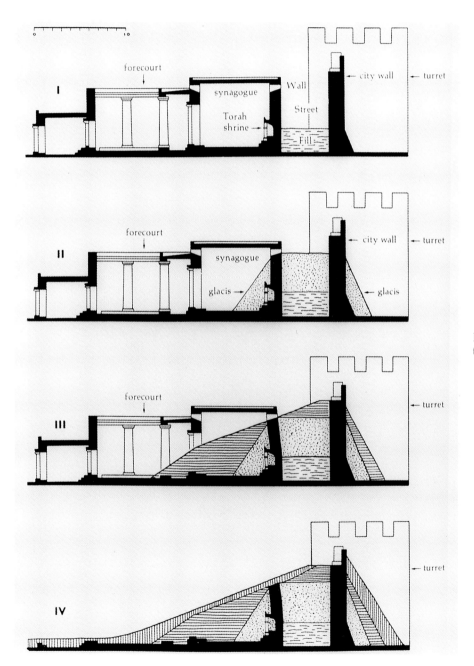

Fig. 4.9. Stages of ramp construction in the Dura Europos synagogue, 256 C.E.

Fig. 4.10. The consecration of the Tabernacle and its priests from the synagogue wall paintings at Dura Europos.

the original geometric decoration almost entirely. Although not all the paintings done at this time have been preserved, 60 percent, or twenty-eight panels, survive that contain as many as fifty-eight episodes or stories, which were all taken from the Hebrew Bible. Although scholars sometimes disagree as to which biblical stories are represented, accompanying painted inscriptions (Fig. 4.10) in Greek and Aramaic help facilitate identifications in a number of cases. Scholars also disagree over the question of whether a single theme or idea underlies all these panels. Pointing to the panel representing Ezekiel and the valley of dry bones (Ezek. 37), which takes up no less than 7.5 meters of wall space, or the one portraying the story of Moses being rescued from the Nile (Exod. 2) (Plate XVa), some scholars say that the overriding theme in Dura is eschatological, salvivic, or messianic. Relying on representations of the story of Mordecai and Esther, the Ark (Fig. 4.11) causing damage to the Temple of Dagon in Ashdod (1 Sam. 5 and 6), or the story of Elijah and the priests of Baal on Mount Carmel (1 Kings 18), other scholars maintain that these paintings were polemical-propagandistic and that they were meant to show how the oppressors and persecutors of the Jews would meet their end. Still others believe that the pictorial program of the Dura synagogue was determined by mystical concerns. Carl H. Kraeling, one of the most prolific American archaeologists of our century and author of a masterful study on the Dura synagogue, rightly observes, however, that "a consistent progression of scenes can be established for the register as a whole only by doing violence to the subject matter of certain panels and is in effect impossible." Kraeling considers the purpose of the paintings as generally didactic in that these paintings were "intended to testify to, or remind the believers of the grounds for and the subsistence of, the faith they profess." In that sense the Dura paintings were meant, in Kraeling's words, "to express an interest in the actual continuity of Israel's sacred history."[27]

The discovery of roof tiles in the Delos synagogue, as well as a long Greek inscription from Acmonia in Roman Turkey that commemorates the renovation of the roof of a synagogue, shows that Diaspora synagogues were roofed structures (as opposed to pagan temples

(a)

Plate XV. (a) Baby Moses in the Bulrushes, from the synagogue wall paintings at Dura Europos. (b) Moses holding a biblical scroll.

(b)

where the nave was sometimes left open). It is again the Dura synagogue, where many painted roof tiles (Fig. 4.12) were found, that enables us to reconstruct the physical appearance of the ceiling of a Diaspora synagogue. Like the paintings on the wall of the Dura synagogue, the roof tiles display various figural (Fig. 4.13a), animal (Fig. 4.13b and c), and vegetal (Fig. 4.13d) motifs in particular. Rather than deriving from the Hebrew Bible, this time the motifs are purely conventional and seem to have been taken from the stock repertoire of motifs (Fig. 4.14) current in this part of the Roman world. Most interesting, perhaps, are representations of a human eye, believed to be apotropaic (Fig. 2.20), and six inscriptions commemorating, in Greek and Aramaic (Fig. 4.15), respectively, several people who in one capacity or another supervised the work in the Dura synagogue.[28] Some of these tiles are exhibited here (Cats. 28–32).

Diaspora synagogues were not entirely uniform in terms of interior arrangement, but the remaining archaeological evidence prevents us from being very specific on this matter. Like some synagogues in Israel, the synagogues of Gerasa, Dura Europos, Delos, Stobi, Bova, and perhaps also Apamea had benches arranged along some or all of their walls. In Sardis benches were arranged in a semicircle that filled an apse located at the back of the building. While a richly sculpted marble table, probably used for the reading of the Torah, was placed centrally in the main hall of the Sardis synagogue, in

Fig. 4.11. The Ark in the Land of the Philistines from the synagogue wall paintings at Dura Europos.

Fig. 4.12. Reconstructed ceiling of the synagogue at Dura Europos in the Damascus Museum.

Ostia the reading of the Law seems to have taken place on a raised platform built against the back wall of the synagogue. In Stobi a smaller yet comparable structure (bema) may have served the same purpose. The existence of such raised platforms is also known from inscriptions, such as the one found in Syracuse on Sicily, and from Rabbinic literature. In a famous passage preserved in the Tosefta as well as in the Jerusalem and Babylonian Talmuds, Rabbi Judah b. Ilai recounts the splendors of the great synagogue of Alexandria. He observes, among other things, that the Alexandrian synagogue was so large that the leader had to climb on a raised platform (bema) and wave with a flag in order to communicate with the community.[29]

About the appurtenances of the Diaspora synagogue we know next to nothing. The pottery lamps found in the Ḥamman Lif, Ostia (Fig. 4.16), and Delos synagogues certainly served to light the synagogue. The excavators of the Dura synagogue noticed in the floor of this synagogue holes that were arranged in a pattern suggesting that they served to keep upright various lamp stands. The extraordinary discovery in the Sardis synagogue of a fragmentary menorah (and perhaps fragments of a bronze one as well) suggests that the large menorahs on the mosaic floors of the Diaspora synagogue had three-dimensional counterparts (see Plate X). An inscription from Side (Turkey) suggests, furthermore, that such monumental menorahs were more widespread than one would perhaps have anticipated. In this inscription a certain Isaac, administrator of the synagogue, prides himself on having ordered (and paid for) the cleaning of just two such "candelabra with seven branches."[30]

Although the interior arrangement of one Diaspora synagogue differed somewhat from the interior arrangements of the next, there was one important feature many Diaspora synagogues shared: a niche or apse. Sometimes, as in the synagogues of Ḥamman Lif, Elche, Bova, and Dura, these niches were rounded and quite small. At other times, as in the Priene synagogue, the niche was square. At still other times, as in the Ostia, Aegina, and Apamea synagogues, it is more

(a)

(b)

(c)   (d)

appropriate to speak of an apse (that is, a large, rounded niche). In the Sardis synagogue, finally, two large square niches (aediculae) can be found. While not enough archaeological evidence has survived in the case of the remaining Diaspora synagogues (Stobi, Plovdiv, Apamea, and Gerasa) to determine whether the walls of these synagogues also had niches, the only Diaspora synagogue that certainly did not have such a niche was the one on Delos.

Such a state of affairs is significant. It may be recalled that the Delos synagogue is the earliest Diaspora synagogue and that it predates the other Diaspora synagogues by at least three to four centuries. Apparently, then, the insertion of a niche or an apse into the walls of the Diaspora synagogue was a fairly late development in the history of Diaspora synagogue architecture. Diaspora synagogues, such as Dura, Ostia, Bova, and Sardis, provide us with more reliable archaeological evidence to determine when the construction of niches and apses in Diaspora synagogues first got under way.

Fig. 4.13. Ceiling tiles from the Dura Europos synagogue. (a) Ceiling tile with a female bust (Cat. 32). (b) Ceiling tile with an image of Capricorn (Cat. 29). (c) Ceiling tile with an image of a centaur (Cat. 30). (d) Ceiling tile with a flower (Cat. 31).

(c)

(a)   (b)

Fig. 4.14. (a) Tile with a female bust from the House of the Roman Scribes at Dura Europos, c. 240 C.E. (Cat.33). (b) Ianthos male figure from the House of the Roman Scribes at Dura Europos (Cat. 34). (c) Painting of Mithras from the Late Mithraeum at Dura Europos (Cat. 35).

We have seen that the niche of the Dura synagogue came into existence when, at an undetermined point in the course of the second century C.E., a house was turned into a synagogue. When the Dura synagogue was elaborately repainted in the middle of the third century C.E., the niche and the area surrounding it were also redone. The large painted Tree of Life that had once decorated this part of the synagogue was replaced by paintings showing the facade of the Temple in Jerusalem, a large menorah that was rendered in detail, and the Binding of Isaac (Gen. 22) (Fig. 4.17a). The niche itself was called *beit arona* in an Aramaic inscription that records the work done at this time. The four holes still visible in the Torah Shrine today are probably to be seen as fixtures that served to attach a *parokhet*, or fabric cover, to veil off the scrolls of the Torah.

In Ostia, the large monumental apse (Plate XVI) had not been part of the original building, as is evident from the formal appearance of this apse. While the main walls of the synagogue were constructed in the second half of the first century C.E. and consisted of rubble with a tuffa facing, the apse was built in a technique known as *opus vittatum mixtum* (that is, consisting of alternating blocks of brick and tuffa). We know that this particular type of *opus vittatum* wall construction started to enjoy popularity in Ostia and in nearby Rome during the third century C.E., but not earlier. Consequently, the monumental apse of the Ostia synagogue must have been constructed in this period, perhaps toward the end of the third century C.E. The apse of the Ostia synagogue was preceded by a steep staircase, which was decorated with a multicolored marble facing. At the sides of the platform that stood before the apse were two finely carved columns, the capitals of which were made of Luna marble. These capitals have been dated by specialists to the early fourth century C.E. Thus, they provide further evidence to reconstruct the chronology of the apse of the Ostia synagogue.[31] On top of these capitals rested two architraves (Plate XVIIa and b) or horizontally arranged blocks of stone.

Fig. 4.15. Ceiling tile with an Aramaic inscription from the synagogue at Dura Europos (Cat. 28).

Fig. 4.16. Oil lamp with an image of a Torah Shrine from the synagogue at Ostia (Cat. 17).

(a)

Fig. 4.17. (a) Detail of the Torah Shrine from the synagogue at Dura Europos; (b) seal of the Binding of Isaac (Cat. 36).

(b)

85

Plate XVI. Aedicula of the synagogue at Ostia.

(a)

Plate XVII. (a) Detail of an architrave with an image of a menorah from the synagogue at Ostia (Cat. 16). (b) Architrave in situ at Ostia.

(b)

(a)   (b)

Plate XVIIIa and b. Fragments of Jewish gold glasses from Rome (Cat. 14).

Plate XIX. Gem with
the image of a menorah
from Italy (Cat. 13).

Plate XX. Torah Shrine flanked by two menorahs from a
wall painting in the Villa Torlonia Catacomb, Rome.

Fig. 4.18. Incense burner from Egypt (Cat. 2).

These were decorated in relief and displayed a large menorah flanked by a lulav, an etrog, and a shofar—yet another example of the practice in Diaspora synagogues to place the menorah (Plates XVIII–XX, Fig. 4.18) in the visually most conspicuous position.

In Bova, a synagogue consisting of a main hall surrounded by several other rooms was constructed during the fourth century. At the beginning of the sixth century this synagogue was redone in its entirety. On that occasion a niche, preceded by a bench, was added.

In Sardis, the excavators were able to distinguish four stages (Fig. 4.19) in the building history of the synagogue. The two large niches, or aediculae (Fig. 4.20), installed on the western wall of the main hall of the Sardis synagogue were erected during stage four, that is, in the years following 360 C.E.

To summarize these data, the "emergence" of the niche or apse in the Diaspora synagogue was a gradual development. Originally, synagogues in the Diaspora did not contain a niche or an apse. Such niches were built only at a later stage, usually when the syna-

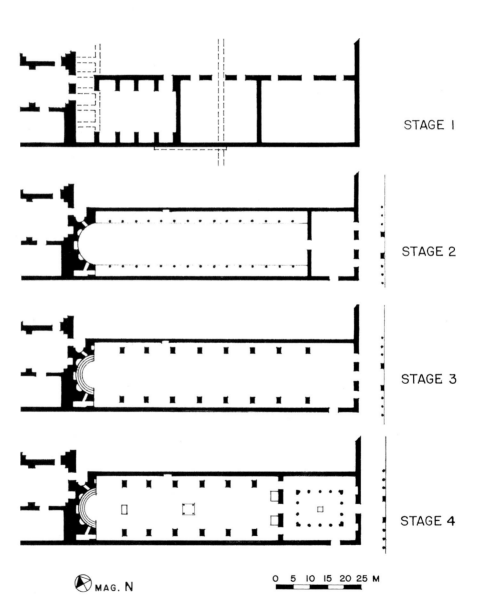

Fig. 4.19. Building stages of the synagogue at Sardis.

STAGE 1

STAGE 2

STAGE 3

STAGE 4

MAG. N

0 5 10 15 20 25 M

gogue was modified to better adapt it to the needs of the community. The evidence from Dura suggests that as early as the third century C.E. niches were added to existing structures. The evidence from Ostia and Sardis suggests that in the Diaspora synagogue the construction of niches became standard practice in the fourth century C.E. The finds in Bova show that even in the fourth century synagogues that did not have a niche could still be built. But the finds in Bova also indicate that even there the absence of a niche was eventually felt to be a drawback. This explains why a niche was added in the sixth century when the Bova synagogue was rebuilt.

It is highly likely that these niches and apses in the Diaspora synagogue served to preserve copies of the Torah. A Greek inscription from the Sardis synagogue records the marble inlaying of a *nomophylakeion*, or place where the Law is guarded. A third-century bilingual inscription in Greek and Latin found in the Ostia synagogue records how a certain Mindi[u]s Faustus set up the "ark [*kibotos*] for the holy law" (see Fig. 2.18). Inasmuch as the inscription was reused in the synagogue's pavement, and inasmuch as the word *kibotos* was normally used for wooden, portable containers, scholars believe that Mindi[u]s Faustus's inscription refers to the installation of an earlier Torah Shrine that was utilized before the more permanent stone apse described earlier replaced it.[32] Wall paintings, glasses with decoration executed in gold leaf, and funerary inscriptions, all found in the Jewish catacombs of Rome, give us some idea of how the Torah Shrine in the synagogues of the Diaspora may have looked: large cupboards with wooden doors that were internally subdivided so as to offer space for the deposition of several scrolls.

Fig. 4.20. Reconstructed aedicula in the synagogue at Sardis.

The Mindi[u]s Faustus inscription from Ostia is interesting for still another reason. It refers to the Law as "holy." It was exactly because the Torah was held in such high esteem by the Jewish communities of the Diaspora that the buildings in which the scrolls of the Torah were kept were also considered to possess a certain degree of holiness. Just as the Diaspora synagogues of late antiquity were equipped with Torah Shrines, so the inscriptions relating to Diaspora synagogues quite consistently refer to the building as a "holy place." While Greek inscriptions from Gerasa and Stobi and Latin inscriptions from Ḥamman Lif add the adjective "holy" when mentioning the synagogue, several Greek inscriptions from Asia Minor (Turkey) and Greece prefer to refer to the synagogue in superlative form as "the most holy."[33] An inscription found in the synagogue of Apamea goes so far as to designate the community that worships in this building "holy." In short, the architectural and epigraphical evidence complement each another in that they indicate that in many Diaspora synagogues the Torah was of central importance.

As noted earlier, many Diaspora synagogues consisted of a complex of buildings rather than a single congregational hall. Although some of these complexes have been excavated, for example, at Ḥamman Lif, Dura Europos, and Ostia, the excavated remains usually tell us little about how these rooms were used. The ovens discovered in the Ostia and Stobi synagogue complexes give us an idea of the types of activities associated with the daily life of the Diaspora synagogue, but they cannot help us solve the question of how the adjacent rooms were used. Fortunately, literary sources and inscriptions survive in sufficient numbers to reconstruct with some degree of precision the role synagogues played in the lives of the Jewish communities of the Diaspora. This evidence also helps us to understand what functions the rooms surrounding the main hall might have fulfilled.

While studying the architectural features of the main hall of the Diaspora synagogue, we have seen that one of its main functions was religious—more specifically, that it set the stage for the reading of the Torah (and perhaps also the *Haftarah*, or writings of the Prophets). Literary sources relating to the synagogues of Greece show that the reading of Scripture played a central role in the synagogue services of the Diaspora.[34] The archaeological evidence points in the same direction. The menorah represented on the mosaic floor of the Plovdiv synagogue, for example, is rendered in such painstaking detail that one scholar has suggested that such a rendering documents an intimate knowledge of Exodus, that is, the biblical book that contains a minute description of the Tabernacle menorah.[35] We might also add that in many Diaspora synagogues the menorah was also rendered to conform to the specifications in Exodus, in that it was often represented in yellow or gold. This holds true, for example, for the large menorah painted on the Torah Shrine of the Dura synagogue; for the menorah reliefs of the Ostia synagogue, which were originally gilded; and for the mosaic floor of the Plovdiv synagogue, on which the menorah is rendered in the form of small yellow mosaic stones and pieces of glass (tesserae).

We see that the artists of the Diaspora synagogue and their patrons were familiar with many books of the Hebrew Bible, and not just Exodus, when we turn once again to the most extraordinary Diaspora synagogue: the synagogue of Dura Europos. The wall paintings of the Dura synagogue were taken from many biblical books, including Genesis, Exodus, Numbers, 1 and 2 Samuel, 1 and 2 Kings, Jeremiah, Ezekiel, Daniel, Nehemiah, and Esther. What is even more remarkable about the wall paintings of the Dura synagogue than the representation of biblical stories, however, is that certain iconographic details in these stories can be explained only by resorting to *targumim* (translations of the Hebrew Bible into Aramaic) and to Rabbinic *midrashim* (commentaries on the Hebrew Bible). The presence of such elements suggests that the synagogue was felt to provide an appropriate setting for the representation (and discussion) of ideas that also made their way into Rabbinic literature.

It is no longer possible to reconstruct in detail the liturgy practiced in the Diaspora synagogue. What we do know, however, is that besides reading from their sacred writings, the Jews of the Diaspora also went to their synagogues to pray. The earliest evidence documenting the existence of synagogues in the Diaspora consists of a collection of inscriptions from Lower (northern) Egypt that refer to the synagogue as *proseuche*, or "house of prayer." These inscriptions date to the third century B.C.E.[36] Although in inscriptions dating to a later period the word *synagoge* almost completely replaces the word *proseuche*, it is nonetheless remarkable to note that the term *proseuche* never disappeared entirely but that it continued to enjoy some degree of popularity well into late antiquity, and throughout the entire Diaspora at that. A first-century inscription from Rome refers to it; Greek and Latin authors used it during the second century C.E., as did early Christian authors during the fourth century; and the term also occurs in second- and third-century Jewish papyri from Egypt and in late antique Jewish inscriptions from Greece, Turkey, the northern coast of the Black Sea, Hungary, and Spain. That prayers were said aloud, at least sometimes, follows from a letter that reached Pope Gregory the Great in 591 C.E. In it, the bishop of Terracina (Italy) com-plained that in the synagogue of that town Jews "recited psalms" so fervently that it was felt to interfere with the services held in a Christian church next door.

It was on the Sabbath that the building attracted the largest number of people. On one occasion Josephus calls the synagogue a *sabbateion,* and this same term appears later in a funerary inscription from Thyatira in Turkey.[37] Describing the lives and customs of the Roman Jewish community, Philo observes that the Jews of first-century Rome "have houses of prayer in which they meet, particularly on the holy Sabbaths when they receive as a body a training in their ancestral philosophy." Jews in Alexandria behaved similarly.[38] Early Christian authors confirm that Jews attended synagogue on the Sabbath.[39] Even Christians observed the Sabbath, for example, when in their churches they read the Gospels on Saturday instead of on Sunday. Such timing was a direct imitation of Jewish liturgical prac-tices. The practice of reading the New Testament on Saturdays was so widespread among some early Christian communities that church authorities attempted to formally forbid it. Church leaders soon discovered, however, that it was no easy task to prevent Christians from "judaizing." The "canons" accepted at the Council of Laodicea (Turkey), which took place in 364 C.E., show that as late as the later fourth century C.E. church authorities had not yet been entirely successful in bringing all Christian communities back on the desired track.

Although the evidence is largely circumstantial, it is fair to say that the Diaspora syna-gogue also provided the setting for the celebration of Jewish holidays other than the Sabbath. An inscription from North Africa tells us, for example, that during Sukkot the Jewish community of Berenice (Libya) agreed, in 25 C.E., to honor a certain Marcus Tittius, "a good and worthy man" and a benefactor of the community.[40] The depiction of the lulav, etrog, and shofar on the mosaic floors of several Diaspora synagogues, and espe-cially on one of the painted panels of the Dura synagogue, suggests that the celebration of Sukkot and of Rosh ha-Shanah must have been quite common among the Jews of the Diaspora. In a fairly enigmatic passage describing the destruction of a synagogue in Kalesh (Armenia), John of Ephesus, a sixth-century early Christian author who wrote in Syriac, relates how "trumpets" (perhaps a reference to the shofar of the Jewish New Year) were taken out of this building before it was put to ashes.[41] Among the paintings of the Dura synagogue one panel represents the story of Mordecai, Esther, and Ahasuerus. It suggests that the Jews of the Diaspora were familiar with Purim, the feast of Esther. Evidence from a slightly later period indicates that in the Diaspora Jews indeed celebrated Purim and that they did so with enthusiasm.[42] As is evident from John Chrysostom's eight homilies, or ser-mons, "Against the Jews," which reflect the situation at Antioch in the 380s C.E., Passover was celebrated by the local Jewish community in a nearby synagogue in such a manner that it attracted considerable numbers of Christians. That Christians in fourth-century Syria would have been attracted to the Jewish Passover is less surprising than it might seem. Many Christian communities, especially those of Roman Turkey, had long depended on the Jewish communities of the Diaspora to establish the date on which to celebrate Easter. The fact that Christian theologians and church leaders ran into serious opposition when they repeatedly tried to prohibit the celebration of Easter on the four-teenth day of Nisan tells us much about the influence the Jewish communities of the Diaspora exerted on early Christian religious practices. It also shows that in the Diaspora Jews must have been rigorous in the observance of Passover.

The rooms surrounding the main hall where the celebration of the holidays took place served several ancillary purposes. The oven discovered in Ostia indicates that food could be prepared on the grounds of the Diaspora synagogue. A Greek inscription found in the

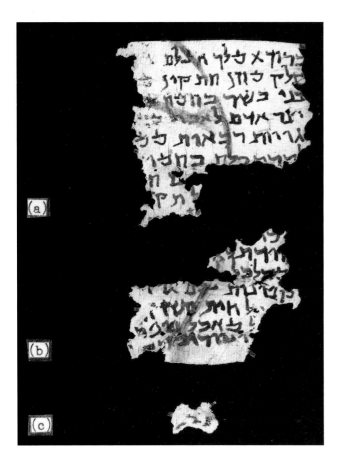

Fig. 4.21. Fragments of a
Hebrew papyrus found near
the Dura Europos
synagogue.

Stobi synagogue, which also mentions an oven, shows that within the synagogue complex there existed *triclinia*, or rooms in which meals were served. References to *triclinia* also appear in inscriptions from synagogues found in Israel.[43] The discovery, near the Dura synagogue, of fragments of parchment (Fig. 4.21) containing in Hebrew specifications concerning food not unlike those known from the Rabbinic *Birkat ha-Mazon* (Grace after Meals) should be understood similarly.[44]

Evidence indicates that the Diaspora synagogue complex provided an architectural setting that fulfilled still other social needs. On the coast of the Black Sea, synagogues served as official locales for the manumission of slaves.[45] Inscriptions from Sardis, Apamea, and Intercisa (Hungary) indicate that people sometimes had an inscription installed in the synagogue in fulfillment of a vow. In Hellenistic Egypt the synagogue building could offer a place of refuge to those guilty of various kinds of crimes (asylum).[46] In fourth-century Antioch, even non-Jews frequented the synagogue because justice was administered there in fairer ways than was normally the case in the later Roman Empire. Some non-Jews also believed that one who had sworn an oath in the synagogue (as opposed to elsewhere) was less likely to break it. It is again John Chrysostom who informs us that in the synagogue of Daphne, near Antioch, people were healed of their sicknesses by a procedure known as incubation: they would stay in the synagogue overnight, and then God would appear in a dream to heal them. Incubation was not commonly associated with the Diaspora synagogue but with the cult of Asklepios, the Greek god of healing. There is isolated evidence to suggest that at least some Jews believed in its efficacy.[47]

Taking all this evidence together, one sees that it is no exaggeration to say that from an urban and a socioreligious perspective, the synagogue was among the most noticeable institutions in the late ancient city. Even though some scholars continue to maintain that synagogues typically "developed on the undesirable periphery" of ancient towns, nothing could be further from the truth.[48] It is undeniable, for example, that the synagogue of Ostia is located in what now appears to be a deserted spot. Yet even a most superficial look at the general architectural history of Ostia reveals that it was exactly in the area surrounding the Ostia synagogue, near the Mediterranean coast, that the most intensive building activities took place over the course of the third and fourth centuries C.E.[49] Many of the other Diaspora synagogues mentioned earlier conform to the same pattern. Being an integral part of the late ancient urban landscape, these buildings fulfilled many needs of the Jewish community. In addition, they attracted the interest of pagans, who donated money to the synagogue. That such willingness existed at all on the part of non-Jews is highly significant. Inasmuch as in the ancient world status depended to a large extent on the sums of money one was able to spend for the benefit of the entire urban community—normally in the form of building projects—the donation of money to the Diaspora synagogue indicates that the Jewish communities of the Diaspora commanded much respect. It seems that one of the ways to augment one's status within ancient society as a whole was by becoming a benefactor of the local synagogue.

No less important, the Diaspora synagogue exerted a powerful influence on both the liturgical practices and the organizational structure of the early Christian communities as they formed during the first few centuries of the Common Era. It is because the Jewish communities of the Diaspora were so much a part of the fabric of late antique urban life that early Christian writers fulminated against the Jews in ways that leave little room for the imagination. Verbal and later physical attacks against the Jews took place not because the Jewish communities of the Diaspora were isolated and easy scapegoats, but rather because the Jews of late antiquity were religiously self-confident and because they were so well integrated into the sociopolitical structure of late ancient society. Late Roman laws forbidding Jews to build new synagogues have to be understood in the same light. Such laws were promulgated not merely to hassle the Jews but also to help effect the Christianization of the late ancient city through the forceful suppression of Jewish public-religious architecture.[50]

The Jews of the Diaspora and their synagogues were in a position that early Christian theologians and legislators found all too enviable. Diaspora synagogues became popular objects of attack as soon as Christianity started to spread more evenly through the provinces of the Roman Empire during the fourth century C.E. Students of late Roman law usually maintain that well into the fifth century the Jews and the buildings in which they worshipped were better off than were other non–Orthodox Christian groups. Yet reality was more complex than such an otherwise correct statement is capable of allowing for. As Jews in all parts of the Diaspora were to discover soon, legal and de facto protection were two very different things. Better than any other ancient source, it is the archaeology of the Diaspora synagogue that provides us, once again, with the means to determine what happened when Diaspora synagogues were destroyed.

In Gerasa, the foundation walls of the church destroyed, in 530 C.E., much of the synagogue below it; more important, the direction of the new building that was constructed on top of the synagogue was changed 180 degrees from an easterly into a westerly one. In Apamea, the foundation walls of the synagogue appear to have been reused when a church was erected in this spot, but the mosaic floor of the synagogue was covered entirely when the building was transformed into a Christian house of worship. In Stobi, foundation trenching for the Christian basilica constructed on top of the synagogue cut right through the walls of the synagogue; a thick layer of fill, which also contained fragments of fresco that had once decorated the synagogue, separated the original Jewish building from the Christian one on top of it. Such archaeological evidence suggests, in short, that even though Christian churches were built on the exact spot on which synagogues had once stood, neither in Gerasa nor in Stobi nor in Apamea can any architectural or structural continuity have been observed between the earlier Jewish and the later Christian building.

Contrary to what early Christian authors state when they observe that synagogues were frequently transformed into Christian churches, the archaeological evidence thus presents us with a more exact understanding to reconstruct how at the end of antiquity synagogues were turned into churches: while usurping the exact spot on which a synagogue had once fulfilled the needs of the Jewish community and attracted the attention of both pagans and Christians, church authorities normally obliterated every architectural trace that could remind one even vaguely of the one-time existence of a Jewish synagogue. Such a policy was strictly in conformance with early Christian theology. It reflects that most irresolvable of ambiguities that stands at the basis of so much of early Christian theology concerning the Jews and Judaism: the idea that the church is *verus Israel* or "the true Israel." According to this approach, the church replaced Judaism once and for all, and is the heir to the whole of the Jewish tradition.

CONCLUSION

Having discussed the most important archaeological evidence bearing on the Diaspora synagogue, we are now in a position to draw several brief conclusions concerning the development of ancient synagogue architecture in the Diaspora.

Scholars have often theorized about the possible origin of the Diaspora synagogue. A. Thomas Kraabel, a well-known authority on the Diaspora synagogue, observes that "ideologically and sociologically the Babylonian exile was where the synagogue began in its earliest sense, as a community assembly rather than a building. There is no archaeological evidence from that date, of course, and even the literary references are fragmentary."[51] We have seen that the earliest archaeological evidence regarding the Diaspora synagogue indeed dates to a later period (after 300 B.C.E.) and that it consists of inscriptions that were found in Egypt and refer to "houses of prayer." The reason we cannot identify these "houses of prayer" archaeologically is that, unlike the Diaspora synagogues of late antiquity, initially synagogues do not appear to have had those architectural features that make identification as a synagogue possible. The archaeological evidence suggests that many Diaspora synagogues first came into existence within the context of domestic architecture: the synagogues at Stobi, Delos, Priene, and Dura, for example, had all been private houses before they were monumentalized and turned into synagogues.

It is this process of transformation and monumentalization that makes the architectural history of the Diaspora synagogue so fascinating. On the one hand, the Jewish communities of the Diaspora made use of what was locally available. This explains why the mosaic floors of the Ḥamman Lif synagogue find their closest stylistic parallels in contemporary (non-Jewish) North African mosaic floors, just as the mosaic floors of the Elche synagogue are similar to those uncovered in nearby (non-Jewish) Roman villas, and the walls of the Ostia synagogue were built to conform to local, that is, non-Jewish, architectural practice. Similarly, the style of the Dura paintings is best understood by comparing them with the wall paintings (see Fig. 4.4) discovered elsewhere in Dura Europos. The bones found at two different locations within the Dura synagogue complex can finally also be explained by taking into account local factors. The excavations of other buildings in Dura have shown that the inclusion of such (invisible!) foundation deposits was common practice among Dura's architects. Supposing that the Dura synagogue too was constructed by local, non-Jewish architects, it is more than likely that the Jews of Dura did not even know that impure objects such as human bones were hidden away in the walls of their communal center.

On the other hand, and no less important, we have noted that in the Diaspora synagogue numerous local techniques and artistic traditions were used to decorate buildings that were unmistakably Jewish. The main architectural characteristic of the fully developed Diaspora synagogue was the Torah Shrine. The Torah was housed in a niche or an apse that was especially constructed for this purpose and that was located in the spot that was visually most prominent. Special platforms and tables were constructed for the reading of the Torah, and sometimes even special chairs were carved where Torah scrolls could be kept before they were returned to the Torah Shrine. The architectural characteristics of the

Diaspora synagogue all participate in making the main hall of the Diaspora synagogue into a space that served a well-defined purpose: Jewish religious worship in general and devotion to the Torah in particular.

Surveying the plans of the synagogues we have discussed in this chapter, we have discovered, in short, that structurally and functionally these buildings have surprisingly much in common. It is therefore incorrect to say, as many scholars do nowadays, that "a stunning diversity" characterizes the architecture of the Diaspora synagogue. It is even more incorrect to infer from this supposed diversity that the Jewish communities of the Diaspora all practiced different forms of Judaism. Insofar as they existed, the differences between the various Diaspora synagogues were in degree and not in nature. What is, in fact, stunning about the Diaspora synagogues is that even though these buildings were erected by Jewish communities that were completely separated in both place and time, such buildings nonetheless shared a common architectural language. For that reason Jews from North Africa who visited, say, their brethren in the Balkans could feel at home almost immediately (in terms of architectural space) when they attended services in synagogues in such faraway places as Stobi and Plovdiv. Liturgical practices may have differed somewhat from one Diaspora synagogue to the next. But Diaspora Jews agreed that what mattered most to them was the one element that united them all: observance of the holy Torah, which was written on scrolls that were preserved in a building they called "the holy" or even "the most holy synagogue."

Synagogues in the Land of Israel

The Art and Architecture of Late Antique Synagogues

RACHEL HACHLILI
University of Haifa

One of the main contributions of this exhibition is that, for the first time, material evidence for synagogues in the Land of Israel has been assembled in a single place. Pieces that left their homeland over a century ago only to reside in European collections have been brought together with artifacts that were excavated only a few years ago to tell the story of the synagogue and its development in the Land of Israel during the Roman and Byzantine periods. This chapter surveys the remains of ancient synagogues in the Land of Israel, stressing both the unifying features of these buildings and the uniqueness of each building. I will also suggest parallels with Christian and pagan architecture and art. We will begin by briefly presenting the architecture of Second Temple period synagogues and then move on to the architecture and art of synagogues during late antiquity.

SYNAGOGUES DURING THE SECOND TEMPLE PERIOD

Though synagogues during the Second Temple period are mentioned in a number of literary sources, and even in an inscription from Jerusalem,[1] no building was identified as a synagogue until the excavation of Masada by Yigael Yadin, son of E.L. Sukenik, during the early 1960s.[2] Since then structures at Herodium,[3] Gamla,[4] Migdal,[5] and Capernaum (Plate XXI)[6] have been interpreted as synagogues.[7]

The structures at Masada, Herodium, and Gamla are all somewhat similar in architecture. The largest is Gamla, 18.5 × 24.2 meters. All are rectangular halls divided by rows of columns into a central nave and side aisles. At Masada, Herodium, and Gamla stepped benches were erected on all four walls of the hall facing the center. The focal point of

Plate XXI. The synagogue at Capernaum.

each of these structures seems to have been the center of the room. Each building dates to the first century C.E. except for Gamla, which dates to the end of the previous century. The free-standing structure at Gamla was the only building that was constructed as a public house of assembly (see Plate III). This building was adorned with architectural ornamentation on its lintels and capitals. A ritual bath was constructed adjacent to it on the northeast corner. It is likely that the Gamla synagogue, constructed with four-tiered benches on all four walls, followed the triclinium plan common in the Herodian palaces of Jericho and elsewhere.[8] The preexisting buildings at Masada and Herodium were converted by the Jewish defenders into meeting houses during the course of the First Jewish Revolt against Rome of 66–74 C.E. The interior arrangement of these synagogue halls was the result of local improvisation. At Masada (see Fig. 2.1), the hall was reconstructed through the relocation of columns and the addition of tiered benches on all four walls. A small room was constructed in the northwest corner of the hall that served as a repository (*genizah*).[9] Similarly at Herodium, a triclinium was converted through the addition of columns and the construction of tiered benches on all four walls.

The identity of the structure at Migdal is unclear. Netzer and Maoz[10] suggest that it was a nympheum. A first-century synagogue has been identified under the fourth- to fifth-century synagogue at Capernaum.[11] This structure follows the main contours of the later building. Benches are assumed to have lined the walls. The dating of this structure to the first century is based upon pottery that was found under the pavement. If the structure could be identified as a synagogue, it would be the only Second Temple period synagogue to have been discovered buried under a late antique synagogue.

The rarity of Second Temple period synagogues may be attributed to a number of factors, not the least of which is the fact that there are no distinguishing architectural features or symbols that aid in the identification of these earliest synagogue buildings. Distinctive Jewish symbols within synagogues did not appear until the second to third centuries, nor did Torah Shrines. Synagogues have been identified by scholars based upon circumstantial evidence. All of the buildings that are said to be synagogues have similar architectural plans, which scholars assume reflect similarities in function. In fact, there is no firm proof that any of these assembly halls served as synagogues in the sense that we might expect from later centuries.[12]

SYNAGOGUES DURING LATE ANTIQUITY

Modern archaeological study of ancient synagogues began in the nineteenth century with surveys of Palestine by British, German, and French scholars.[13] These early explorers discovered remains of ancient synagogues in many regions, particularly in the Upper Galilee. Archaeological excavation of synagogues in the region north of the Sea of Galilee was undertaken by Heinrich Kohl and Carl Watzinger between 1905 and 1907. Eleven sites in all were surveyed, including Capernaum, Chorazin, Umm el-Kanatir, Horvat Ammudim, Baram, Meiron, and Nabratein. The excavators dated these synagogues to the second century C.E. The results of their research, published as *Antike Synagogen in Galilaea*, appeared in Leipzig in 1916, and established the field of synagogue studies on firm foundations. The most important work by these scholars was carried out at Tel Hum, ancient Capernaum (Fig. 5.1), on the northern shore of the Sea of Galilee.[14] Kohl and Watzinger dated synagogues in the Galilee to the second century through art historical comparison with pagan temple architecture in Syria and Lebanon.

The next major synagogue discovery in the Land of Israel came in 1918 when a shell accidentally exposed a mosaic during the battle between British and Ottoman troops near Ain al-Duq, ancient Naaran. Naaran is located 7.5 kilometers north of Jericho. The synagogue was subsequently excavated by the Dominican Fathers of the Ecole Biblique,

Fig. 5.1. Frieze with an image of a carriage from the synagogue at Capernaum.

Jerusalem, in 1919 and 1921.[15] This building was of a different type, having been built as a basilica with a carpet mosaic. A Torah Shrine may have stood in an apse, aligned with Jerusalem. Naaran was dated to the sixth century, and its mosaic bore images of menorahs, a Torah Shrine, Daniel in the lion's den, and the zodiac. The appearance of human beings in the mosaic was particularly surprising to the excavators, since the human form had never been seen before in early Jewish art. This synagogue discovery was soon followed by a similar mosaic in the Beth Shean valley. The Beth Alpha floor mosaic was uncovered in 1928–29 and excavated by E.L. Sukenik on behalf of the recently established Hebrew University of Jerusalem.[16] The beauty of this floor, which bore images of a Torah Shrine, a zodiac wheel, and the Binding of Isaac, sent waves of excitement throughout the Jewish community in the Land of Israel.

Plate XXII. Ashlar with an image of a menorah from the synagogue of Eshtemoa.

After the Beth Alpha discovery, two synagogues with a similar interior arrangement were excavated, one in Syria, the other in Judea. The synagogue of Dura Europos on the Euphrates, discovered in 1932, was completed in its final form in 244–45 C.E.[17] The synagogue of Eshtemoa (Plate XXII), in Judea, was discovered in 1935–36. It was dated to the fourth century by the excavators. In both of these buildings a Torah Shrine was built in the form of a niche on the wide wall of the synagogue.[18] Buildings of this form are generally called broadhouses.

SYNAGOGUE ARCHITECTURE

A major breakthrough in synagogue archaeology was the typology of synagogue architecture developed by the eminent archaeologist Michael Avi-Yonah. Avi-Yonah divided the evidence into three types (Fig. 5.2).[19] He suggests that the Galilean-type predominated during the late second to third centuries. It was at this time, during the period of growth and security when Rabbi Judah the Prince completed the Mishnah and ruled over Jewish Palestine, that the synagogues of Capernaum, Baram, and the others were built. The next group Avi-Yonah termed "transitional synagogues." This group included the broadhouses as well as basilicas with a central nave and two side aisles, like Ḥammath Tiberias B (Fig. 5.3), which he dated to the fourth and fifth centuries. The last group consisted of apsidal basilicas like Beth Alpha and Naaran that date to the sixth century.

This typology was ultimately discarded after a reevaluation of the Capernaum synagogue and the excavation of a synagogue at Khirbet Shema in the Upper Galilee. Scholars had long noted some anomalies in the dating of the Capernaum synagogue. Sukenik had dated an Aramaic inscription found on a column to the fourth century or later, and Avi-Yonah had noted that Byzantine period capitals had been used in the building. In 1971, V. Corbo, S. Loffrada, and A. Spijkerman, working on behalf of the Franciscan Protectorate of the Holy Land, discovered several coin hoards beneath the stone pavement of the synagogue in several places. These coins date from the Hellenistic period through the mid-fifth

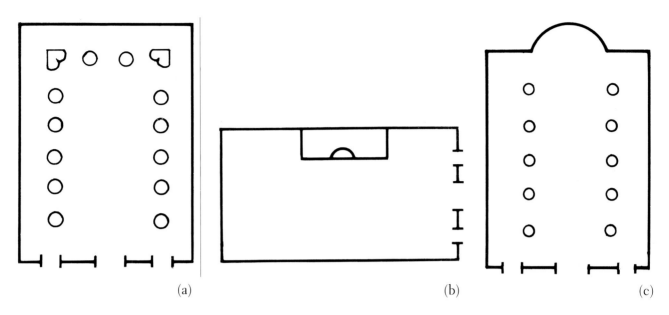

(a)   (b)   (c)

Fig. 5.2. Plans of the three synagogue types:
(a) Galilean-type basilica, (b) broadhouse,
and (c) apsical basilica.

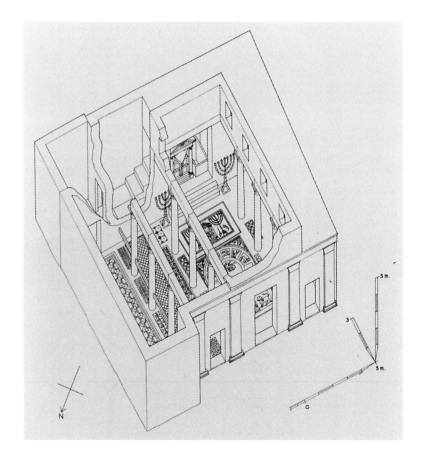

Fig. 5.3. Reconstructed drawing of the synagogue at
Ḥammath Tiberias B.

century C.E.: "Several of these Late Roman coins were still firmly imbedded in the thick layer of mortar, making their chronological significance unquestionable."[20]

These scholars argued that the synagogue must, therefore, be dated to this period. This discovery caused a paradigm shift in scholarship on ancient synagogues. Even Avi-Yonah, who at first attacked this finding, was moving toward its acceptance shortly before his death in 1974. He writes:

> Formerly regarded as the earliest of the existing Galilee synagogues, the building [Capernaum] was now dated some two hundred years later on account of the large coin hoards of the fourth and fifth centuries found buried under the pavements or near the walls. . . . Other scholars have so far been skeptical of this opinion, which indeed leaves a great deal to be explained.[21]

In the continuation of this discussion, Avi-Yonah's main difficulties with this new approach are essentially historical. His objection to it is that this synagogue is so unlike the Hammath Tiberias synagogue "ten miles to the south," with its lavish mosaics. How is it possible, he asks, for two buildings, so radically different, to be contemporary? Slowly a new consensus has emerged suggesting that synagogue architecture developed principally along regional lines.[22] In answer to Avi-Yonah, scholars who accept this approach argue that the synagogue of Capernaum belongs to a different regional tradition of synagogue architecture than Hammath Tiberias, despite their geographical proximity. More pointedly, the third-century synagogue of Khirbet Shema, a broadhouse of the "transitional" type, was constructed 600 meters away from the Meiron synagogue (Fig. 5.4), a roughly contemporaneous "Galilean-type" synagogue![23] This discovery clearly cast doubt upon the typological approach. Remains of over one hundred synagogues have been uncovered in the Land of Israel, and numerous others are mentioned in literary sources. Synagogues were constructed continuously during the Late Roman-Byzantine periods. Synagogue building seems to have been most prolific during two periods: the mid- or late third and early fourth centuries C.E.,

Fig. 5.4. The synagogue at Meiron photographed by Kohl and Watzinger, 1905–7.

when most of the Galilean synagogues were erected, and the sixth century, when many of the characteristic Byzantine synagogues were built. Each synagogue should be examined separately to determine its date, by analysis of the data revealed as the result of excavation and by its ornamentation, style, and historical content.[24]

No universal or uniform synagogue plan existed in the Land of Israel during late antiquity. A common feature of all types was a spacious hall that was used to serve the congregation for reading the Torah and for prayer, with specific features of Torah Shrine, benches, and gallery to suit their particular needs. Differing architectural types usually reflect regional and local traditions as well as the social standing of the synagogue builders or differing religious conceptions.

As Kohl and Watzinger first suggested, synagogues in the region north of the Sea of Galilee, extending in the west to the Mount Meiron region and in the east into the Golan Heights, bear strong affinities. In the territory north of the Sea of Galilee and the Golan Heights we find a longitudinal colonnaded stone structure with benches, characterized by a richly decorated stone facade. The use of the structure as an assembly center determined its architectural plan, which usually consists of an oblong hall divided by two rows of stone columns running lengthwise into a central nave and two side aisles. Other characteristic features of these buildings are a permanent Torah Shrine and a second-story galley.[25]

Synagogues of the Galilean-type—Capernaum (Fig. 5.5), Chorazin (Plate XXIII), Merot (Plate XXIV), Meiron (Fig. 5.4), and Baram (see Plate i)—all had gabled facades that were usually built on the short side of the structure. They had a high central portal with two smaller doorways flanking it.[26] Most of the Galilean synagogues had triple portal facades richly ornamented in relief, although at Nabratein and Merot we find a single portal. Synagogues in the Golan Heights usually had only one portal. Facades with both triple and single entryways appear in pagan architecture from Syria, whose rich surface decoration is also similar to that which we find in synagogue art. Several pagan temples in Syria have triple

Fig. 5.5. A reconstructed model of the synagogue at Capernaum by Kohl and Watzinger.

תה דכר לטב יוסחבר חלקן ברחו

Fig. 5.6. Drawing of the lintel from the synagogue at Kanef.

portals.[27] As in Galilean synagogues, the central portals of these buildings are wider and higher than the two smaller side entrances. Other temples have a single entrance, sometimes flanked by niches or windows.[28] The Jewish preference for the triple entrance may have had some connection with the tradition of the triple Nicanor Gate, the portal to the south of the Temple Mount that served as the main entrance to the Jerusalem Temple.

The main feature of Galilean and Golan Heights synagogues is their finely ornamented facades. Facade decoration was focused upon the frames of the entrance portals and sometimes a central heraldic design on the lintel. This decoration encompassed the entire surface of the portal frames and consisted of both geometric and floral patterns (Fig. 5.6).[29] Synagogues in the Galilee and the Golan were generally built of indigenous stone. Those of the Galilean type were built of limestone, except for Chorazin, which, like the Golan synagogues, was built of basalt. It is worth noting that the white limestone used at Capernaum was imported to the site from a location farther to the west. The differences in consistency between soft limestone and hard basalt led to the development of differing artistic traditions, as reflected in extant lintels, arches, architraves, friezes, gables, and capitals. Synagogue portal ornamentation is frequently compared with the portals of first- to second-century C.E. pagan temples in Syria. This decorative tradition continued in the churches of northern Syria during the fourth century.

Kohl and Watzinger reconstructed the gables of Galilean synagogues in the light of fragmentary evidence, suggesting that the gables of these structures resembled second-century Roman temple architecture in Syria. This reconstruction, based upon minimal evidence, places the gable along the entire width of the synagogue facade. It is more likely that the gable was constructed as a "narrow facade," encompassing only the center of the building. This form is common in contemporaneous Syrian churches. Shrivel Yeivin argued that the Beth Shearim synagogue had a narrow facade, and Ze'ev Yeivin has suggested both possibilities, both the "wide" and the "narrow" gable, in his reconstruction of the Chorazin synagogue (Plate XXIII, Fig. 5.7).[30]

Plate XXIII. The synagogue at Chorazin.

Fig. 5.7. Aedicula from the synagogue at Chorazin (Cat. 44).

Plate XXIV. The synagogue at Merot.

Fig. 5.8. Coin hoard from the synagogue at Merot, with scale (Cat. 47).

The columns that supported galleries in most Galilean-type synagogues were constructed in a "U" pattern on the north, east, and west sides of the building. This arrangement further emphasized the facade wall of the synagogue, which was aligned toward the south, toward Jerusalem. On the interior of this wall were one or two aediculae. Remains of single platforms for Torah Shrines beside the main portal of the synagogue were uncovered at Gush Ḥalav, Meiron, and Ḥorvat Ammudim. At Capernaum, Chorazin, Nabratein, and Merot (Plate XXIV, Fig. 5.8), two aediculae flanked the central portal of the synagogue on the south (Jerusalem-aligned) wall. They probably had separate functions. One of these aediculae undoubtedly served as a Torah Shrine, and the other may have held a menorah. Free-standing seven-branched menorahs have been uncovered at a number of sites, including Ḥammath Tiberias A (Plate XXV) and Maon in Judea. In the Golan Heights the Torah Shrine was constructed as an aedicula. It stood either on the wall opposite the portal, aligned with Jerusalem, as at Qasrin, or beside the entrance, as at En Nashut and in Galilean-type synagogues. The aedicula form was used in the Galilee and in the Golan from the second through the sixth century C.E. It should be noted that no apse has been found in any of the Galilean-type or Golan Heights synagogues. Most of the Galilean synagogues were paved with flagstones, though mosaic pavements were uncovered at Ḥorvat Ammudim and Merot (Plates XXVI and XLb).

Plate XXV. Menorah from the synagogue at Ḥammath Tiberias A (Cat. 57).

Plate XXVI. Mosaic with pomegranates and shofars from the synagogue at Merot (Cat. 48).

The remains of small columns and capitals that probably belonged to the gallery on an upper floor were recovered by excavators. Scholars are divided as to the function of such a gallery. Some regard it as the women's section, implying that segregation existed between the sexes. Others maintain that many synagogues in Israel did not possess a gallery and that Rabbinic literature does not indicate such segregation.[31] The only fact is that from the upper gallery floor an unhindered view of the main hall was possible, so that the worshippers could follow and observe the ceremonies conducted below.

The synagogue of Khirbet Shema has a unique plan. The orientation of the building makes it a broadhouse. It had two rows of interior columns on pedestals. The main and side entrances are on the north wall, and a raised platform for an aedicula was built on the south, Jerusalem-oriented wall. This is different from the plans of all other Galilean synagogues, and, as we have noted, is noteworthy because of its proximity to Meiron and Gush Ḥalav.[32]

Synagogues in the hill country of Judea form a distinct group among late antique Palestinian synagogues. Torah Shrines in the form of niches that extend into the wall of the synagogue have been found in synagogues throughout the Land of Israel. Two are located in Ḥammath Tiberias (synagogues A and B) and four in Judea (Susiya, Eshtemoa, Maon, and Rimmon), suggesting that choice of this type of Torah Shrine had regional implications. The Torah Shrine at Khirbet Susiya is particularly elaborate. It is constructed as a niche on the north, Jerusalem-aligned wall. A bema protrudes into the hall before it. This bema was constructed of three benches ending in rounded edges. At the center of the bema are five steps, possibly for ascent to the Torah Shrine. Depressions were discovered around the bema in which ten chancel posts and elaborately decorated screens were erected.[33]

The apsidal basilica became a dominant architectural feature in synagogue architecture in the Lower Galilee, the Jordan Rift Valley, and the coastal plane during the late fifth or early sixth century. The apse was constructed as an integral part of the structure, becoming a dominant feature of synagogue architecture. A good example of this sort of building is the synagogue at Maoz Ḥayyim.[34] In the earliest phase the synagogue was constructed as a simple hall with a nave and two side aisles, a platform that undoubtedly bore a Torah Shrine at its focal point. The entrance to the synagogue was from the east. In the second phase at Maoz Ḥayyim, during the fifth century, the hall was greatly enlarged and an apse added. This architectural form focuses attention on the contents of the apse, the Torah Shrine. The synagogue was paved with a carpet mosaic (Plate XXVII) that bore images of the menorah, birds, and floral images. In the final sixth-century phase the bema, in front of the apse, was enlarged into the hall itself and enclosed by a chancel screen. The focal point of this hall was the Torah Shrine, the base of which is extant.

Synagogue chancel screens have been discovered at a number of sites.[35] These are

Plate XXVII. Mosaic pavement from the synagogue at Maoz Ḥayyim.

Plate XXVIII. Chancel post from the synagogue at Ḥammath Tiberias A (Cat. 56).

Fig. 5.9. (a) Chancel screen from the synagogue at Reḥov (Cat. 63). (b) Christian chancel screen from Massout Itzhak.

(a)

(b)

usually decorated with Jewish symbols (Plate XXVIII, Fig. 5.9, Plates XXIXa and XXIXb), including seven-branched menorahs. The chancel arrangement was borrowed directly from church architecture (Fig. 5.9b). Within the Christian context the separation between the nave and the platform was designed to differentiate between the laity and the clergy. Within the synagogue, its purpose was to separate the Torah Shrine from the prayer hall.

All known Torah Shrines were constructed of stone, elevated on bases, and approached by steps. The stone lintel of a Torah Shrine was uncovered at Nabratein in the Upper Galilee (see Plate V). The Nabratein relief has a broad gable with a conch design in its arch. The gable is topped with two heraldic lions. At Nabratein the Torah Shrine is constructed as an aedicula, with a hole that was probably used to suspend a lamp at its pinnacle. Torah Shrines that appear in carpet mosaics are often flanked by two free-standing

Plate XXIXa. Chancel screen fragment with menorah from Gaza (Cat. 79).

Plate XXIXb. Open-work chancel screen, Tiberias (Cat. 55).

menorahs. This arrangement is first seen at Ḥammath Tiberias B (Plate XXX) and in relief and graffiti in the Beth Shearim necropolis (Fig. 5.10), both dating to the fourth century. This iconography appeared during the sixth century at Susiya, Naaran, and Beth Alpha. The image of a Shrine flanked by menorahs also appeared on a plaque (Plate XXXI), which

Plate XXX. Torah Shrine panel from the synagogue at Ḥammath Tiberias B.

Plate XXXI. Plaque in the form of a Torah Shrine (Cat. 40).

Fig. 5.10. Relief of a Torah Shrine from catacomb 4 at Beth Shearim.

110

Plate XXXII. Torah Shrine panel from the synagogue mosaic at Beth Alpha.

was apparently directed against the evil eye, that has been acquired by Hebrew University. At Beth Alpha (Plate XXXII) a conch also appears, and a lamp (called today an eternal lamp) is shown hanging from the gable of the shrine. There two animals, in this case birds, flank the gable of the aedicula. At Ḥammath Tiberias B wooden doors of the ark are portrayed inside the Torah Shrine. In at least a few synagogues a wooden cabinet that housed the Torah scrolls stood within a stone aedicula much like that discovered at Nabratein and portrayed at Ḥammath Tiberias.

It is likely that, as in the visual depictions, synagogue Torah Shrines were often flanked by two seven-branched menorahs. Remains of four large menorahs have been uncovered. The menorah from Ḥammath Tiberias A in 1921 and a recently reconstructed menorah from Maon in Judea in 1987[36] (see Fig. 2.12) are the most impressive. Lamps are illustrated suspended from the branches of the menorah images from Naaran (Fig. 5.11), Susiya, and other sites (Plate XXXIII). This undoubtedly reflects lighting practices in late antique synagogues.

SYNAGOGUE ART DURING LATE ANTIQUITY

Throughout the nineteenth century scholars were convinced that the Jews as a people were artistically deprived. For this reason Kohl and Watzinger assumed that the Galilean-type synagogues were built by the Roman authorities for the Jews, who certainly would (or could) not build these fine structures on their own. During this period, it was often said, the Jewish "genius" was expressed through the Word, not through the image. This attitude was expressed even in so thoroughly Jewish a publication as *The Jewish Encyclopedia* in 1902:

Plate XXXIII. Detail of mosaic floor depicting a menorah with hanging lamps from the synagogue at Beth Shean B.

Fig. 5.11. (a) Drawing of the mosaic floor depicting two menorahs with hanging lamps from the synagogue at Naaran. (b) Lintel fragment with a menorah in a wreath (Cat. 43).

(a)

(b)

112

It was the religion of the Jews that precluded the full development of the art of sculpture. . . . In the most ancient times, when images were not proscribed, the technical ability to make them artistically was lacking; and when in later periods this artistic skill might have been acquired from others, images were forbidden. . . . Such a command as that of the Decalogue (Ex. 20:4, Deut. 5:8) would have been impossible to a nation possessed of such artistic gifts as the Greeks, and was carried out to its ultimate consequences—as to-day in Islam—only because the people lacked artistic imagination, with its creative power and formative imagination. The same reason, to which is to be added a defective sense of color . . . prevented any development of painting.[37]

As this text notes, the source of this Jewish lack was thought to have been the Second Commandment:

You shall not make for yourself a sculptured image, or any likeness of what is in the heavens above, or on the earth below, or in the waters under the earth. You shall not bow down to them or serve them. . . . (Exod. 20:4–5)

In fact, these verses are open to interpretation. It may be read strictly as a prohibition against all images. Alternatively, the Second Commandment may be seen as restricting images when there is fear that "you shall not bow down to them or serve them." Other sorts of images, then, may be permitted. These two interpretations set the contours of Jewish attitudes toward art from antiquity into the modern period.

Jewish art of the latter Second Temple, for example, seems to have functioned under a strict and widely held interpretation of the Second Commandment. Artistic creations from this period are characterized by their focus upon geometric and floral patterns. This phenomenon is well reflected in Nachman Avigad's excavations of aristocratic villas in what is today the Jewish Quarter of Jerusalem, where the only image of a living creature is a single bird in a fresco. This bird is the image that proves the rule, for throughout Jerusalem no other such images have been found. In fact, the only images known from outside Jerusalem are birds alighted upon vines that were discovered in the "Goliath" family tomb in Jericho.[38]

The situation is radically different in Jewish art of the third century and onward. A broad repertoire of images appear within Jewish contexts, including both Jewish symbols and blatantly pagan images. Discovery of the synagogues of Naaran, Beth Alpha, the necropolis of Beth Shearim, and, most important, the synagogue of Dura Europos in Syria has provided evidence that Jews during late antiquity often interpreted the Second Commandment in a more liberal manner. Some scholars, particularly the eminent historian E.R. Goodenough in his monumental history *Jewish Symbols in the Greco-Roman Period*, interpret the development of art as evidence for a non-Rabbinic mystery religion that developed with the "breakdown" of the authority of the aniconic Rabbis when the Temple was destroyed. Owing to Goodenough's provocative counterhistory, the most important scholars of Jewish history, literature, and art have turned to the question of art in Judaism during late antiquity.[39] A consensus has developed that the appearance of art among Jews is reflective of the overall accommodation with Hellenism that Judaism made during the later Roman and Byzantine periods.[40] Many Jews seem to have interpreted the Second Commandment rather loosely, apparently not considering images to be idolatrous. This attitude is expressed in an Aramaic paraphrase in Targum Pseudo-Jonathan of Leviticus 26:1, which modifies the Bible's stern prohibition against making and bowing down to "carved stone":

. . . nor shall you place a figured stone in your land to bow down upon it. But a pavement figured with images and likenesses you may make on the floor of your synagogue[s]. And do not bow down [idolatrously] to it, for I am the Lord your God.[41]

Plate XXXIV. Mosaic from the synagogue at Ein-Gedi.

Attitudes within the Rabbinic community were mixed in regard to art. Some Sages were vehemently against art, even refusing to look upon the image of the emperor on a coin. Others considered it to be relatively harmless. A statement in the Jerusalem Talmud that was preserved in its entirety only in a manuscript discovered in the Cairo Geniza reflects a more tolerant (if somewhat ambivalent) position:

Fig. 5.12. Mosaic inscription from the central hall of the synagogue at Ein-Gedi (Cat. 81).

In the days of Rabbi Johanan they permitted images *[tzayirin]* on its walls, and he did not stop them.

In the days of R. Abun they permitted images on mosaics and he did not stop them.[42]

Toward the close of antiquity, attitudes that were less tolerant of artistic presentations resurfaced. During the mid-sixth century C.E. synagogue art in the Jordan Rift Valley and in Judaea seems to have taken an aniconic turn. For instance, at Ein-Gedi (Plate XXXIV) no figurative zodiac appears. Rather, a list of the zodiac signs appears in a floor inscription (Fig. 5.12). Similarly, the Reḥov inscription, with twenty-nine lines of text, is by definition aniconic. This is in marked contrast to the nearby Beth Alpha floor, and it reflects the sensibilities of a very different community. Biblical scenes and the zodiac are replaced by a floral and geometric carpet at Khirbet Susiya. In other late-sixth–century synagogues the design now consists of floral and geometric carpets (Jericho, Maoz Ḥayyim, and Ein-Gedi). It is important to note that a Jewish symbol, usually the menorah, was integrated into the decorated synagogue pavement. Jewish iconoclastic activity is clearly felt in the Naaran synagogue (Fig. 5.13), where images of the zodiac signs were carefully removed by iconoclasts sometime after its sixth-century construction. Winged figures on the facade of the Capernaum synagogue were also carefully removed in antiquity.

The most common Jewish symbols during late antiquity were the menorah, the Torah Shrine, ritual appurtenances such as the lulav and etrog, the shofar, and the incense shovel.[43] These Jewish symbols derived from the symbolism of the Jerusalem Temple, per-

Fig. 5.13. Sections of the defaced zodiac wheel mosaic from the synagogue at Naaran: (a) Scorpio; (b) Virgo.

(a)

(b)

Plate XXXV. Oil lamp with a menorah handle (Cat. 41).

Fig. 5.14. Lamp handle in the form of a menorah from the synagogue at Beth Shean A (Cat. 61).

haps explaining why they are so pervasive yet so limited in number. They are to be found in synagogue art, in funerary art, and sometimes within domestic contexts.

The menorah was by far the most important and widespread Jewish symbol during this period. The history of Jewish use of this symbol can be traced to the Second Temple period. The first occurrence was on a bronze coin of Mattathias Antigonus (reigned 40–37 B.C.E.), the last of the Hasmonean kings. Here two Temple implements are represented: the menorah appears on one side, the table of the showbread on the other. The menorah next appears inscribed on a stucco fragment from a house in the Jewish Quarter of Jerusalem that dates from the first century B.C.E. to the first century C.E. It again appears on the triumphal Arch of Titus in Rome, constructed in 80 C.E. to commemorate the Roman defeat of Judea in the Jewish War of 66–74 C.E. The menorah and the showbread table were the most sacred Temple vessels. They most likely represented the professional signs of the Jerusalem priesthood during the Second Temple period. Between the destruction of the Temple in 70 C.E. and the Bar Kokhba Revolt of 132–35, menorahs appeared on oil lamps from Judea, the so-called *darom* (southern) type, and inscribed on two ossuaries. From the late third century onward the menorah appeared in Jewish art, most commonly in synagogue ornamentation (Plate XXXV, Fig. 5.14), mosaic pavements (Plate XXXVI), columns and capitals (Plates XXXVII and XXXVIII), lintels, and doors. As we have seen, seven-branched menorahs were also used to illuminate synagogues. The menorah became the most important Jewish symbol, symbolizing both Judaism and the Jewish people. This choice of a Temple-based image reflects a distinctly Greco-Roman aesthetic. Most localities chose

Plate XXXVI. Detail of the Torah Shrine panel from the synagogue mosaic at Beth Shean A.

Plate XXXVII. Capital with a menorah from the synagogue at Ḥammath Tiberias A (Cat. 58).

Plate XXXVIII. Detail of a capital with a menorah from the synagogue at Capernaum.

Fig. 5.15. Plate with a menorah and Torah Shrine from Naanah (Cat. 73).

symbols from their local temples. The Jews chose a symbol from their God-given cult, which they perceived as being in temporary abeyance.

Renditions of the Torah Shrine encountered in synagogue art appear on mosaic floors and reliefs, as well as on tomb walls and doors, on a ceramic bowl from Nabratein, on a bronze plate from Naanah (Fig. 5.15) in Judea, and on oil lamps.[44] The Torah Shrine was also part of the symbolic repertoire of Jewish art. It was perceived as the focal point of synagogue worship, symbolizing the place of Scripture par excellence.

Depictions of the menorah flanked by ritual objects (Plate XXXIX), the shofar, lulav,

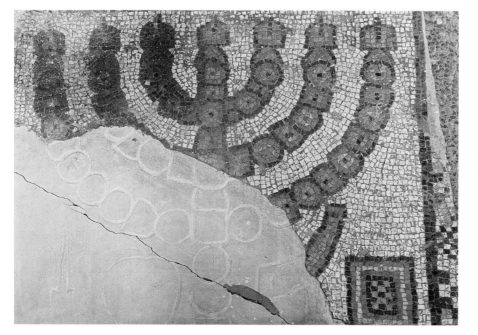

Plate XXXIX. Menorah panel from the synagogue at Ḥuseifa (Cat. 59).

Fig. 5.16. Drawing of Gerasa synagogue mosaic, Jordan, c. fifth century, by N. Avigad (Cat. 66).

etrog, and incense shovel, or the more elaborate Torah Shrine flanked by menorahs and ritual objects, are frequently represented in synagogal art.[45] These motifs came to symbolize the Temple cult, where the shofar was sounded on the New Year and the lulav and etrog taken up on Tabernacles. Many scholars see the incense shovel as representing the service of the Day of Atonement. Significantly, the shofar, lulav, etrog, and possibly even the incense shovel were important elements of synagogue liturgy. Their representation thus makes an important connection between the Temple and the synagogue.

Another common symbol is the conch, which appears in synagogue art in the form of a stylized scallop ornamentation with other motifs. It is portrayed frequently as an ornamented architectural element of the gable of the Torah shrine. The conch in this connotation seems to symbolize the synagogal Torah Shrine itself and has developed characteristics of a religious symbol in Jewish art.[46]

The biblical themes depicted on synagogue mosaic pavements in the Land of Israel were selected from a relatively small number of biblical stories: Noah's ark, the Binding of Isaac, the Twelve Tribes, King David, and Daniel in the lions' den.[47] The themes were depicted in simple narratives, although some of the scenes may have had symbolic interpretation—such as salvation—and they might have been associated with prayers offered within the synagogue context. Noteworthy is the recurrence of biblical scenes in more than one synagogue mosaic pavement in the Land of Israel and on mosaics and wall paintings in the Diaspora: Noah's ark at Gerasa (Fig. 5.16) and Misis-Mopsuestia (in Cilicia);[48] the Binding of Isaac at Beth Alpha, Sepphoris, and Dura Europos; David/Orpheus at Gaza (Plate XLa) and Dura Europos; David with Goliath's weapons at Merot (Plate XLb); and Daniel in the lions' den at Naaran (Fig. 5.17) and Susiya. The choice of themes was derived from the sociocultural climate of the period and was meant to be a reminder of and reference to traditional historical events. Some scholars[49] maintain that these themes were used for symbolic or didactic purposes. The biblical scenes found so far do not seem to have a common denominator in regard to style or origins. The style, form, and artistic depiction on each of these floors is completely different, and each scene may be traced back to a distinct influence or source. The Binding of Isaac at Beth Alpha is an example of local popular art. Joseph Gutmann has recently suggested important Christian parallels to this scene.[50] Noah's ark in Gerasa is more realistic, probably deriving from lists of animals in a pattern book. The image of David as Orpheus, portrayed on the mosaic pavement of the synagogue of Gaza, shows in its depiction and iconography Hellenistic and Byzantine influences. Daniel in the lions' den at Naaran is similar to the same theme in Christian iconography.

Plate XLa. David mosaic from the synagogue at Gaza.

Plate XLb. Mosaic depiction of a Roman soldier from the synagogue at Merot (Cat. 49).

Fig. 5.17. Drawing of Daniel in the lion's den from the synagogue at Naaran.

Some similarity does exist in the arrangement of the three connecting panels and in biblical subject matter both at Beth Alpha and Naaran, which may suggest a common model.

The origin of the biblical themes in Jewish and Christian art has been the subject of heated discussions by art historians. Some maintain that these images originated in illuminated biblical manuscripts and were taken over into mosaic depictions.[51] No proof, however, exists of early illuminated manuscripts dating before the sixth century, and then only within Christian contexts. If such illustration existed, a uniformity of design and pattern would be expected. It is quite possible that the biblical themes might have originated in pattern books where they would be included as subject matter for the decoration of synagogues.[52]

Images that appear in both synagogues and non-Jewish religious buildings often share visual motifs (Plate XLI). Even when the form of the pagan motif was appropriated, it would be wrong to assume that its symbolic value was also transferred. On the contrary, a symbol has a certain value that is applicable only within its own context. It loses its original significance when it is transplanted into another milieu. Once taken over into a Jewish context new symbolic associations were made. Thus the zodiac motif (Plates XLII and XLIII), so common in ancient synagogue art, was used by Jews primarily for its calendrical functions.

Plate XLI. Mosaic panel with a Gorgon head from the synagogue at Yafia (Cat. 67).

Plate XLII. Mosaic of a zodiac wheel from the synagogue at Ḥammath Tiberias B.

Plate XLIII. Fragment of zodiac wheel from the synagogue at Ḥuseifa (Cat. 60).

Fig. 5.18. Ashlar with a double meander from the synagogue at Kefar Baram (Cat. 42).

Fig. 5.19. Lintel with an image of an eagle from the synagogue at Gush Ḥalav.

Numerous visual motifs that were shared with other Greco-Roman groups appear in synagogue art. These included both floral and faunal motifs (Figs. 5.18 and 5.19). Plant ornaments were popular on architectural elements and on mosaic pavements. The repertoire of plant ornaments includes vines, wreaths, and garlands, sometimes depicted as repetitive all-over motifs or decorative compositions. Plant motifs were common in Jewish art of the Second Temple as well. The prevalence of these forms in later periods may be indicative of the continuation of a popular motif from the Second Temple period. Selected secular decorative patterns and motifs were taken from contemporary arts, especially from Syrian and Nabatean art. Some motifs were emphasized because they were given uniquely Jewish interpretations. These include, for example, the eagle and lions.[53] Pattern books were most probably a source for the motifs in Jewish art. This is indicated by the stylization of pose and posture as well as the patterning for the representations of animals, plants, and other ornaments; it is less likely that the motifs were copied directly from nature.

Geometric motifs, such as the rosette, were already a popular and frequent motif in Jewish art of the Second Temple period. They probably served as decorative designs, devoid of symbolic meaning. Animal motifs were common in late antique synagogue art (Fig. 5.20). Lions, eagles, and bulls all appear regularly and, though devoid of their pagan religious symbolism, had some significance in Jewish art. It is interesting to note that the placement of the image of a Roman eagle in the facade of the Jerusalem Temple was cause for a riot in the last days of Herod the Great in 4 B.C.E., while in late antiquity eagles appear regularly in synagogues. The new era of tolerance clearly spread even to the symbol of imperial might.[54] Lions and unidentified birds appear flanking Torah Shrines, suggesting that this three-dimensional image was not religiously problematic for some synagogue communities. The lion may have been seen as a guardian or symbolic protector of the Torah Shrine. Other animal motifs appearing in synagogal art are fishes, dolphins, horned animals, and peacocks and other birds.

Human figures are represented in a stylized manner and are characteristic of "Oriental"[55] art during this period. Body proportions are disregarded, and each body part is rendered separately. Faces are usually portrayed in a frontal pose. Human figures are portrayed on architectural reliefs and mosaic floors (Plate XLIV). Few mythological motifs are

Fig. 5.20. She-wolf feeding her young from the synagogue at Chorazin (Cat. 45).

Plate XLIV. Detail of Helios from the zodiac wheel at Ḥammath Tiberias B.

depicted in synagogal art. Jews persistently selected heraldic and symmetrical designs, such as lions, bulls, Nikae, eagles, peacocks and other birds, horned animals, dolphins, and rosettes. These are depicted on sarcophagi, synagogue lintels, friezes, and mosaic floors. A kind of asymmetrical symmetry was employed, meaning that while the basic images were symmetrical, details of each were distinctly different.

Six ancient synagogue mosaics containing images of the zodiac have been discovered in Israel. These pavements date from the fourth to the sixth century and include Ḥammath Tiberias, Beth Alpha, Ḥuseifa, Susiya, Naaran, and the recently discovered mosaic at Sepphoris.[56] A mosaic from Ein Gedi contains an inscription that includes the names of the zodiac signs followed by the names of the corresponding Jewish months (as does the figurative zodiac at Sepphoris). Representations of the zodiac are presented within a square frame, two concentric circles forming a zodiac wheel. In the corners of the frame are busts personifying the four seasons. The outer, larger circle depicts the zodiac divided into twelve radial units; each one renders one of the signs and bears its Hebrew name. At Sepphoris, human figures personifying the months are also presented, together with the name of each Hebrew month. The innermost circle generally contains the image of the sun god Helios (see Plate XLIV) riding in a chariot drawn by four horses. At Sepphoris the sun god does not appear, but rather a column topped by a sun disk is presented (see Plate VIII).

Fig. 5.21. Mosaic from the Shellal church in the Gaza region.

The zodiac was adapted from pagan art to represent the yearly calendrical cycle. This is made explicit at Sepphoris, where both the zodiac signs and personifications of the months are illustrated. In the Jewish calendar the months follow the signs exactly. The image of the sun god symbolizes the day; the background of the crescent moon and stars represent the night. Thus, the zodiac calendar was employed as a significant framework for the annual synagogue rituals. This recurrence of the zodiac design in a number of synagogue mosaics indicates its relevance to religious thought and its importance in synagogal art. The zodiac signs in the Roman world are of cosmic and astronomical significance. In Christian as in Roman art the calendar design is represented by the personifications of the labors of the months. The zodiac is not represented in Christian mosaics from Palestine, although the labors of the months do appear in the Monastery of the Lady Mary in Beth Shean. Whereas Jewish art generally preferred a symbolic zodiac, the naturalistic representation of human activity is most common in Christian examples. An eighth-century Christian manuscript of Ptolemy's *Astronomy* in the Vatican collection bears an image of a zodiac wheel that is similar to those in synagogue mosaics.[57] Both the zodiac signs and the labors appear in this image, which is thought to be based upon a fourth-century model.

The ways in which Jews and Christians decorated their Sacred Realms reflect the unique religious conceptions of each community. The similarities between Jewish and Christian art are many, and numerous motifs are shared. A good example is the inhabited scroll, a form of mosaic depiction common among both Christians and Jews. In fact, a church near Gaza, Shellal (Fig. 5.21), and a synagogue several kilometers away at Nirim (Maon) (Plate XLV) had virtually the same mosaic pavements, based upon a model in a shared pattern book.

Another common theme in Jewish and Christian mosaics is the nilotic scene. Such a scene is represented in the Leontis synagogue-house complex (Plate XLVIa) in Beth Shean.[58] It also appears in the church of Tabigha,[59] the traditional site of Jesus's multiplication of the loaves; in the church of Haditha;[60] and in the recently discovered fifth-century House of the Celebration of the Nile (Plate XLVIb) at Sepphoris.[61] The iconography of these scenes includes a walled structure, identified with an inscription: in Beth Shean, "Alexandria," at Haditha, "Egypt." In all four examples in the Land of Israel is a nilometer, a device to measure the yearly rise of the Nile. Combat between a crocodile, symbol of Egypt, and either a cow or a man appears in each, as do various birds, plants, and fish that represent the bounty of the Nile. These nilotic motifs were apparently common in mosaic pattern books.[62]

Plate XLV. Mosaic from the synagogue at Maon (Nirim).

Plate XLVIa. Mosaic pavement of the House of Leontis at Beth Shean.

Plate XLVIb. Mosaic from the House of the Celebration of the Nile at Sepphoris.

Fig. 5.22. Corinthian capital with a menorah from Caesarea.

Plate XLVII. Capital with three menorahs from Caesarea (Cat. 68).

Smaller appurtenances within synagogues and churches also reflect important relations between these institutions. Corinthian-type capitals made of marble were discovered in the Caesarea synagogue.[63] They are ornamented with a menorah in place of the central boss (Fig. 5.22, Plate XLVII). Christians chose a similar solution. A Corinthian-type capital from a Byzantine church from Caesarea was decorated with a cross (Fig. 5.23).[64] Similarly, chancel screens found in synagogues and churches show similarities in design and execution. A premiere example of this phenomenon is the chancel screen of the Ḥammath Gader synagogue. This marble screen is decorated with a stylized wreath that encloses a menorah. A chancel screen from a Beth Shean church has a cross at its center. Similarities in carving and design indicate that the pieces were probably crafted in the same workshop, which catered to clients of different religions. One should also recall the synagogue mosaics of Beth Alpha and the synagogue of Beth Shean A, which appears to have served a Samaritan community. Both floors were laid by "Marianos and his son Anina."

Fig. 5.23. Corinthian capital with a cross from a church at Caesarea.

Jewish and Christian perceptions of what constitutes an appropriate decoration for a religious building were at times quite different. Figurative art is introduced into the design on synagogue pavements beginning in the fourth century C.E. We have seen that this art was quite often ornate, with images of sacred symbols such as the menorah. In contrast, early churches were generally decorated with geometric, floral, and faunal carpets. This is in marked contrast to secular mosaics from private dwellings from the same period. This difference between the church and other contexts may be in part a response to an imperial decree dated 427 C.E. that forbade the representation of sacred symbols on church mosaic pavements.[65] According to the Theodosian Code, images of the cross, and perhaps by extension other biblical images, should be forbidden within Christian contexts. This is generally borne out in Christian mosaics from the Holy Land. Within synagogue contexts, however, narratives drawn from the Bible appear on a number of synagogue mosaic pavements. This seems to reflect a fundamental difference between Jewish and Christian notions of visual imagery. For Jews, art seems to have been merely a means of communication, even when short biblical passages are set in the floor. The ornamentation of synagogue pavements with images, ritual objects, and even the hand of God at Beth Alpha might suggest that an image, stepped upon, had no sacred quality. For Christians, however, images had great religious value. They were perceived as windows to eternity. More surprising within the synagogue context is the twenty-nine-line mosaic pavement inscription from Reḥov, which extensively parallels legal traditions that appear in Rabbinic sources and deals with the application of biblical agricultural laws.[66] This extensive citation reflects a different attitude toward the words of the Rabbinic Sages among the Jews of Beth Shean than that which we find evidenced a few centuries later in the Cairo Genizah or today. In Cairo, Rabbinic texts that were no longer usable were set aside so as to avoid desecration. At Reḥov, the words of the Sages were regularly walked upon.

In the sixth century church pavements begin to portray figurative designs composed mostly of subjects such as vintage, hunting, and village scenes. Even though figurative themes are employed, the negative attitude toward portrayal of religious subjects is evident in these mosaics. Interestingly, while scenes of animal fights and hunting are not uncommon in church contexts, they do not appear in synagogues. This too may reflect a difference in religious attitudes that separated these communities in antiquity. During the eighth and ninth centuries elements of Orthodox Christianity became strongly iconoclastic, removing images from churches throughout the Land of Israel. This tendency, toward the close of our period, parallels stringent Jewish attitudes toward images that we have discussed earlier as well as Muslim iconoclasm. In fact, Jewish, Christian, and Muslim iconoclasm may be contemporaneous and reflect a common trend toward the close of antiquity.

CONCLUSION

With roots during the Second Temple period, the synagogue during late antiquity became the most important institution in Jewish life. Fine synagogue buildings were constructed throughout the Land of Israel that reflected the religious lives of the Jews who built them. The destruction of the Jerusalem Temple in 70 C.E. and the removal of the center of Jewish life to the Galilee were pivotal for the history of Jewish art and architecture. The strictly aniconic and nonsymbolic art of the Second Temple period gave way to a more open and varied approach to art from the third century on. The decline of paganism and the rise and expansion of Christianity most certainly influenced the Jewish attitude toward art. During this period Temple implements, like the menorah, took on a symbolic significance in synagogal and funerary art. A limited selection of symbols and subjects were chosen by the Jewish community and by its donors, who apparently made their choices from available pattern books. The art and architecture of the ancient synagogue set in stone the beliefs, aspirations, customs, and traditions of the Jews in their land at the very time when the literature of the Rabbinic Sages was being written and edited.

Synagogues in the Land of Israel

The Literature of the Ancient Synagogue
and Synagogue Archaeology

AVIGDOR SHINAN
Hebrew University of Jerusalem

Scholars of Jewish literature from late antiquity, particularly those of us who deal with the literary record of life in the ancient synagogue, often wonder what it must have been like to visit an ancient synagogue on the Sabbath or on a holiday. We would like nothing more than to be transported to a synagogue in ancient Palestine and hear one of the sermons that we know from literary sources when it was first delivered. How did the Sage stand as he spoke, or perhaps he sat? What was his body language, and how did he modulate his voice? How was the sermon received by his audience? Our desire to experience ancient synagogue life becomes even more intense when we visit one of the many well-preserved ancient synagogues in the Land of Israel. The remains of ancient synagogues include floors and alcoves, pillars, and the rubble of walls, mosaics, and inscriptions. When read together, ancient Jewish literature and the remains of ancient synagogues provide a window into the religious life of that institution. We can sense the pulse of the life that flowed through both the archaeological and the literary remains of ancient synagogues.

This chapter describes the liturgical activity that took place in Palestinian synagogues during late antiquity. I will emphasize themes that appear in the Beth Alpha floor mosaic, a masterpiece of ancient Jewish art that has been discussed by both Eric Meyers and Rachel Hachlili in this volume. In particular, I will focus upon the Binding of Isaac panel at Beth Alpha (Plate XLVIII) and treatments of Genesis 22:1–19 in the literature of the ancient synagogue. I will also make reference to synagogue practice in the large Diaspora community of Babylonia, modern Iraq. Ancient Palestinian practice has left few imprints upon modern Jewish liturgies. This is not the case with Babylonian practice, which is the basis of modern synagogue practice. By contrast, the literature of the ancient synagogue in the Land of Israel was far more varied and vibrant than its Babylonian counterpart.

Plate XLVIII. Binding of Isaac panel from the synagogue mosaic at Beth Alpha.

The textual record of religious life within ancient synagogues is preserved in the literature of the synagogue. This literature consists of translations of Scripture into Aramaic (*targumim*), public sermons (*derashot*), prose liturgical texts, and liturgical poetry (*piyyutim*).[1] All were used primarily (or perhaps exclusively) on the Sabbath and holidays, and all shared connection to the core religious activity in the synagogue: the public reading of Scripture. The reading of the Torah was regularly accompanied by translation into Aramaic (Fig. 6.1). The scriptural readings were integrated into the works of those who offered sermons and liturgical poetry before and after the Torah reading. Finally, the liturgy that was recited by the assembly was built upon biblical themes and verses, particularly verses from the book of Psalms.

Fig. 6.1. Targum fragment of Genesis 37:15 from Cairo Genizah.

SCRIPTURE IN THE ANCIENT SYNAGOGUE

Scriptural reading was an essential part of synagogue life in antiquity. This is expressed visually in the internal arrangement of late antique synagogue buildings, where a Torah Shrine stood at the focal point of the hall and Scripture was read aloud on a podium (bema). The centrality of Scripture within the synagogue is first evidenced during the Second Temple period.[2] The ancient

Rabbis saw the centrality reflected in the covenant renewal ceremony prescribed by Ezra, "the priest and scribe" for those who had returned to Jerusalem from the Babylonian Captivity:

> And when the seventh month had come, the children of Israel were in their towns. And all the people gathered as one in the square before the Water Gate; and they told Ezra the Scribe to bring the book of the Torah of Moses which the Lord had given to Israel. And Ezra the priest brought the Torah before the assembly, both men and women and all who could understand to hear on the first day of the seventh month. And he read it facing the square before the Water Gate from the first light until noon, in the presence of the men and the women and those who could understand. And the ears of all the people were fixed on the book of the Torah. And Ezra the Scribe stood on a wooden stand which they had made for the purpose. . . . And Ezra opened the book in the sight of all the people, for he was above all the people, and when he opened it all the people stood. And Ezra blessed the Lord, the great God, and all the people answered "Amen, Amen," lifting their hands; and they bowed their heads and worshipped the Lord with their faces to the ground. . . . (Neh. 8:1–6).

In later generations this text was the model for communal scriptural reading, which has influenced the development of Jewish liturgy to this day.[3] The public reading and study of Scripture was a feature of all brands of Second Temple period Judaism and was the common legacy of all. This was especially the case in the Judaism of the Rabbinic Sages, the self-perceived descendants of the Second Temple period Pharisees. The Sages believed that prophecy had ceased.[4] They believed that other paths to the Divine Will had also been blocked: dreams speak falsehoods and a *bat kol* (Divine Voice) was not to be trusted, while the *urim ve-tumim* (the oracular breastplate) worn by the High Priest during the First Temple period had been long lost. All that was left to the Sages was the Sacred Scriptures, the collection of twenty-four books through which God had chosen, they believed, to reveal Himself eternally, in every generation. God's will could be unlocked from Scripture, they held, through the unique hermeneutical approach that they possessed and believed had been handed down to them by Moses. The Rabbinic Sages called their unique perspective the Oral Torah.[5] Many hundreds and even thousands of teachers and preachers, exegetes and translators, working in Hebrew, Aramaic, and Greek, took part over centuries in the Rabbinic project of teaching and interpreting the Bible. Rabbinic culture developed and was transmitted within the Rabbinic academies, the *batei midrash* and the synagogues, in elementary schools, through public eulogies, and at festive meals. It was transmitted on the roads of ancient Israel as the Sages and their students traveled from place to place.[6] In all these contexts, the Bible was explained, new ideas were expounded, and answers were found to the questions of the day.

The ancient synagogue was the place of Scripture reading par excellence. Josephus, the Acts of the Apostles, and the Talmudic Sages all agree that public Torah reading every Sabbath was instituted by Moses himself.[7] According to the Talmudic Sages, three days were not to pass without a public reading of the Torah: each Monday and Thursday in addition to the Sabbath.[8] This innovation was ascribed to none other than Ezra the Scribe. Torah was also read on holidays, on the first day of the lunar month (*Rosh Ḥodesh*), and on fast days. Sections of the prophetic books were read each Sabbath and on festivals. In addition, books from the third section of the Bible, the "Writings," were recited on different occasions. Lamentations was read on the Ninth of Av and Esther on Purim.[9]

Considerable variation in the practice of public Scripture reading can be discerned from Rabbinic literature. In Babylonia the Torah was read in an established uniform annual cycle. The Babylonian practice is today the standard for synagogal Torah reading.

In Babylonia the Torah reading was read in fifty-four well-defined weekly portions. According to this system, fixed weekly portions were read in all synagogues, beginning and ending the Torah on the ninth day of the Sukkot festival.[10] This day came to be called *Simhat Torah*, the festival of "Joy of the Torah."[11]

By contrast, in most Palestinian synagogues a more flexible and nonuniform Torah reading cycle was followed. Each synagogue and each community established the length of its weekly Torah reading. The length of the reading and the total number of Torah portions varied according to local custom. An early tradition preserved in Mishnah Berakhot 4:4 requires that each Torah reader recite at least three verses, although no maximum is stipulated. The Mishnah[12] further instructs that at least seven people were to read from the Torah on the Sabbath. Thus, at least twenty-one verses were read each week. At this rate each synagogue concluded its reading of the Torah in about three years The shortest known lectionary cycle contains 141 Sabbath readings and the longest 167.[13] For the sake of convenience this approach is called by scholars the triennial lectionary cycle.[14] An early medieval Babylonian source contrasts this practice with Palestinian synagogues that followed the triennial cycle, stating:

> The sons of the west [= Palestine] only celebrate *Simhat Torah* after three years and a bit. . . .[15]

The diversity of Torah reading practices in late antiquity is exemplified in regard to the Binding of Isaac, a text that appears in Genesis 22:1–19. Known as the *Aqedat Yitzhak*, or simply the *Aqedah* in Hebrew, this Torah portion is read in modern synagogues that follow the ancient Babylonian rite each fall on the fourth Sabbath after the festival of Sukkot. The contemporary practice of Torah reading encompasses five chapters, beginning with Genesis 18:1 and concluding with Genesis 22:24. In late antique Palestine, however, there were places where only the Binding of Isaac (Gen. 22:1–19) was read. In other synagogues the next scriptural section, the death of Sarah (22:1–23:20), was read together with the Binding of Isaac. According to Babylonian practice the death of Sarah is read a week after the Binding of Isaac. The Palestinian reading relates to the midrashic tradition that Sarah, Isaac's mother, died upon hearing an incorrect report that Isaac had been killed by Abraham on Mount Moriah.[16]

A similar pattern emerges in regard to the prophetic reading that accompanies the weekly Torah reading, the *haftarah*.[17] *Haftarah* means "completion" or "summation." The custom of appending verses from the Prophets to the Torah reading may date as early as the latter Second Temple period. From an early date verses were chosen primarily from the books of Isaiah, Jeremiah, Ezekiel, and the Minor Prophets.[18] The choice of verses to be read and their exact number was left to reader. In Acts 13:14–15 we have a description of the reading of a prophetic text in a Diaspora synagogue:

> . . . and on the Sabbath day they [Paul and his entourage] went into the synagogue and sat down. After the reading of Torah [*nomos*] and the Prophets, the rulers of the synagogue sent to them saying, "Brethren, if you have any word of exhortation for the people, say it." . . .[19]

Palestinian Jewry did not develop a uniform lectionary of prophetic readings as their Babylonian brothers did. Rather, the *haftarah* in the Land of Israel was generally chosen on an ad hoc basis by the reader of the prophetic section and his community. The Binding of Isaac was often accompanied by a prophetic reading from Isaiah 33:7ff., a passage that begins with the words "Hark, the Arielites [= angels] cry aloud; Shalom's messengers weep bitterly." Later we will show the exegetical relationship between this verse to the Binding of

Plate XLIX. Lintel from the synagogue at Merot inscribed with Deuteronomy 28:6.

Isaac. Another prophetic reading was Judges 3:1ff.: "These are the nations that the Lord left so that He might test by them all the Israelites."[20] The Torah reading and the *haftarah*, then, varied from place to place and from time to time. Their length, and the specific readings, were not standardized in most Palestinian synagogues.

The central place of Scripture in the ancient synagogue is also expressed in extant synagogue art and inscriptions.[21] On the lintel at Merot (Plate XLIX), for example, is engraved a verse from Deuteronomy (28:6): "Blessed are you when you come and blessed are you when you go." To this, the Midrash Tanhuma interprets:

> "Blessed are you when you come" to the synagogues and study houses "and blessed are you when you go" from the synagogues and study houses.[22]

In numerous inscriptions, including one from a synagogue in Jericho (Plate L), we find Psalm 125:5 (and parallels): "Peace unto Israel." Of particular interest are images of biblical episodes that appear in floor mosaics. The story of the Binding of Isaac appears in the sixth-century synagogue mosaic from Beth Alpha. In this image all of the central characters of the story appear: Abraham, Isaac, the two lads who accompanied Abraham and Isaac, the ram caught in the thicket, and a manifestation of God Himself, a hand extended from heaven calling on Abraham not to harm Isaac. The mosaic also depicts Abraham holding the knife in his hand, Isaac held aloft above the altar, and the fire burning on the altar. Labels drawn from the biblical narrative identify Isaac and Abraham. The biblical phrases "Do not raise [your hand]" (Gen. 22:12) and "here is the ram" (Gen. 22:13) appear as labels for the relevant scenes. The decision to illustrate the mosaic floor with this picture undoubtedly stems from the centrality of the Binding of Isaac in Jewish thought and piety.

In 1966 the image of a young man playing a harp while surrounded by animals was discovered in Gaza. The figure (see Plate XLa)), appearing to be the god Orpheus, bears a label in Hebrew that reads "David." The image of the youthful David, "sweet singer of

Plate L. Mosaic from the synagogue at Jericho.

Israel," graced the floor of a sixth-century synagogue in Gaza. In a synagogue discovered in Gerasa, in modern Jordan, remains of a mosaic bearing Noah's ark can be seen. A dove (Fig. 6.2) bearing a branch in its mouth and other animals survived antiquity, as did the names of Noah's sons, Shem and Jafeth. At Naaran, Daniel in the lion's den is portrayed. Alongside that mosaic is preserved the fragmentary inscription that apparently should be read as "Danie[l]." All of these themes are well known from the literature of the synagogue.

Fig. 6.2. Detail of a dove with an olive branch from the synagogue mosaic at Gerasa.

Their appearance in the art of the ancient synagogue is important evidence for the continuity between the extant literature and archaeological evidence for this institution.

THE LITERATURE OF THE SYNAGOGUE

Synagogue Torah reading was accompanied by public teaching. Just as Ezra and the Levites "gave the sense" of Scripture so that "the people understood the reading" (Neh. 8:8), so the "literature of the synagogue" was often intended to make Scripture accessible. The recitation of an expansive Aramaic translation (*targum*) made the text comprehensible and meaningful to Aramaic speakers, particularly when complemented with a homiletical sermon. Prayer and *piyyut* translated God's word into a vehicle for communication with the God of Israel and for adoration of Him.

The Palestinian literature of the synagogue has four unifying characteristics: the languages in which it was composed, its variety and vitality, its popular character, and its geographical spread. During late antiquity the divine service in Palestinian synagogues was conducted in three languages: Hebrew, Aramaic, and Greek (and in small amounts of Latin). The Torah, the Prophets, and the Scrolls were generally read in their original Hebrew, accompanied by Aramaic *targum* smattered with a few Greek and Latin words. The liturgy itself was composed in Hebrew, with some Aramaic. *Piyyut* was almost entirely in Hebrew, but the sermons were a mixture of Hebrew and Aramaic interwoven with Greek and Latin words.

An essential characteristic of the literature of the ancient synagogue was its variety and vitality. The visitor to an ancient synagogue in the Land of Israel could expect to hear a new composition that had never before been heard. Whether in the Aramaic translation, the sermon, the form of the prayer, or perhaps in an artful liturgical poem, the visitor might be treated to a new and varied aesthetic and religious experience. An element of surprise thus awaited one who entered a synagogue for Sabbath or holiday prayers. This is in marked contrast to the situation in late antique Babylonia. Babylonian synagogue practice tended to be more standardized from an earlier date. The Palestinian and Babylonian centers developed very different conceptions of synagogue liturgy. These centers were in heated competition with one another during late antiquity for leadership of the Jewish

Fig. 6.3. Aramaic dedicatory inscription mentioning the Holy Community and the Holy Place, from the synagogue at Beth Shean B (Cat. 62).

people. This contest is often manifested in issues of religious practice. In this chapter, I will compare synagogue life in the Babylonian center with that of the Land of Israel, and in so doing shed light upon the religious life of each community.

The ancient synagogue was a meeting place for all segments of late antique Jewish society.[23] It was attended not only by scholars but by the masses of Jews as well, old and young, men, women, and children. This fact is reflected both in synagogue dedicatory inscriptions (Fig. 6.3.) and in the literature of this institution.[24] The synagogue service thus had to take into account the needs of the masses: their perceptions, problems, and beliefs. These are expressed in different degrees in all the components of the literature of the synagogue.

The four facets of the literature of the late antique Palestinian synagogue—*targum*, the public sermon, a unique liturgy, and liturgical poetry—were the essence of the synagogue service in all regions that were under Palestinian influence during late antiquity. This came to include the entire Byzantine sphere of influence, from Tiberias to Cairo to southern Italy and eventually into early medieval Ashkenaz (the Franco-German cultural realm in northern Europe). In what follows I will describe, one by one, the component literatures of the literature of the synagogue.

THE ARAMAIC *TARGUM*

At the entrance to the Beth Alpha synagogue is a dedicatory inscription (Fig. 6.4) in Aramaic that dates the construction of the mosaic floor ("in the time of Justin Caesar") and mentions by name the people who donated funds to the project.[25] The use of Aramaic, the language in which the majority of synagogue inscriptions were composed, attests to the broad importance of that language among Jews in Roman Palestine.[26] The Torah reading, and apparently also the *haftarah*, was regularly translated into Aramaic for the benefit of

Fig. 6.4. Greek and Aramaic dedicatory inscriptions from the synagogue at Beth Alpha.

this population.[27] As in the spoken language, the *targumim* are sprinkled with Greek and Latin loan words.

The translator into Aramaic, known as the *meturgeman*,[28] stood beside the Torah reader, perhaps on the podium (bema) at the focal point of the synagogue. The reader and the *meturgeman* worked in tandem. Some translators were professionals, while others were skilled members of the community. After the reader pronounced one verse of the Torah, the *meturgeman* translated it. For the prophetic reading, groups of verses were read and translated consecutively. The reader and the translator had to be careful not to begin before the other had completed his task.

Palestinian *targum* traditions wove exegetical traditions into the fabric of the biblical text. These traditions reflect the full range of Rabbinic exegesis, both the Law (*halakhah*) and the lore (*aggadah*). Through expansive translations and emphasis upon specific verses, the *meturgeman* was able to make the ancient biblical text meaningful for his community. Translators differed in their formulations, some producing literal correspondence translations, others expansive homiletical presentations. Both approaches are expressed in Aramaic *targum* texts that have been uncovered in the Cairo Genizah, as well as in texts that were copied during the Middle Ages. Targumic treatments of the Binding of Isaac reflect the methods used by late antique targumists.

One of the most important and, in fact, latest Aramaic *targum* texts, *Targum Pseudo-Jonathan* (Fig. 6.5),[29] tells of an argument between Isaac and Ishmael over which of the

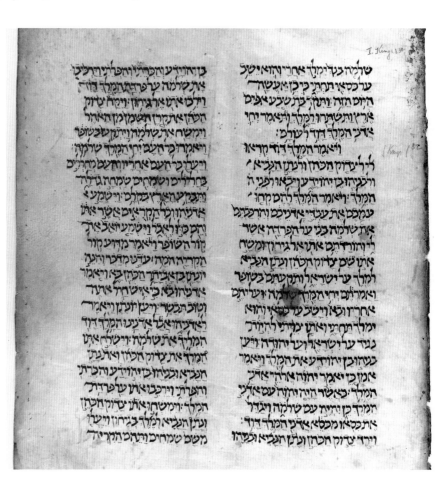

Fig. 6.5. *Targum Jonathan* to I Kings 1:30 from the Cairo Genizah.

two is worthy of the birthright. Expanding upon the opening verse of the Binding of Isaac, "And it came to pass after these *devarim* [=things/events/words] that God put Abraham to the test," the *Targum* clarifies what the *devarim* are. Ishmael would say, "I am worthy of being my father's heir, since I am the firstborn son." Then Isaac would retort, "I am worthy of being my father's heir, since I am the son of Sarah, his wife, while you are the son of Hagar the handmaiden." Similarly, Ishmael would say, "I am more righteous than you, for I was circumcised at thirteen years old, and had I wanted to refuse, I would not have agreed to allow myself to be circumcised," to which Isaac's retort was that he would be prepared to sacrifice all the parts of his body and his life as well if God were to ask it of him. These words reached God's ear, and as a result God asked Abraham to slaughter his son Isaac. In this tradition, Isaac is the protagonist of the story. More than testing Abraham's faith, God is trying to find out whether Isaac can withstand this difficult test. This conception of the biblical story reflects Second Temple and early Rabbinic notions of martyrdom, whereby one is willing to die on the altar of faith. Isaac, who represents the Jewish people, is a willing martyr. Ishmael represents Abraham's descendants, who were not found worthy of being heirs to his divine promises and his status. This text is probably a polemic against Islam and its claim that the Abrahamic covenant was made with Ishmael.[30]

The *Targum Pseudo-Jonathan* identifies the anonymous lads who went with Abraham to the place of the Binding of Isaac (verse 3) as Abraham's servant Eliezer and his son Ishmael. The choice of Isaac is thus stressed, since Ishmael is found worthy enough only to remain far from the place of the event, along with Abraham's ass (verse 5). Again we find here a polemic against pretenders to the Abrahamic covenant. It is possible that a similar perception is expressed in the Beth Alpha image of the Binding of Isaac. There, considerable space is devoted to a depiction of Abraham's two lads, who remain behind with the ass, distant from the sacrificial altar. The *Targum* and the mosaic are but two expressions of an anti-Gentile polemic tradition that sees in the Binding of Isaac a clear act of preference for Isaac, the Israelite patriarch, over any other descendant of the first monotheist.

A tradition preserved in a text known as the *Fragment Targum* (or *Targum Yerushalmi*) adds to the verse "And Abraham picked up the knife to slay his son" (verse 10) an extended portrayal of God's angels observing the dramatic event and extolling Abraham and his son as:

> The only two righteous persons in the world
> one slaying, the other being slain
> the slayer not delaying and the slain extending his neck.[31]

The angelic voice magnifies the sense of exaltation for the patriarchs that the *meturgeman* intended to arouse in his listeners.

Another *Targum* passage, discovered in the Genizah of the Cairo synagogue, focuses on the passage in the story, "On the third day Abraham looked up and saw the place from afar" (verse 4). It is not clear from the biblical narrative how Abraham identified the place where he was to sacrifice his son. The *Targum* relates that Abraham saw there "a pillar of cloud from the sky to the earth." When he questioned the two lads, it became clear to him that they did not see a thing, while Isaac saw quite clearly the divine revelation symbolized by the cloud. The *Targum* continues: "At that moment, Abraham knew that Isaac had been chosen as a burnt offering," if he had harbored any shadow of a doubt about the issue.

At pivotal moments in the Pentateuchal narrative, long dramatic poems were sometimes interjected within targumic translations to increase the pathos of the audience.

These include the crossing of the Red Sea (Exod. 12) and the death of Moses (Deut. 34). A poem is inserted within the *Aqedah* as well, at the point where Abraham raises his knife to slaughter his son (Gen. 22:10). Taking the role of a willing martyr, Isaac pleads with his father not to tarry in fulfilling the Divine Will:

> Isaac said to Abraham, his father:
> How lovely is the altar you have built for me, Father.
> Hurry, pick up your knife
> While I yet pray to my God . . .
> Splatter my blood on the altar,
> And take my ashes and bring them to my mother.
> My life and death are in the Lord's hands,
> And I thank Him for having chosen me. . . .[32]

Later in this poem the heavenly angels enter to request Divine mercy for Isaac. Their request is granted, and the dramatic tension eases.

The diversity of Palestinian targumic expression is striking when it is contrasted with the Aramaic translation that was pronounced in Babylonian synagogues during late antiquity. In Babylonia there was one official translation, *Targum Onqelos*. This text is much more literal in its translations, although it too contains important, if limited, midrashic departures from the biblical narrative. The wealth of Palestinian targumic traditions reflects the special importance of Torah reading and the translation of the Sacred Writ within the late antique Palestinian synagogue. One can imagine that Jews who were assembled in Beth Alpha on a Sabbath or festival when the Binding of Isaac was read and translated might have looked down on the floor and seen the image of the Binding of Isaac. Their understanding of the biblical text might thus have been enriched by the image of the *Aqedah* that was before them.

THE SERMON

Public sermons (*derashot*) were an important part of synagogue life during late antiquity. Homilies were delivered at various times on the Sabbath, festivals, and other occasions. They were given both before and after the Torah reading, during morning and afternoon services. The homilist, called a *darshan* in Hebrew, might have been a local authority or a visiting guest lecturer.[33] Sermons were both pedagogic and exegetical, sometimes touching on issues of local interest. The homilist had considerable flexibility in his presentation, as did the targumist. Homilies generally dealt with the scriptural reading, often using a literary model known as the proem, or *petiḥta*. The proem structure is rather uniform, the homily opening with a verse from the Prophets or the Writings that seems to be unrelated to the Torah reading. It then moves through a succession of topics that lead ultimately to the opening verse of the Torah reading. This model allowed the homilist to shed light on several different issues in his progression from the prophetic or hagiographic verse to the opening line of the Torah reading. It also allowed for a certain amount of suspense as the audience tried to figure out how the homilist would traverse the space between the two unrelated verses.

The *petiḥta* form employed a range of rhetorical devices. It was replete with stories, fables, parables, folk sayings, appeals to the audience, imaginary dialogues between biblical characters, and the like. The homily was often aimed at the broadest segment of Jewish society, both the scholars and the illiterate, women and children. This accounts for the didactic and rhetorical qualities of this literature. These characteristics are expressed in the following homily on the Binding of Isaac:

> "The Lord tests the righteous. . . . (Psalm 11:5)."
> Rabbi Jonathan said: This potter does not examine defective vessels, because he cannot give them a single blow without breaking them.
> What does he examine?
> Sound vessels, even if he hits them a few times for he will not break them.
> Thus, the Holy One, blessed be He, does not test the wicked but the righteous.
>
> Rabbi Jose son of R. Hanina said: This flax worker, when he knows that his flax is of good quality, the more he beats it the more it improves and the more it glistens.
> When it is of poor quality, he cannot give it one knock without it splitting.
> Thus, the Holy One, blessed be He, does not test the wicked but the righteous, for it is said: "The Lord tests the righteous. . . . (Psalm 11:5)."
>
> Rabbi Lazar said: Regarding a householder who possesses two cows, one strong and the other feeble, upon which does he put the yoke?
> Upon the strong one.
> Thus, the Holy One, blessed be He, tests the righteous, for it is said: "The Lord tests the righteous. . . . (Psalm 11:5)."
> Another interpretation: "The Lord tests the righteous."
> This is Abraham:
> "And God tested Abraham (Gen. 22:1)."[34]

Through a series of analogies, the homilist communicates to his audience that God tests only the righteous. This testing is done for a number of reasons. Sometimes it is intended to make the righteous praiseworthy, like the clay vessel. At other times, the testing is used to improve the qualities of the righteous, like the flax in our homily. In still other times, testing is necessary so that the world can continue to exist, as in the case of the cows plowing the field. In all cases, the homilist asserts, the Binding of Isaac was not to prove to God Abraham's righteousness. Just as the potter knows which vessels to examine, the flax worker knows the quality of his flax before he beats it, and just as the householder can distinguish among his cows before he sends them out to the field, so God knew in advance that Abraham was righteous. He asserts that the Binding of Isaac was done for the benefit of Abraham, and through him, for all humanity. To our author, the Binding of Isaac was not just a one-time historical event, but an allegory for Jewish and personal existence in all difficult times.

Other proem-type homilies begin with a question of Jewish Law (*halakhah*). The answer to this question served as a jumping-off point for the homily, which would conclude with the opening verse of the Torah reading. So we read:

> Let our Master teach us: One who sees a person of unusual appearance, what blessing is he to offer?
> Our Masters have taught: One who sees a person of unusual appearance must bless and praise the Holy One, Blessed be He.
> And what formula is he to employ?
> "Praised be You, Lord, who makes people different."[35]

The homilist continues that, in contradistinction to human beings, God can create innumerable individuals, all different from one another, including the most unusual people. He then enumerates other differences between humans and God. One difference is that

God knows human thoughts, whereas humans do not know what their fellows are thinking. The homilist connects this discussion seamlessly to Isaac's thoughts before the Binding of Isaac, which only God could know. Over two thousand proem-type homilies are preserved in Rabbinic literature. While some were clearly literary creations,[36] this large number obviously reflects the popularity of this genre among synagogue audiences.

In the course of his sermon the homilist would address the congregation in Aramaic, in Hebrew, or sometimes in both languages interspersed. Greek and sometimes Latin were used, and loan words from these languages abound. Words such as *bema* (podium), *pesifas* (mosaic), *safsal* (bench), and *qatedra* (a special seat) (Fig. 6.6a) are all loan words from Greek that were used for the furnishings of ancient synagogues.

In fact, approximately thirty inscriptions in Greek have been uncovered in the Land of Israel. This is clear evidence of the importance of this language among Jewish communities in certain parts of Palestine. An inscription in Greek from Beth Alpha recognizes the work of the artisans Marianos and his son Aninas. This pair of artisans is recognized in a inscription from the first synagogue that was discovered in Beth Shean as well. There, as in Beth Alpha, these apparently well-known craftsmen are recognized for their work. It is possible that these workers were more comfortable in Greek than in either Aramaic or Hebrew! The influence of Greek upon Aramaic and Hebrew is evident in subtle and less subtle ways. A tradition in the Jerusalem Talmud[37] rules that

Fig. 6.6. (a) Stone chair from the synagogue at Chorazin; (b) chancel screen post with Aramaic inscription from the synagogue at Dalton (Cat. 50).

(a)

(b)

the men of Haifa, Beth Shean and Tivon are not "passed before the cabinet" (that is, they may not lead prayers before the Torah shrine), for they make [the letter] *hay* into a *het* and *ayin* into *alef*.

The pronunciation of the guttural *ayin*, as the silent *alef*, reflects the influence of the Greek language on the Jews of these three towns in northern Israel, all of which were influenced linguistically by Greek, which has no sound that parallels *ayin*. An inscription that was unearthed in a second synagogue in Beth Shean contains exactly the error envisioned by our Talmudic tradition. In this inscription we read: "Remembered for good the artisan who made this work." The word "work" in our inscription, *avedata*, begins with an *alef*. The correct spelling, of course, begins with an *ayin*! Similar features appear in great numbers in the Hebrew and Aramaic of late antique Palestine and can often be attributed to Greek influences. The linguistic richness of late antique Palestine is thus reflected in both archaeological discoveries from the Land of Israel and in the languages of ancient synagogue literature.

PRAYER

For the Rabbinic Sages prayer was an essential element of the synagogue service. The Sages ordained that prayer be recited two or three times a day. While the morning (*shaharit*) and afternoon (*minhah*) services were considered to be obligatory by the early Rabbinic Sages, the evening service (*aravit*) was originally optional.[38] Prayer was localized within the synagogue during the period after the Temple's destruction. Though private prayer was acceptable, communal devotions in the presence of a community of ten or more men (a *minyan*) was preferable.

Synagogue prayer was conducted orally and from memory. There were no written prayer books at that time. Prayer was variegated, flexible, and changing. With the composition of authoritative prayer books in Babylonia, beginning with that of Rav Amram Gaon in the ninth century, the text began to stabilize, taking on more and more unified formulae. This process of standardization was accelerated by the printing press, although it has not been completely successful even today.[39] During late antiquity the Palestinian liturgy was fixed and unvarying only in regard to its general outline. This outline included the number of blessings said in this or that context, the subjects these blessings addressed, and certain key phrases (such as opening and closing formulae). The final wording, which was left open, was shaped according to the understanding and needs of each worshipper or prayer leader.

The variation and creativity that we encountered in *targum* and in homilies can be seen in late antique prayer texts as well. They are reflected in both Rabbinic discussions of liturgical practice in antiquity and documents discovered in the Cairo Genizah. The liturgical texts from the Genizah number in the tens of thousands. A single example of liturgical diversity will suffice. The Rabbinic Sages assigned a central position to a text they called The Prayer par excellence, the *Tefillah*. This prayer is today called the standing prayer, the *Amidah*, or the *Shemoneh-esreh*, the "eighteen benedictions." It opens with praise to God, followed by requests addressed to Him and expressions of thanks. It is known as the *Shemoneh-esreh* (eighteen benedictions) because the original number of its component parts was eighteen. The eighth blessing, which requests health for the worshipper and those dear to him, illustrates the variety of literary forms in ancient Jewish liturgical texts. The concluding formula is the same in all the versions, having been set at an

early date.[40] The remainder of the blessing was originally left to the worshipper to formu-
late himself. The Sages encouraged innovation, stating explicitly that "one who makes his
prayer a fixed routine, his prayer is no plea,"[41] and thus does not achieve its goal.[42]
Eventually communities developed standardized language for these blessings. We will cite
three examples:

> Heal us, Lord, and we shall be healed; save us and we shall be saved. Praised are You, Lord,
> who heals the sick of His people Israel. (*Siddur Rav Saadya Gaon*, tenth century)[43]

> Heal us, Lord, and we shall be healed; save us and we shall be saved. For You are our glory,
> and grant relief and healing to all our illnesses, all our pains, and all our wounds, for You are
> a merciful and reliable healing God. Praised are You, Lord, who heals the sick of His people
> Israel. (Liturgy of Middle Eastern Jewish communities)[44]

> Heal us, Lord our God, from the pains of our heart, remove from us sorrow and sighing and
> pestilence, and grant healing to our wounds. Praised are You, Lord, who heals the sick of
> His people Israel. (Cairo Genizah fragment)[45]

While similar in their formulations, these versions reflect varying concerns. The first version, from the *Siddur Rav Saadya Gaon*, speaks briefly about healing and salvation in general, while the second speaks at greater length about healing that is mainly physical. The
third version, preserved in the Cairo Genizah, speaks explicitly about psychological healing. Numerous blessing formulae undoubtedly existed in antiquity, most of which were not
written down. The supplicant was able to use whatever formula seemed most fitting to him
and to emphasize that part of the liturgy that seemed most important at the time. He could
choose whether to be inventive or to use one version consistently. The openness that we
have demonstrated in regard to the benediction for healing of the *Tefillah* was the case
with all Rabbinic prayer formulations. These included the Grace after Meals, the blessings
before and after recitation of the *shema*, and many others.

The openness of the Palestinian liturgy continued well into the Middle Ages. Prayers
were composed in both Hebrew and Aramaic, with the most important prayers composed
in a somewhat biblicized Hebrew, while the Kaddish (whose roots extend at least into the
Talmudic period), a prayer stressing God's holiness and offering Him praise, was composed
both in a Hebrew version and a mixture of Aramaic and Hebrew.[46]

The language of the liturgy and the language of inscriptions (Hebrew, Aramaic, and
Greek) discovered in ancient synagogues (Fig. 6.7) sometimes display a great similarity.
Thus, for example, we find that in several Aramaic and Greek inscriptions the synagogue is
called a "holy place" (*atra qedisha, hagios topos*),[47] an expression that appears in one version
of the Kaddish as well. Close liturgical connections can be seen between extant versions of
the Kaddish and a synagogue dedicatory inscription from Jericho. The inscription reads:

> Remembered for good, may their memory be for good, all of the holy community, the elders
> and the youths, whom the King of the Universe helped and who donated and made the
> mosaic.

> He who knows their names and the names of their sons and the people of their households
> will write them in the book of life [with all] the righteous [ones].

> All of Israel is interconnected [*haverim*]. Peace, [Amen].[48]

The Kaddish prayer of the communities of Cochin, India, and Kaffa (Feodosiya) in
Crimea share a Palestinian source with this text. In the version from Kaffa we read:

Fig. 6.7. Mosaic inscription from the synagogue at Jericho that parallels the Kaddish prayer.

Remembered for good and may their memory be for good . . .
All of this holy community, the elders and the youths.
He who knows their names will write them in the book of life with the righteous [ones]. . . .

In Cochin the Kaddish concludes with: "All of the house of Israel is interconnected [*haverim*], amen. . . ." These similarities point to a long subterranean liturgical development. A text that influenced the composition of the mosaic inscription in Jericho was transmitted to and preserved in two distinct and geographically distant liturgical traditions that were influenced by ancient Palestinian modes of prayer. As in our Jericho inscription, the liturgical term "amen" appears in a number of Aramaic and Greek dedicatory inscriptions. Elsewhere God is called "King of the universe,"[49] just as He is called in the standard formula for benedictions "Praised are You, Lord, King of the universe. . . ." The same is true for the divine epithet "Master of the high heavens,"

Fig. 6.8. Dedicatory inscription from a synagogue at Ashkelon (Cat. 74).

which appears in inscriptions (Fig. 6.8) and the benediction recited for the assembled worshippers on Sabbath: "May the Master who is in the high heavens be your help at all times."[50]

The Binding of Isaac appears in numerous liturgical texts. It has a particularly important position in the Rosh ha-Shanah liturgy as a sign of the covenant between God and Israel. This is, in fact, a central feature of the day, when the Binding of Isaac appeared in all genres of synagogue literature. In the liturgy God is asked to remember

> the covenant and the oath that You swore to our father Abraham at Mt. Moriah, and bring to mind the binding of his son Isaac upon the altar by our father Abraham.[51]

The fact that the patriarchs fulfilled God's will at the *Aqedah* is the basis of the artist's request for mercy for their children on the Day of Judgment, Rosh ha-Shanah.

A Palestinian text preserved in the Cairo Genizah contains a tradition which ordains that a worshipper prostrate himself before God when requesting forgiveness for sins. He is directed there to lie on his left side,

> like a lamb bound for slaughter so that he sacrificed his impulse [*yitsro*] before his Creator [*yotzro*] . . . and remember the binding of our father Isaac.[52]

This is another usage of the Binding of Isaac within late antique Jewish liturgy that sets the context for the Beth Alpha mosaic presentation. The central significance of divine intervention in the Binding of Isaac is clearly evidenced in the Beth Alpha mosaic, where the "hand of God" injects itself into the scene from heaven at the very center of the upper register. Below it is the ram, "caught in a tree" at the center of the composition with his horn prominently displayed. This scene does not emphasize the piety of Abraham, as the Rosh ha-Shanah liturgy and most Christian representations of this scene do. Rather, its interest is divine intervention as symbolized in the ram (a shofar prominent upon his head) that replaced Isaac upon the altar.

In the synagogue mosaic from Gaza David appears playing his harp. The Book of Psalms, which was ascribed to David, plays a central role in Jewish liturgy. The appearance of David the poet on the synagogue floor paralleled the recitation of Psalms, a literature that was primarily ascribed to David, within the synagogue. We have already mentioned the phrase "Peace upon Israel," which originates in Psalms and which appears in several synagogue inscriptions. The importance of David's psalms within the synagogue is reflected in an Aramaic *piyyut* that was discovered in the Cairo Genizah. This text describes Jews congregating in synagogues to sing the "hundred and fifty psalms" of David; the poet continues:

> Songs of Songs of prophecy sweet like honey
> The meaning they interpret in the language of the holy house He loved and made him
> [David] holy the holy king
> And He gave him his kingdom and the Divine name.[53]

"Language of the holy house" refers to synagogues, the "holy house" where Scripture was read and prayer recited principally in Hebrew. In this section, then, we have seen that the prayer conducted in ancient Palestinian synagogues was consonant in its design, multifaceted nature, and language with the other activities of the synagogue we have surveyed.

LITURGICAL POETRY: *PIYYUT*

The term *piyyut* refers to religious poetry, largely in Hebrew, employed in liturgical contexts in the synagogue as well as in wedding ceremonies, festive meals, and the like.[54] *Piyyut* is a Greek loan word in Hebrew, based upon the Greek *poietas*. It is related, through Greek, to the English word "poetry." In fact, *piyyutim* share much with contemporaneous Christian liturgical poetry.[55] Synagogue poetry displays characteristics that are typical of poetry in general, such as the use of rhyme, meter, refrains, and acrostics of various types.

Today, *piyyutim* are generally used as poetic additions to a prescribed and authoritative prayer book, a usage that follows medieval Babylonian practice. In late antique Palestine, by contrast, recitation of a *piyyut* was seen as an equally valid choice for fulfilling the public religious obligation of offering prayers at fixed times. A congregation and its leaders could choose whether to pronounce the types of prose prayers described in the previous section or to recite *piyyutim*. A poetic alternative to the benediction for healing, for example, reads: "Merciful One, quickly bind our wounds. Praised are You, Lord who heals the ill among His people, Israel." In this text, which was discovered in the Cairo Genizah, the alliteration of the letter "ḥet," which cannot be reproduced in translation, is the central poetic vehicle.[56] Hundreds and indeed thousands of *piyyutim* were composed by numerous poets, only some of whom are known to us by name. Many of these works were discovered in the Cairo Genizah, although others have been recited by Jews from antiquity to the present.

In many cases the poets chose to devote their poems to themes in the Torah portion for that Sabbath or festival, writing a sort of poetic sermon on the scriptural reading. Sometimes the poet was accompanied by a modest choir, which added a dimension to the *piyyut* experience.[57] A Palestinian poet of the fifth century, Yose son of Yose, composed, for example, a *piyyut* for Yom Kippur that reflects upon the ancient service of the High Priest in the Jerusalem Temple before 70 C.E. on that holy day. This poem, of a genre known as *Avodah*, a Hebrew term meaning "Temple service," treats the Temple sacrifices of Yom Kippur as the climax of history. Yose recounts the history of the world from Creation to the construction of the Tabernacle in the wilderness of Sinai and the offering of sacrifices in it. In the context of this poetic retelling of universal history, the poet comes to the story of the Binding of Isaac:

> A basket of first-fruits he brought as an offering,
> The father showed no mercy and the son did not delay.
> While slaughtering the lamb, he [the father] took up the sword.
> The angels of peace cried out in bitter weeping.
> The Good and Merciful One said: "Do not harm the lad!"
> Your [plural] action is desirable, both as offerer and as sacrificed."[58]

Naturally, the alphabetical acrostic, the rhythm, and the exalted language of the original Hebrew cannot be successfully replicated in English. It is evident even from our translation, however, that the story has been reworked here using several traditions we have already encountered. These include the portrayal of Isaac as a willing participant in the *Aqedah* and the depiction of angelic prayer on behalf of Isaac. The poet paraphrases the biblical phrase "Do not raise your hand against the lad!" as "Do not harm the lad!." The artist (or source) of the Beth Alpha mosaic, too, regarded this to be a pivotal point of the biblical story, and he included in his work not only the words "Do not raise" but also the visual depiction of a heavenly hand coming down to intervene in the action and stop Abraham from carrying out the sacrifice.

The Binding of Isaac was a particularly popular theme in *piyyutim* for Rosh ha-Shanah. We shall cite as an example a *piyyut* composed for that holiday's *shaḥarit* service. This work, of the genre called *silluk* (a Hebrew term meaning "conclusion") was, in fact, composed in medieval Ashkenaz by R. Shimon bar Yitzhak (c. 1000 C.E.), but it imitates earlier Palestinian forms and themes:

> [Abraham] rose early and was not lax.
> He gladly saddled his ass himself
> the very ass ridden by the one who drew water for Jethro's daughters [=Moses]
> and the same one that the poor one [=Messiah] will ride at Redemption.
> They rode off in a straight path.
> When they arrived at Scopus [=Jerusalem] they beheld a flame aloft.[59]

Here too the English translation cannot transmit the full lyric force of the original. Within this poem we find the statement, familiar from Rabbinic literature, that the ass upon which Abraham rode is the same ass that Moses rode when he returned from Midian to rescue the Israelites from Egypt and the same ass that the Messiah will ride when he reveals himself at the end of days. This never-dying animal connects central historical events: the Binding of Isaac, redemption from Egypt, and the future redemption.[60] Who knows whether this relationship was known to the artist (or the source) of the artist who designed the Beth Alpha floor, or perhaps of one of the numerous *paytanim* who prayed upon it?

One of the most interesting and alluring themes in ancient Jewish art is the zodiac wheel, which appears in synagogue mosaics throughout the Land of Israel from the fourth century onward.[61] In these images, the most famous of which was discovered in Beth Alpha, the zodiac wheel contains images of the twelve signs of the zodiac labeled by name (Aries, Taurus, Gemini, and so on). The theme of the zodiac appears in numerous *piyyutim* for various occasions, providing a partial context for interpreting zodiac images. We see this in the following elegy, an early anonymous poetic composition written for use on *Tisha be-Av* (the ninth of the Hebrew month of Av), the day when Jews mourn the destruction of the Jerusalem Temple:

> Then, because of our sins, the Temple was destroyed
> And the Sanctuary was burnt because of our iniquities.
>
> The tribes of Jacob cried in sorrow
> And even the constellations shed tears
>
> The Lamb cried first, its soul saddened
> Because its little lambs were led to slaughter.
>
> The Bull made its cry heard in the heavens
> Because we were all pursued to the very neck. . . .
>
> Heaven shook from the roar of the Lion
> Because our roar [of supplication?] did not rise to heaven
> Virgins and young men were killed
>
> And therefore the Virgin's face was darkened. . . .[62]

The poem encompasses the entire zodiac. The heavens themselves mourned when the Temple was destroyed. One who recited this elegy, or one like it, in a synagogue in which there was a zodiac mosaic could visualize the heavens by looking beneath his feet.

A premiere case of the close relationship between synagogue decoration and the *piyyut* literature is a series of synagogue inscriptions of 1 Chronicles: 24, the twenty-four priestly watches that served in the Temple during the Second Temple period in rotation.[63] During late antiquity *piyyutim* were recited in synagogues that were based upon the priestly watches. Like many elements of Rabbinic Judaism, particularly the synagogue liturgy, these poems served to recall the Temple and its glory and as a way of marking the hope of its restoration. It may also be that the priestly families, who guarded their pedigrees even after the destruction, hoped to demonstrate their special status by calling to mind the priestly watches.[64] The watches are mentioned in elegies composed for the ninth of Av. One example of this phenomenon is a poem by the prolific seventh-century poet Eleazar son of Qallir, who mentions the watches (Petaḥiah, Yakhin, Gamul, and others) at the end of each of the poem's stanzas:

I called to the One who opens His hand
but to me He closed His hand
And sank [in the earth] the gates of Yah [God],
So they weep, the watch of Petaḥiah.
All the kings heard
That angels had disappeared
and the Temple pillars had fallen, Boaz and Yakhin,
So they weep, the watch of Yakhin.
For evil I paid the price
So my heart I will circumcise
Over infant and child His mercy did not rule,
So they weep, the watch of Gamul.[65]

The list of watches in liturgical poetry generally matches the list as it appears in synagogue ruins.[66] These lists have been discovered in Ashkelon, Caesarea (Fig. 6.9), Reḥov, and the area of Nazareth.[67] Perhaps the inscription even acted as a mnemonic aid to the *paytan*, who recited his piece aloud from memory.

משמרת ראשונה יהויריב מסרביי מירון
משמרת שניה ידעיה עמוק צפורים
משמרת שלישית יחרים מפשטה
משמרת רביעית שערים עיתהלי
משמרת חמישית מלכיה הב'ית לחם
משמרת ששית ימין יודפת
משמרת שביעית הקוץ עילבו
משמרת שמינית אביה כפר עוזיה
משמרת תשיעית ישוע ארבל
משמרת עשירית שכניה חבורת כבול
משמרת אחת עשרה אלישיב כהן קנה
משמרת שתים עשרה יקים פשחור צפת
משמרת שלוש עשרה חופה בית מעון
משמרת ארבע עשרה ישבאב צלצח תשיחין
משמרת חמש עשרה בילגה בל גזי יונית
משמרת שש עשרה אימר כפר נמרה
משמרת שבע עשרה חזיר מ'מליח
משמרת שמונה עשרה הפיצץ ערית
משמרת תשע עשרה פתחיה אכלו ערב
משמרת עשרים יחזקאל כי זל ונא
משמרת עשרים ואחת יכין כפר יוחנה
משמרת עשרים ושתים גמול בית חביה
משמרת עשרים ושלוש דליה גנתון צלמין
משמרת עשרים וארבע מעזיה חמת אריח

Fig. 6.9. Plaque listing priestly courses (*Mishmarot*) from the synagogue at Caesarea (Cat. 70).

Fig. 6.10. Mosaic inscription from the synagogue at Reḥov.

One of the most important inscriptions to have been uncovered in a synagogue in the Land of Israel was found in the narthex of the sixth-century synagogue at Reḥov (Fig. 6.10) in the Beth Shean Valley. This twenty-nine-line inscription deals with the application of biblical agricultural law in late antique Palestine.[68] It details the religious responsibilities of Jews in various parts of the country as far as tithing and seventh-year produce. This issue was particularly important in the region of Beth Shean, which was a mainly non-Jewish city during the Greco-Roman period. Rabbinical law since at least the third century had exempted regions that were mainly Gentile from the biblical agricultural laws. These included Beth Shean. It was necessary, however, for Jews who lived in this and similar regions to know exactly where and when the agricultural rules were in force. The inscription opens as follows:

> Shalom! These fruits are forbidden at Beth Shean in the Seventh year, and in the other sabbatical cycle years they are tithed as *demai*:[69] the marrows and the cucumbers and the parsnips and the mint which is bound by itself and the Egyptian beans which are bound in shavings and the leeks from the holiday [of Sukkot] until Hanukkah, and seeds and dried figs and sesame and mustard and rice and cumin and dry lupine. . . .

> These are the places which are permitted around Beth Shean: On the south which is the "campus" gate till the "whitefield" on the west which is the gate of the [oil] press till the end of the pavement (?) on the north which is the gate of the watchtower [or the Sekuta] till Kefar Qarnos and Kefar Qarnos is Beth Shean. . . .[70]

The text goes on to discuss the rules for other regions as well as other issues. It closely parallels Rabbinic traditions that are known from medieval manuscripts of ancient Jewish literary sources.[71] It is the oldest extant copy of a Rabbinic source to have come down to us.

The Reḥov inscription is not part of the corpus that we call the literature of the synagogue. Rather, it is important evidence for Rabbinic legal tradition and its influence in late antique Palestine. The text does, however, bear important relationships with *piyyutim* from this period. Eleazar son of Qallir composed numerous extant poems for Passover, in which God is asked for abundant dew during the spring and summer. In one, intended to be recited on Passover that falls on the Sabbath, he prays for the success of thirty-six varieties of foodstuffs. Each verse opens with a stanza from Song of Songs, which was recited in the synagogue on Passover:

> "I will lead you"—You who look into my dwelling place when it is like clear heat
> [in the sunlight and like the cloud of dew in the heat of the harvest].
> "Dew of rest"—Blossom forth those whose song is pleasant [=Israel]"
> "And bless"—and make bountiful sesame seeds and mustard and cumin and fennel.[72]

Other foods that are mentioned in this poem include lentils, wheat, barley, millet, coriander, Egyptian beans, white beans, onions, turnips, and garlic. The editor of this text, Menahem Zulay, wrote with obvious delight that "before us is a Palestinian *paytan* who invites us on a short stroll in the food market of his day." The parallels between this poem and the Reḥov inscription are clear, since many of the same foodstuffs are listed in each. The religious concern for the continued agricultural bounty of the Land of Israel unifies the Rabbinic author of the text that appears at Reḥov, the community that commissioned the floor, and the author of our *piyyut*.

The *piyyutim* dealing with the Binding of Isaac, the zodiac cycle, the priestly watches, and the fecundity of the Land of Israel are just a few examples of close relationships

Fig. 6.11. Chancel screen fragment inscribed with *Shalom*, Tiberias (Cat.54).

Plate LI. "Peace upon Israel" from the mosaic pavement of the Ḥuseifa synagogue (Cat. 59).

between synagogue liturgical poetry and archaeological remains. Read together, the literary and the archaeological evidence makes it possible to come a bit closer to the living context of the late antique synagogue.

CONCLUSION

A Babylonian Jew of the fifth century who visited a Palestinian synagogue would certainly have been surprised by the ritual he experienced there, particularly on the Sabbath. The public reading of the Torah took place in a manner that was entirely foreign to him. He would certainly question the "shortness" of the triennial Torah reading and the expansive nature of the Aramaic translation. The liturgy would be quite different from the more standardized prayers to which he was accustomed. It was flexible and lacking in standardization, changing according to the needs and perceptions of the worshippers. Poetic works of a variety of types were accorded an important position in the Palestinian synagogue. This literary superstructure would be difficult for him to follow, since the Jewish Aramaic of Palestine was much different from Jewish Babylonian Aramaic.[73] He would not understand the Greek spoken by many of his Palestinian brethren and may not have known Hebrew quite as well.

This said, we might assume that our visitor might have sensed that a single spirit informed the several components of the literature of the synagogue. Could that same Babylonian Jew draw connections, as we have, between what he heard in the synagogue and the inscriptions and mosaics he saw there? Until we find remnants of ancient synagogues in Babylonia from the period of formative Judaism, we cannot answer that question. (The synagogue of Dura Europos, on the Euphrates, which was destroyed in 256 C.E., does not, as far as we know, reflect the world of Babylonian Jewry.) This lack gives us another good reason to look forward to the day when it will be possible to excavate ancient synagogues in Syria and Iraq. Perhaps we will find on the floors or walls of these synagogues the biblical phrase that graced so many late antique Palestinian synagogues: "Peace upon Israel" (Fig. 6.11, Plate LI).[74]

Contributors

Steven Fine, Guest Curator
Assistant Professor of Rabbinic Literature and History, Baltimore Hebrew University,
Baltimore, Maryland

Rhoda Terry
Adjunct Assistant Curator, Yeshiva University Museum, New York

Louis H. Feldman
Abraham Wouk Family Chair of Classics and Literature,
Yeshiva University, New York

Gabriel M. Goldstein
Curator, Yeshiva University Museum, New York

Rachel Hachlili
Professor of Archaeology and Director of the Museum Studies Program,
University of Haifa, Israel

Sylvia A. Herskowitz
Director, Yeshiva University Museum, New York

Eric M. Meyers
Professor of Religion, Duke University, Durham, North Carolina

Bonni-Dara Michaels
Curator/Registrar, Yeshiva University Museum, New York

153

Leonard Victor Rutgers
Fellow of the Royal Dutch Academy, University of Utrecht, the Netherlands

Lawrence H. Schiffman
Professor of Hebrew and Judaic Studies, Skirball Department,
New York University, New York

Andrew R. Seager
Professor of Architecture, Ball State University, Muncie, Indiana

Avigal Sheffer
Textile Archaeologist, Hebrew University of Jerusalem, Israel

Avigdor Shinan
Professor of Hebrew Literature, Hebrew University of Jerusalem, Israel

Gerdy Trachtman
Graduate Research Assistant, Baltimore Hebrew University,
Baltimore, Maryland

Catalogue of Objects in the Exhibition

1 Dedicatory Inscription for Prayer Hall (Fig. 3.1)
Egypt, c. first or second century C.E.
Sandstone
40.7 × 33.7 cm
Toronto, Royal Ontario Museum 916.1.15, Walter Massey Gift

Παποῦς οἰκοδόμηση τὴν προσευχὴν ὑπὲρ αὐτοῦ καὶ τῆς
<γ>υναικὸς καὶ τῶν τέκνων· (ἔτους) δ΄ Φαρμοῦθι <ζ>΄.

Papous built the place of prayer on behalf of himself and his
wife and children. In the 4th year, Pharmouthi 7.

Numerous Greek inscriptions from Egypt mention Jewish
prayer places, the *proseuche*. The earliest date to the third century B.C.E. The Royal Ontario Museum inscription has been
dated to the first or second century C.E. on epigraphic grounds.
Many scholars consider the Egyptian *proseuche* inscriptions to
be the earliest evidence for the history of the synagogue. Based
upon them J.G. Griffiths posits that the synagogue originated in
Ptolemaic Egypt. The title *proseuche* suggests that at least in its
origins the most important feature of the "prayer place" was
prayer. It is possible, however, that some other sort of worship
(perhaps sacrificial) occurred in "prayer places." We know virtually nothing about this institution in its early stages other than
that it had rights of asylum and architectural affinities to contemporaneous polytheistic temples and associations in Egypt.
By the first century C.E. the term *proseuche* was essentially a

synonym for "synagogue" in Egypt and other areas of the
Greek-speaking Diaspora. Philo of Alexandria provides considerable evidence for "prayer places," of which "there are many
in each section of the city" (*Embassy to Gaius*, line 132).

SF

Fox 1917: 411, no. 11; Horbury and Noy 1992: 214–16; Noy 1992:
118–22; Griffiths 1995; Fine and Della Pergola 1995: 50–52; Fine
1996.

2 Incense Burner (Fig. 4.18)
Egypt, fourth to fifth century C.E.
Bronze
28.3 × 14 cm
Brooklyn, Brooklyn Museum, Charles Edwin Wilbour Fund,
41.684

This fine Egyptian incense burner was cast in three separate
parts: a tripod base with claw feet, a baluster, and a bowl. The
rim of the bowl is composed of open-work rings, a bird standing
atop each (two are missing). Three lines of a crude, almost
unintelligible Greek (dedicatory?) inscription were added to
the exterior of the bowl. The first line is preceded by a seven-
branched menorah, which suggests that this piece was used
within a Jewish context. The inscription has been reconstructed by K. Herbert as:

ὑπὲρ εὐχῆς Αὐξάνοντος εὔλογα, Κ(ύρι)ε, χαριτόν
ΟΣΤΑ καὶ ΑΝ

On behalf of a vow of Auxanon, Blessed, O Lord [thou who is] gracious (?) and . . . .

The name Auxanon was used by Jews in both Rome and Asia Minor during late antiquity. This piece was apparently dedicated to a Jewish public institution, most likely a synagogue. Herbert suggests that this text is a poor rendering in Greek of a Rabbinic prayer formula, though the reading of the inscription is too conjectural to substantiate this.

SF

Herbert 1972: 61, no. 32; Horbury and Noy 1992: 225–26; Weitzmann 1979: 330, fig. 347.

3 Mosaic Lozenge with Menorah (Fig. 4.3b)
Ḥamman Lif (Naro), Tunisia, second half of the fifth century C.E.
Stone tesserae
57 × 89.5 cm
Brooklyn, Brooklyn Museum 05.27

The synagogue of Ḥamman Lif was discovered in 1883. The structure was constructed as a broadhouse with an apse and an elaborate mosaic pavement. A Latin inscription, which divided the central hall in half, reads:

> Thy servant, Juliana P, at her own expense paved with mosaic this holy synagogue of Naro for her salvation.

The inscription is flanked by two menorahs, each within a lozenge. The lozenge to the right is exhibited here. The inscription and the lozenges identify this building as a synagogue. The remainder of the mosaic represents local fauna; above the inscription is an aquatic scene and below a fountain flanked by two peacocks and two palm trees. To the right is an inhabited scroll with a lion and a duck. Within the inhabited scroll to the left are sea birds, a quadruped, a lion, and two wicker baskets holding fruit.

RT

Renan 1883: 157–63; Biebel 1936: 541–43; Goodenough 1953: 2: 89–100, 3: fig. 890; Weitzmann 1979: 378.

4 Funerary Inscription for a Synagogue Official with Image of a Torah Shrine (Fig. 3.8)
Rome, Monteverde Catacomb, fourth century C.E.
Marble, inscribed
30.0 × 23.2 × 2.6 cm
Rome, Museo Nazionale delle Terme 77645

ἐνθάδε κῖτε Ἵλαρος ἄρχων ἀπὸ συναγωγῆς
Βολυμνησίων
ζήσας ἔτη λε· ἐν ἰρήνη ἡ κοίμησις αὐτοῦ. μνία <α>ὐτοῦ.

Here lies Hilarus, archon of the synagogue of Volumnenses, having lived for 35 years. In peace his sleep. His Memory [for a blessing?].

No synagogue building has been discovered within the city of Rome. Literary and epigraphic sources suggest that approximately twelve synagogues served the Jewish communities of Rome between the first and the fourth century C.E. Extensive evidence for synagogue life in Rome is extant from the fourth-century Jewish burial catacombs of Monteverde and the Villa Torlonia. The centrality of the synagogue in the lives of Roman Jews is also reflected in funerary inscriptions, which preserve the titles of synagogue functionaries and social relationships. Wall paintings and carvings preserve images of Torah Shrines, menorahs, and occasionally biblical scrolls. These constitute important evidence of synagogue life in Rome.

This inscription memorializes Hilarus, a synagogue leader. The lower right corner of the inscription is missing. Below the inscription is a Torah Shrine flanked by a shofar and lulav branch on the left and an amphora on the right. In the foreground are two circular elements. The Torah Shrine's open doors reveal nine scrolls on three shelves. All extant inscribed images of Torah Shrines were discovered in the Monteverde catacomb.

RT

Frey 1936: no. 343; Leon 1960: 314, no. 343; Noy 1995: 133, no. 167; Westenholz 1995: 23–24, 104, no. 6.

5 Funerary Inscription for a Synagogue Official with Image of a Torah Shrine (Fig. 3.10)
Rome, Monteverde Catacomb, fourth century C.E.
Marble
23.5 × 82.0 × 2.2 cm
Rome, Museo Nazionale delle Terme 77642

οἶκος αἰώνιος. ἐνθάδε κεῖτε
Εὔψυχος δὶς ἄρχ(ων), ἄρχ(ων) πάσης τειμῆς καὶ
φροντιστής· ἐν εἰρήνη κοίμησις αὐτοῦ. ἐτῶν νε′.

Eternal Home. Here lies Eupsychus, twice Archon, Archon of all dignity and Phrontistes. In peace his sleep Aged 55 years.

Eupsychus was twice a synagogue *archon* (leader). The phrase "*archon* of dignity" perhaps denotes a higher title than archon. The name Eupsychus appears in a non-Jewish inscription from Naples. An image of a Torah Shrine is inscribed to the right of the first line of the inscription.

RT

Frey 1936: no. 337; Leon 1960: 314, no. 337; Noy 1995: 130–31, no. 164.

6 Depiction of a Torah Shrine Flanked by Two Menorahs (Fig. 3.12)
Rome, Monteverde Catacomb, fourth century C.E.
Marble
25.4 × 45.5 × 2 cm
Naples, Museo Archeologico Nazionale 4521

Εὐλογία

The image of the Torah Shrine is highly stylized. The Shrine's roof is gabled and its doors are open to reveal six scrolls. Two seven-branched menorahs with square bases flank the Torah Shrine. The Greek word *Eulogia* appears above the Shrine. It is not clear whether this is a personal name or simply the Greek word for "blessing."

SF

Frey 1936: no. 327; Leon 1960: 213, no. 327; Noy 1995: 147–48, no. 185; Westenholz 1995: 110, no. 20.

7 Funerary Inscription for a Woman with Image of a Torah Shrine and Two Menorahs (Fig. 3.7c)
Rome, Monteverde Catacomb, fourth century C.E.
Marble
22 × 22 × 1.5 cm
Naples, Museo Archeologico Nazionale 4522

λοκου Βεσουλες ἀνουϱο ϱεκεσηϯ κε′

Burial place of Besula, she died at the age of 25 years.

This is a Latin inscription transliterated into Greek script. Besula is apparently the name of a young woman, as in the Hebrew *Betula*. The lower half of the marble is dominated by a Torah Shrine flanked by two seven-branched menorahs with square bases. Within the Shrine are nine scrolls.

RT

Frey 1936: no. 460; Leon 1960: 332, no. 460; Noy 1995: 158, no. 195; Westenholtz 1995: 122, no. 45.

8 Burial Inscription Mentioning a Synagogue Official (Fig. 3.9)
Rome, Vigna Randanini Catacomb, fourth century C.E.
Marble
26 × 16 × 5 cm
Los Angeles, Simon Wiesenthal Center

The upper-left corner of the inscription is missing but can be reconstructed to read:

[ἐνθ]άδε κεῖτε [E]ὐθυχιάνο ἄϱχοντι σινβίο ἀξίῳ {ν}·
εὐψύχι· μετὰ τῶν δικέων ἡ κύμησις αὐτοῦ.

Here lies, Euthychianus Archon, a worthy husband. Be of good spirit. With the just his sleep.

The upper half of a menorah is engraved on the lower-right corner of this piece. The branches are topped with small horizontal lines, possibly meant to represent lamps. *Archon* was a title used by synagogue officials in Rome. The left side of the inscription is in situ.

RT

Frey 1936: 77, no. 110; Leon 1960: 280, no. 110; Noy 1995: 207–8, no. 235.

9 Funerary Inscription for a Child, "Lover of the Law" (Fig. 3.11)
Rome, Vigna Randanini Catacomb, c. fourth century C.E.
Marble
29.5 × 27.5 cm

New York, Rare Book and Manuscript Library, Columbia University, Epigraphy 412

The left half of a funerary inscription was discovered near the Basilica of St. Paul on the Via Ostiensis in 1898. A menorah is crudely inscribed on its upper-left corner. H. Leon discovered the matching right half of this inscription in situ in the Vigna Randanini catacomb. The complete inscription reads:

ἐνθάδε κεῖτε Εὔκαϱπος νήπιος ὅσιος φιλόνομος· ἐν εἰϱήνη κοίμησίς σου.

Here lies Eukarpos, pious child, Lover of the Law. In peace be your sleep

The term "Lover of the Law" appears in no other epigraphic or literary context. Rutgers suggests that this phrase, and others such as *philosynagogos* (lover of the synagogue), reflect a particularly Jewish religious consciousness.

SF

Frey 1936: 78, no. 111; Leon 1924: 251–52; 1960: 280, no. 111; Noy 1995: 190–91, no. 212; Rutgers 1995: 195.

10 Funerary Inscription for a Priestess with Image of a Menorah and a Torah Shrine (facsimile) (Fig. 3.7b)
Rome, Monteverde Catacomb, fourth century C.E.
Marble, inscribed
19 × 35 × 3.7 cm
Original: Vatican City, Museo Vaticano 30771
Boston, International Catacomb Society

ἐνθάδε κῖτε Γαυδεντία ἱέϱισα ετῶν κδ′· ἐν ἰϱήνη ἡ κοίμησις αὐτῆς.

Here lies Gaudentia, priestess, aged 24 years. In peace be her sleep

This fragmentary inscription memorializes Gaudentia, a priestess. It is likely that Gaudentia belonged to a family that traced its lineage to the priests of the Jerusalem Temple. To the left of the inscription are a menorah with a square base and a Torah Shrine with its doors open.

RT

Frey 1936: 247–48, no. 315; Leon 1960: 311, no. 315; Brettman 1985: 17, no. 64; Noy 1995: 18, no. 11; Westenholtz 1995: 11, no. 21.

11 Sarcophagus Fragment with Inscription "Mother of the Synagogue" (facsimile) (Fig. 3.7a)
Rome, Via Anicia, perhaps Monteverde Catacomb, fourth century C.E.
52 × 48 cm
Original: Rome, Palazzo dei Conservatori
Boston, International Catacomb Society

[ἐνθά]δε κεῖτε [...]ια Μαϱκέλ[λα μή]τηϱ συνα[γωγῆς]
Αὐγουστη[σίων μ]νησθῆ [... ἐ]ν εἰϱήνη [ἡκοίμη]σις αὐτῆς.

Here lies [. . .], a Marcella, Mother of the Synagogue of the Augustesians
May [. . .] be remembered (?). In peace her sleep.

Women as synagogue leaders are mentioned in a number of inscriptions in Greek and Latin from various localities. Scholars debate as to whether the title "Mother of the Synagogue" here or "elder" and *archisynagogas* (synagogue leader) elsewhere are honorific or whether they reflect the roles served by women in Greco-Roman Diaspora synagogues. Six funerary inscriptions bear witness to the synagogue of the Augustesians.

SF

Frey 1936: no. 496; Leon 1960: no. 337; Brooten 1982: 59; Brettman 1985: no. 54; Rutgers 1995: 134–35.

12 Menorah Plaque
Rome (?), fourth century C.E.
Marble
19 × 12.5 cm
Collection of Dr. David Jeselsohn, Zurich

A seven-branched menorah is carved on this marble tablet. The menorah is very similar to images that appear in the Roman catacombs, where individual oil lamps are portrayed resting atop the branches.

SF

Westenholz 1995: 107, no. 11.

13 Gem with the Image of a Menorah (Plate XIX)
Italy, third to fifth century C.E.
Red stone
2.0 × 1.4 cm
Collection of Dr. David Jeselsohn, Zurich

Engraved on the surface of the gem is a seven-branched menorah with an ornate tripod base. The branches and the stem are marked with fine lines, as in menorahs on wall paintings of the Villa Torlonia catacomb. Oil lamps sit on each of the branches. Two large amphorae flank the menorah. A palm branch stands in each amphora. A horizontal line defines the ground, giving the scene a sense of space. A similar gem is in the collection of the British Museum.

RT

Westenholz 1995: 108, no. 13; Goodenough 1953: 2: 221, no. 1033.

14 Fragments of a Jewish Gold Glass (Plate XVIII)
Rome, c. 300–350 C.E.
Gold glass
Fragment A: 8.9 × 3.8 cm, B: 3.8 × 3.2 cm
New York, Metropolitan Museum of Art,
Rogers Fund 18.145.1a, b

Two fragments from the base of this drinking vessel are extant. The composition is divided into two registers, though little of the lower register remains. In the center of the upper register is a Torah Shrine, with two acroteria. The gable is supported by two columns with Corinthian capitals. Its doors are open, revealing four shelves containing a total of six scrolls. The columns are reminiscent of those that appear in the Torah

Shrine from Ostia. A cloth is suspended within the Shrine, which is flanked by two seven-branched menorahs. The branches of each lamp stand are connected by a crossbar, and individual lighted oil lamps rest atop each branch, their flames focused upon the central shaft. The branches of the menorah on the right are semicircular. To the right of this lamp stand is a ram's horn; to its left is a round object. The branches of the menorah on the left taper downward in an angular fashion. On its right is a scroll. The object on the menorah's left has been identified as an etrog. A similar gold glass in Berlin has the image of a fish on a round tripod table in the lower register. Fragmentary remains of a similar scene can be seen on our piece as well. Elements of a semicircular, strapped bolster can be seen behind the table. A curtain is swagged above. Encircling the composition are the remains of a semicircular inscription in Latin that reads:

> Drink with Eulogia [or with Blessings] in preparation.

The function of this cup is unclear. It is not known whether such cups were used within a domestic context before being placed in the tomb or whether they were made for fellowship meals in honor of the dead as in non-Jewish contexts. Banqueting scenes with tripod tables are known from numerous Christian and pagan funerary contexts. A Torah Shrine with tripod table bearing a fish and other foods on its left was recently uncovered in the Samaritan synagogue of El Khirbe in Samaria.

SF

Frey 1936: 380, no. 518; Goodenough 1953: 2: 111–12; 3: 973; Magen 1991; Weitzmann 1979: 381, fig. 348; Mann 1989: 228, no. 34.

15 Dedicatory Inscription of the Torah Shrine (Fig. 2.18)
Ostia, third century C.E.
Stone
36 × 54.3 × 2.5–3.5 cm
Ostia, Soprintendenza Archeologica, Magazzino epigrafico 8978

> *pro salute Aug(usti).* οἰκοδόμησεν κὲ αἰπο[ί]ησεν ἐκ τῶν αὐτοῦ δομάτων καὶ τὴν κειβωτὸν ἀνέθηκεν νόμῳ ἁγίῳ Μίνδις Φαῦστος με [τα τῶν ἰ]διῶ[ν].

> For the Safety of the Emperor Aug[ustus].
> Mindus Faustos, with his family built and made [it] from his own gifts, and set up the Ark for the Sacred Law.

Though no synagogue has been discovered in Rome, in 1961–62 a synagogue building was uncovered in Ostia, the ancient port of Rome. Originally constructed during the first century C.E., the building was remodeled as a synagogue during the second to third century and underwent further remodeling during the fourth century C.E. This inscription was found incorporated into the flooring of the vestibule. It dates to the third century C.E. The upper-right corner is missing. The first line of the inscription, in Latin, is a loyalty formula to the emperor. This parallels Greek inscriptions from Egypt. The remainder of the inscription is written in Greek. The last two lines were erased, and the name Mindus Faustus was inscribed over the erasure in a later and rougher script. This suggests that

Mindus Faustus may not have been the original donor. This inscription testifies to the existence of a permanent Torah Shrine at Ostia before the construction of the fourth-century Shrine. The term used for the Torah Shrine, *kibotos*, often refers to the Ark of the Covenant in Jewish Greek, just as *nomos* refers to the Torah. *Kibotos* is the equivalent of the Hebrew *aron* and the Aramaic *arona*. The Torah Shrine of the Dura Europos synagogue is called an *arona* in its dedicatory inscription and also dates to the third century.

RT, SF

Zevi 1972: 131–45; Mann 1989: 210–11, no. 8, fig. 61; Noy 1993: 22, pl. 13; Fine and Della Pergola 1995: 50–52; Westenholz 1995: 110, no. 19.

16 Architrave with Image of a Menorah (facsimile)
(Plate XVIIa)
Ostia, fourth to fifth century C.E.
Stone
32 × 48 × 184 cm
Ostia, Soprintendenza Archeologica 1883

Among the fourth-century C.E. renovations to the Ostia synagogue was the construction of a large Torah Shrine in the form of an aedicula. The aedicula was built as a free-standing structure, consisting of a large apse flanked by two marble columns. A broad podium that was ascended by four steps was added sometime after the construction of the aedicula. This Torah Shrine looked much like the images of Shrines that have been recovered from the Roman catacombs and on oil lamps from Ostia. Resting upon the columns of the Ostia Shrine were two architraves. Carved on the corbels of the architraves were menorahs flanked by a shofar on the right and a lulav and ethrog on the left. The menorah is incised with alternating diamond and rectangular patterns, probably meant to imitate jewels. Traces of pigment, possibly glue for gilding, were detected on the relief.

RT, SF

Squarciapino 1963: 194–203; Zevi 1972: 131–45; Fine and Della Pergola 1995: 42–47; Westenholz 1995: 110, no. 19.

17 Oil Lamp with Image of a Torah Shrine (Fig. 4.16)
Ostia, second to fourth century C.E. (?)
Terracotta
9.2 × 6.9 cm
Ostia, Soprintendenza Archeologica, Ostia magazzini 12501

During the fourth-century C.E. renovations to the Ostia synagogue, a large room with an oven was added on the southern side of the building. This single-wick lamp was discovered in the anteroom. It bears the image of a Torah Shrine of a type known from images of Torah Shrines from Rome. The gabled Shrine is rendered with its doors open, with a row of three circles at the bottom that represent the ends of scrolls, a common feature of Jewish art from the catacombs. The image is framed by a bead and reel molding. This lamp and the similar lamp found in Ostia (Cat. 18) form an iconographic bridge between

the Ostia synagogue Torah Shrine and depictions of synagogue Torah Shrines from Rome itself.

SF

Mann 1989: 226, no. 27; Westenholz 1995: 108–9, no. 16; Fine and Della Pergola 1995: 55.

18 Oil Lamp with Image of a Torah Shrine
Ostia, second to fourth century C.E. (?)
Terracotta
9.2 × 6.9 cm
Ostia, Soprintendenza Archeologica, Ostia magazzini 13351

This single-wick lamp was discovered in an early excavation of Ostia at the fortress of Julius II. It is very similar to catalogue number 17.

SF

Mann, 1989: 226, no. 27; Westenholz 1995: 109, no. 17; Fine and Della Pergola 1995: 55.

19 Oil Lamp with Image of a Menorah (Fig. 4.16)
Ostia, second to fourth century C.E.
Terracotta
8.2 × 7 cm
Ostia, Soprintendenza Archeologica, Ostia magazzini 12558

Five ceramic lamps decorated with the image of a seven-branched menorah were discovered within the fourth-century room with the oven in the synagogue. Each menorah has a tripod base and is encircled by a stylized wreath pattern.

SF

Squarciapino 1964; Zevi 1972: 131–45; Westenholz 1995: 108, no. 14.

20 Model of the Sardis Synagogue
Basswood, clay, and plaster
Constructed under the direction of Andrew Seager
Archaeological Exploration of Sardis, 1995

Excavations under the auspices of Harvard and Cornell universities revealed a massive urban complex, including a bath and gymnasium, palaestra, and synagogue. The synagogue site apparently served as a public building before the Jewish community obtained the property in the third century C.E. The synagogue of Sardis is the largest ancient synagogue yet discovered.

This model is a reconstruction of the synagogue building as it probably appeared during the fourth and fifth centuries C.E. It was prepared by Andrew Seager and Joe Henseler specifically for "Sacred Realm." The synagogue consisted of a colonnaded forecourt and a main hall. The forecourt had a roof that covered only the perimeter of the room, leaving the center open. A large marble fountain was found in the center of the court, supplied by underground water pipes. The floors of the court were paved with a geometric carpet mosaic. Some of the mosaic panels contained dedicatory inscriptions. An inscription from the balustrade mentions a reconstruction.

Entry into the main hall was by three doors. The main hall, measuring 54 by 18 meters, contained twelve piers and a large apse at its western wall. Unlike other synagogues, there were no benches along the walls. Three tiers of benches lined the interior of the apse. It is thought that the benches served as seats for the elders of the synagogue. The floor of the main hall was paved with a carpet mosaic. A large marble table was found before the apse, which was flanked by two pairs of marble lions. The exact use of the table is not known; it might have served as a lectern.

Situated at the eastern end of the hall were two aediculae, flanking the central entrance. Reconstructed by the excavators, the aediculae strongly resemble Torah Shrines depicted on gold glass. Each structure featured steps leading to the interior, and two marble columns supported a gable roof. Near the southern aedicula was a plaque depicting a menorah (Cat. 24) and an inscription mentioning the place that protects the Law (Cat. 21). Seager believes that the Torah scrolls were possibly housed within the structures.

The prominent size and position of the Sardis synagogue points to an affluent and somewhat powerful Jewish community. The inclusion of the synagogue within the Roman urban complex demonstrates the peaceful co-existence of the Roman and Jewish communities. The scale is 1:80.

ARS, RT

Seager 1972: 425–35; Seager 1981: 178–84; Seager 1989: 82–92.

21 Inscription Mentioning a Torah Shrine (facsimile) (Fig. 3.13)
Sardis, fourth to fifth century C.E.
Marble
20.5 × 14.5 cm
Archaeological Exploration of Sardis IN63.124, IN63.125

Fragments of a Greek inscription on two ornamented plaques were found scattered between the piers of the southern and western walls of the synagogue. Framed in *tabula ansata*, the plaques were decorated with flowers and tendrils. A horizontal register divides the text, which is carved in shallow relief against a depressed background. Remnants of red paint have given the white marble an orange tint. Two grooves, possibly forming a molding, run across both plaques. The well-carved Greek letters read:

Κἀμὲ τὸ νομοφυλ[ά]κιον ὁ αὐτ[ὸς] Μεμνόνιος
[ὑ]πὲρ ὑγίας [α]ὐτοῦ ἐσσ[κούτλ]ωσεν.

And the same Memnonios, on account of his good health, gave the marble inlay [*skoutlosis*] for me also, the place that protects the Law [*nomophylakion*].

Marble inlay was used in the decoration of the Sardis synagogue. The inscription seems to imply that marble inlay was also employed in the construction of the *nomophylakion*, the "place that protects the Law," a Torah Shrine. Based upon this inscription, J. Kroll believes that the Shrine was made of masonry. The ornateness of the plaques suggests the richness of the Shrine. It is likely that the Torah Shrine to which the inscription refers was housed in, or may even have been one of, the twin aediculae. If so, this inscription may have been affixed to one of the aediculae.

RT

Kroll, forthcoming.

22 Dedicatory Plaque for a Menorah (facsimile) (Fig. 3.4)
Sardis, fourth to fifth century C.E.
Marble
57 × 20.5 cm
Archaeological Exploration of Sardis IN63.48, IN63.49

Found in front of the southwest corner of the main hall were two panels bearing a Greek dedicatory inscription. Kroll transcribes and translates this inscription as:

Αὐρ. Ἑρμογένης Σαρδ. θεοσεβὴς
ἐκ τῶν τῆς Προνοίας εὐξάμενος τὸ ἑπταμύξιον ἐποίησα.

Aurelios Hermogenes, citizen of Sardis, God-fearer, from his gifts of Providence, I made [i.e., donated?] the seven-branched candlestick.

The long and narrow dimensions of the plaque are unusual for a wall revetment. Kroll suggests that the panel was attached to the base of masonry used to support the menorah. The donor of the menorah, Aurelios Hermogenes, describes himself as a *theosebes*, a "God-fearer." God-fearers are considered by most scholars to have been non-Jews who adopted a few practices of Judaism without undergoing formal conversion. The presence of God-fearers within synagogues is well documented during late antiquity. A fragment of a seven-branched stone menorah was discovered in the Sardis synagogue. The term *heptamuxion* (seven-branched candlestick) also appears in a synagogue dedicatory inscription from Side in Pamphylia.

RT, SF

Feldman 1989; Kroll, forthcoming.

23 Molding with Image of a Menorah and Torah Shrine (facsimile) (Fig. 3.15)
Sardis, fourth to fifth century C.E.
Marble
Segment a: 0.06 × 0.31 m
Segment b: 0.55 × 0.285 m
Segment c: 0.12 × 0.23 m
Archaeological Exploration of Sardis IN63.67, IN63.15, IN63.20

This very fragmentary inscribed molding was found in the forecourt, just south of the main entrance of the Sardis synagogue. It was possibly part of a door lintel. A Greek inscription runs across the front:

Εὐχὴ Αὐ[ρ. - -]ιαρου [- - -] N

Vow of Aurelios [—]iaros . . . .

The inscription is flanked by a seven-branched menorah and possibly an etrog to the left and the lower part of a Torah Shrine containing three scrolls to the right. Passing under this molding, the ancient visitor would enter the synagogue. Based upon the images on the molding, it has been conjectured that one of the twin aediculae in the main hall held the Torah Shrine and the other a menorah.

RT

Kroll, forthcoming.

24 Plaque with a Menorah (facsimile) (Fig. 2.19b)
Sardis, fourth to fifth century C.E.
Marble
70 × 70 cm
Archaeological Exploration of Sardis S62.26 (4501)

This plaque was discovered at the southern end of the synagogue, near the twin aediculae. Depicted in the center are a menorah, lulav, and shofar. The menorah is rendered in a linear style. The curved branches are connected at the top by a crossbar. Above the branches are triangular lamps. Directly under the branches are two spirals, a motif that is known to appear four times in Jewish art from Asia Minor. To the left is a smaller linear menorah or frond-shaped motif with eleven uneven branches. To the right is an angular shofar, similar to the horns depicted on the Priene and New York plaques (Cat. 25 and 26). The plaque has fittings for clasps and may have hung from a low balustrade or fit into a screen.

RT

Seager 1972: 425–35; 1981: 178–84; 1989: 82–92; Shilo 1968; Kraabel 1987: 62–73; Fine and Rutgers, forthcoming.

25 Menorah Plaque (Fig. 2.19a)
Priene, c. fourth century C.E.
Stone
60 × 61.5 cm
Berlin, Museum für Spätantike und Byzantinische Kunst 4691

Discovered in the late 1890s, the synagogue of Priene was initially identified as a house church. The building was converted from a private dwelling to a synagogue in the fourth or fifth century C.E. A niche was built into the eastern wall of the small main hall. Benches were located along the northern wall. Entrance into the main hall was through the forecourt to the west.

Three relief plaques carved with menorah motifs have been found in connection with the site. The plaque displayed here was found in a nearby church, though it surely came from the synagogue. A seven-branched menorah with a tripod base dominates the plaque. The curved branches support triangular elements that rest on the horizontal bar. As in the Sardis plaque (Cat. 24), it is likely that the triangles represent clay lamps used as burners for the menorah. Between the tripod base of the menorah and the lowest set of branches are two spirals, each curling in the same direction. Sukenik identified these spirals as the ends of Torah scrolls. It is likely that these spirals are

related to curls of the Sardis and New York plaques (Cat. 24 and 26) and to those of the Nicaea menorah (Fig. 2.16). To the left of the menorah is an etrog and to the right a palm frond and an angular shofar. The angularity of the shofar is reminiscent of the lulav represented on the Sardis plaque.

SF, RT

Weigand and Schrader 1904: 480, fig. 585; Sukenik 1934: 42–43; Goodenough 1953: 2: 77, 3, no. 878; Fine and Rutgers, forthcoming.

26 Plaque with Aedicula with a Menorah (Fig. 2.19c)
Asia Minor, fourth to seventh century C.E.
Stone
34 × 28.5 cm
Collection of Mr. and Mrs. Jonathan P. Rosen, New York

The focal point of this composition is a large aedicula supported by two columns. Within the aedicula is a large seven-branched menorah surmounted by a horizontal cross piece. Triangular burners stand above each branch, a flame burning within each. Similar triangular burners also appear on the Sardis and Priene plaques (Cat. 24 and 25). The base of the menorah is in the shape of a tripod. Beneath the lowest branch of the menorah are two curls. Such curls are known from pieces in Asia Minor such as Sardis and Nicaea. The curls are known from no other region, which suggests that this piece is from Asia Minor. In the recently identified piece from Nicaea the curls are clearly the handles of an amphora.

Flanking the menorah on the left is a horn or shofar. The angular horn is much like one represented on the Sardis and Priene pieces. On the right is a palm frond and an etrog. Aediculae such as this one are known from numerous synagogues, including Sardis. This piece may suggest that menorahs were sometimes housed within aediculae in Asia Minor. A menorah within an aedicula is also illustrated on lead coffins from Beth She'arim. On either side of the aedicula is a lattice screen. In the background the aedicula is flanked by two palm trees laden with dates. The palm tree was often used to represent Judea and Judaism in late Roman art. Above the trees, facing the aedicula, are two birds. Beneath each bird is a twig. Birds flank the Torah Shrine of the Beth Alpha mosaic and appear regularly above aediculae in Coptic art. There is no evidence on the reverse of this piece to suggest its original function.

SF, LVR

Fine 1989; Fine and Rutgers, forthcoming.

27 Model of the Dura Europos Synagogue (Fig. 1.8)
63.5 × 152.4 × 121.9 cm
New York, Yeshiva University Museum 89.83

The Dura Europos synagogue was discovered in 1932 by American and French archaeologists. This model represents the synagogue complex as it appeared after its renovation in 244–45 C.E. and before its destruction during the successful Sassanian siege of Dura Europos in 256 C.E. The design of this model was supervised by art historian Rachel Wischnitzer based mainly upon Carl Kraeling's final report of the synagogue discovery and her own extensive research on the Dura Europos synagogue. The model does not include the anterooms on the eastern side of the synagogue, leaving the impression that the building was a monumental structure. In reality the Dura Europos synagogue was part of a housing complex renovated for use as a synagogue. The renovation of housing complexes for use as synagogues was common in the Diaspora and may be hinted at in early Rabbinic literature from the Land of Israel as well. Christian and polytheistic communities followed this practice at Dura Europos and elsewhere in the Greco-Roman world.

SF

Kraeling 1956; Wischnitzer 1948; Weitzmann 1979: 392–93; White 1990; Meyers and Fine, forthcoming; Brooten 1982: 126–29.

28 Ceiling Tile with Aramaic Inscription (Fig. 4.15)
Dura Europos, c. 244–45 C.E.
Terracotta
42 × 42 cm
New Haven, Yale University Art Gallery 1933.255

The ceiling of the refurbished Dura Synagogue was ornamented with painted tiles. Remains of 234 ceiling tiles were discovered, slightly more than half the original number. Tiles were decorated with a number of themes, which fall into several groups: signs of the zodiac, human faces, animals, floral forms, fruits, vegetal motifs, eyes of apotropaic intent, and inscriptions. Many of the individual motifs were repeated in the decorative arrangement. Six tiles bearing dedicatory inscriptions were discovered within the synagogue. Three of the inscriptions are in Greek and three in Aramaic. The longest of the Aramaic inscriptions, fifteen lines in all, is exhibited here. Our translation is based upon Joseph Naveh's reading of this poorly preserved text:

הדין ביתה אתבני
בשנת חמש מאה חמשין
ושית דאינין שנת תרתן לפלפוס
///// קסר בקשישותה דשמואל
כהנה בר יד[ע]ן ארכונ ודקמו
על עיביתה הדי אברם גיזב
רה ושמואל [בר ס[פרה ו[ארשך]
[גיורה בן
[ ] בשת חדה וחמשין יסדו [ ]
[ ] [מן רהיטי]ן [ ]
[ ] [תה ועמלו בן [ ]
[ ] [ברכתה מן שמיה]
וכל בן[ ] עמלו ולאיו
שלמה [להון ולנ[שיהון ובניהון כלהון
[ ]

This house was built in the year five hundred fifty
and six, which is the second year of Philip
. . . Caesar in the eldership of Samuel
the priest son of Yed[a']ya, the Archon. [Those who] stood (as patrons)

of this work were: Abram the Treasurer
Samuel [son of S]afra, and [Arshakh]
the proselyte in . . . .
In the year fifty and one they established . . .
. . . from the roofing . . .
. . . and toiled in . . .
. . . Blessing from the Heavens
And everything in . . . worked and toiled
Peace [unto them and their wi]ves and their children all
. . .

B-DM, SF

Torrey 1956: 263–66; Naveh 1978: 126–31.

29 Ceiling Tile with Image of Capricorn (Fig. 4.13b)
Dura Europos, c. 244–45 C.E.
Terracotta
40 × 40 cm
New Haven, Yale University Art Gallery 1933.271

Astrological symbols that appear on the synagogue ceiling tiles include Pisces (two examples), Capricorn (seventeen examples), and a centaur (twenty-one examples). The image of Capricorn, a goat with a fishtail, is almost identical to a similar tile from the mithraeum at Dura. This standard representation also appears in the fourth-century mosaic of the Ḥammath Tiberias B synagogue.

B-DM

Kraeling 1956: 41–43.

30 Ceiling Tile with Image of a Centaur (Fig. 4.13c)
Dura Europos, c. 244–45 C.E.
Terracotta
39 × 40 cm
New Haven, Yale University Art Gallery 1933.268

Twenty-one centaurs are depicted on the tiles from the Dura synagogue. In ancient zodiacs the centaur usually represents Sagittarius. The masculine torso of the figure is shown frontally, while the lower half is seen in profile. The frontal presentation is consistent with the Dura style evident in the synagogue murals. The centaur clutches a fish in his left hand.

B-DM

Kraeling 1956: 42–43, pl. IX.

31 Ceiling Tile with Image of a Flower (Fig. 4.13d)
Dura Europos, c. 244–45 C.E.
Terracotta
39 × 39 cm
New Haven, Yale University Art Gallery 1933.258

Twelve of the surviving ceiling tiles from the Dura synagogue depict a flower with four heart-shaped petals between which green leaves are visible, surrounded by a wreath. The petals are outlined in red and radiate from a central red calyx. Flowers without leaves decorate more than twenty other tiles. This flower has been identified as a rose, a common motif in Egypt and Syria.

B-DM

Kraeling 1956: 45.

32 Ceiling Tile with a Female Bust (Fig. 4.13a)
Dura Europos, c. 244–45 C.E.
Terracotta
37 × 39 cm
New Haven, Yale University Art Gallery 1933.267

Twenty-three images of female busts were recovered among the extant ceiling tiles. These images parallel the female busts in the imitation marble dado of the synagogue. The images in the dado are usually identified as theater masks. The images on the tiles are generally interpreted as personifications of fertile forces in nature due to the leaves and flowers twined in their hair. Similar abstract personifications have been found at other ancient sites, including Pompeii, Antioch, and Takh-i Bustan.

B-DM

Kraeling 1956: 41–42.

33 Tile with a Female Bust from the House of the Roman Scribes (Fig. 4.14a)
Dura Europos, c. 240 C.E
Terracotta
29 × 33 cm
New Haven, Yale University Art Gallery 1933.293

This tile was found in the House of the Roman Scribes at Dura. Stylistically it is very similar to the synagogue busts. The Greek inscription mentions a man named Chariton, though the circular motif below the figure's ear may represent a bun or knot of hair, indicating a woman.

B-DM

Rostovtzeff 1936: 6: 294–95, pl. XLV, 6.

34 Ianthos Male Figure from the House of the Roman Scribes (Fig. 4.14b)
Dura Europos, c. 240 C.E.
Terracotta
33 × 35 cm
New Haven, Yale University Art Gallery 1933.294

This tile was found in the House of the Roman Scribes. Only half of the tile is preserved; it depicts a male wearing a belted tunic. He holds a pink object, which appears to be tied with red and yellow ribbons, that has been identified as an unclosed wreath similar to those depicted in Dura's Palmyrene temple. In style and conception this piece is very similar to the synagogue roof tiles and the wall paintings.

B-DM

Rostovtzeff 1936: 6: 295–96, pl. XLV, 5.

35 Painting of Mithras from the Late Mithraeum (Fig. 4.14c)
Dura Europos, c. 240 C.E.
Pigment on plaster
23 × 20 cm
New Haven, Yale University Art Gallery 1935.99B

The Dura Europos mithraeum was constructed in what was originally a private house. The house underwent three phases. During the last phase the hall was adorned with wall paintings of the cycle of the Mithraic mysteries. Near the niche a figure of Mithras was found. Mithras is shown wearing a floppy Phrygian cap encircled by a halo, a crescent pendant, and a flowing cape. This figure of Mithras has many stylistic affinities with painted figures in the Dura synagogue.

RT

Kraeling 1956: 151–58, 223–24; Rostovtzeff 1939: 7–8: 101–4, pl. XIII, 2; White 1990: 47–59.

36 Seal of the Binding of Isaac (Fig. 4.17b)
Provenance unknown, third to sixth century C.E.
Frit
4.5 cm
New York, American Numismatic Society 000.999.35847

The Binding of Isaac (Gen. 22:1–19) is presented on this flat ovoid seal. Abraham is shown approaching an altar, holding a knife in his left hand. A smaller figure of Isaac is shown nude with a cloth hanging over his right shoulder. His open gait suggests that he is running toward the altar. Abraham turns his head toward a Divine hand that reaches from a cloud in the sky toward a tree to the right. A ram is standing to the right of the tree, its head inclined toward Abraham. In the sky above the altar floats a star.

On the reverse of the seal is a four-line inscription written in a square Semitic script. Bonner followed by Campbell suggests if the characters are Hebrew, then part of the inscription was written in an archaic alphabet (most notable in lines 2–4). Due to the illegibility of the text, it is almost impossible to give a translation.

The pictorial representation of the Binding of Isaac first appears in late antique Jewish art on the Torah Shrine at Dura Europos. Though the provenance of the seal is unknown, the style and iconography are similar to the scene on the Dura Torah Shrine. The altar that Bonner terms "unique" is similar in shape to the one on the Elijah panel on the Dura mural. Such altars can be traced back to types known from the ancient Near East. The hand reaching from a cloud appears in both scenes. Abraham's garment is not unlike those of other male figures on the Dura murals. It is not known whether this seal stems from a Jewish or a Christian context.

RT

Goodenough 1953: 2, 224; 3, fig. 1039; Kraeling 1956: 58, pl. 40, 4; Bonner 1950: 226–27, 310–11; Schwartz and Schwartz 1979: 149–82.

37 Theodotos Inscription (facsimile) (Fig. 1.6)
Jerusalem, c. first century B.C.E. to first century C.E.
Limestone
100 × 8 × 20 cm
Jerusalem, Israel Antiquities Authority

Θ[ε]όδοτος Οὐεττήνου, ἱερεὺς καὶ ἀ[ρ]χισυνάγωγος,
υἱὸς ἀρχισυν[αγώ]γ[ο]υ, υἱωνὸς ἀρχισυν[α]γώγου,
ᾠκοδόμησε την συναγωγὴν εἰς
ἀν[άγν]ωσ[ιν] νόμου καὶ εἰς [δ]ιδαχ[ὴ]ν ἐντολῶν,
καὶ τ[ὸ]ν ξενῶνα, κα[ὶ τὰ] δώματα καὶ τὰ
χρησ[τ]ήρια τῶν ὑδάτων εἰς κατάλυμα τοῖς
[χ]ρῄζουσιν ἀπὸ τῆς ξέ[ν]ης, ἥν ἐθεμελ[ίω]σαν οἱ
πατέρες [α]ὐτοῦ καὶ οἱ πρεσ[β]ύτεροι καὶ
Σιμων[ί]δης

Theodotos, son of Vettenos the priest and synagogue leader
[*archisynagogos*], son of a synagogue leader and grandson of a
synagogue leader, built the synagogue for the reading of the
Torah and studying of the commandments, and as a hostel
with chambers and water installations to provide for the needs
of itinerants from abroad, which his fathers, the elders, and
Simonides founded.

This inscription was discovered in 1913–14 by French scholars
in a cistern just south of the Temple Mount in Jerusalem. The
focus upon Torah study within this synagogue accords well
with literary sources from the latter Second Temple period.
Sources in the New Testament and in early Rabbinic literature
mention synagogues in Jerusalem (Acts 6:9; Tosefta Megillah
2:12, ed. Lieberman.). One scholar has recently suggested that
this text dates to the second century C.E., an approach that is
not supported by the evidence for either the latter Second Temple period or by second-century sources.

SF

Levine 1989; Roth-Gerson 1987: 76–86, fig. 19; Kee 1990: 8; Oster
1993.

38 Cloth Wrapper (facsimile) (Fig. 2.3)
Masada, c. first century C.E.
Twill weave wool; tabby weave wool lining
22 × 32 cm
Original: Jerusalem, Israel Antiquities Authority and Hebrew
University, Institute of Archaeology
Facsimile by Bracha Sadowsky
On loan from Avigail Sheffer

This piece was discovered in the Northern Palace on Masada. It
was found rolled and tied, revealing an embroidered exterior.
The unfurled wrapper was discolored and insect damaged. The
main outer cloth is a diamond twill. The original color was pale
blue, as seen in a few spots that were covered by the lining. The
blue color has faded and the wool yellowed. Darning in light
blue thread was apparent in two places. The lining was executed
in a fine weft-faced plain weave. Seven red embroidered triangles were sewn onto the edge of the outer cloth. Red tying cords
with knots were threaded onto the two outer corners of the
embroidery. Other textiles found at Masada were repaired with
patches. It is important to note that the wrapper is constructed

entirely of wool. Residue of parchment or papyrus is not apparent on the fabric, though a brown staining is evident.

Avigail Sheffer believes that the wrapper contained a precious item because of its embroidery. Mishnah Kelim 28:4 mentions "figured" (*mitzuyarot*) wrappers that covered scrolls. Sheffer notes that the wrapper is large enough to hold one of the
smaller Qumran scrolls. Scrolls were often stored within cloth
wrappers like this during the Roman and Byzantine periods.

AS, RT

Yadin 1981: 21–22; Foerster 1981a: 24–29; Sheffer and Granger-Taylor
1994: 223–26, 236, 241.

39 Bar Kokhba Coin (Fig. 2.4)
Year 1, 132 C.E.
Silver tetradrachm
Collection of Dr. David Jeselsohn, Zurich

Obverse: Image of the Jerusalem Temple with a tetra-style
façade. Jerusalem is inscribed above the Temple's façade.
Reverse: Palm frond (lulav) bound with willow and myrtle
twigs, a citron (etrog) to the left. "Year 1 of the freedom
of Israel" is inscribed around the central motif.

39a Bar Kokhba Coin
Year 2, 133–34 C.E.
Silver tetradrachm
Collection of Dr. David Jeselsohn, Zurich

Obverse: Image of the Jerusalem Temple with a tetra-style
façade. The name Shimon is inscribed above the Temple's façade.
Reverse: Palm frond (lulav) bound with willow and myrtle
twigs, a citron (etrog) to the left. "Year 2 of the freedom
of Israel" is inscribed around the central motif.

The palm frond bundle that appears on the obverse of this coin
is reminiscent of the festival of Sukkot (Tabernacles). This festival was of great significance for Simeon bar Kokhba (actually,
bar Kosiba) and his followers. This sentiment is expressed in
two letters discovered in the Judean desert, one in Aramaic and
one in Greek, sent by "Simeon" himself. In both, Bar Kohkba
sees to the proper distribution of lulavs and citrons to his soldiers, using the terminology for the four component species of
plants that is known in Rabbinic sources. The early Rabbis too
considered the lulav to be of great importance to the celebration of Sukkot, expanding its role in the synagogue liturgy during this festival. (e.g., Mishnah Sukkah 3:12–13).

RT, SF

Mildenberg 1984: R 19.14; Meshorer 1982: 96–131.

40 Plaque in the Form of a Torah Shrine (Plate XXXI)
Provenance unknown, c. fifth to sixth century C.E.
Limestone
35 × 25 cm
Jerusalem, Hebrew University, Institute of Archaeology 2473

This plaque is carved as a gabled structure. The central element of the iconography is the image of a large niche, a Torah Shrine, with a rounded top. At the center of the niche is a circular hollow that originally contained a mirror. The upper portion of the niche is articulated with four small columns. Crowning the niche is a smaller arch, with a scalloped inner ring enclosing a semicircular hollow that contained a second mirror. This scalloped ring is reminiscent of the conch motif found in representations of Torah Shrines from Beth Alpha and Beth Shean A and in aediculae from Nabratein, Chorazin (Cat. 44), and elsewhere. The Torah niche is flanked by two seven-branched menorahs that stand on tripod bases. The branches of the menorahs are rendered as globular segments and topped with a crossbar. Four vertical perforations are cut between the branches and the base of the menorahs. Above each menorah is a somewhat smaller semicircular hollow, and above the smaller arch is a suspension hole. The base is articulated as a frieze of three birds. The original purpose of this piece is unknown. A considerable number of plaques with inlaid mirrors have been uncovered, mainly in tombs. Jewish, Christian, and pagan iconography appears on these plaques. The iconography of a Torah Shrine flanked by two menorahs also appears in sarcophogus carvings and in graffiti from the Beth Shearim catacombs. Rahmani has conjectured that these plaques served to ward off the evil eye.

SF

Mayer and Reifenberg 1937: 136–39; Goodenough 1953–68: 1, 174–77; 3, nos. 440–42, 445–46; Rahmani 1964.

41 Oil Lamp with a Menorah Handle (Plate XXXV)
Provenance unknown, fifth to sixth century C.E.
Bronze
11 × 16.5 cm
Jerusalem, Hebrew University, Institute of Archaeology Schloessinger Collection 6654

The body and handle of this large lamp were cast as one unit. There was originally a hinged lid over the filling hole. The handle is formed as a seven-branched menorah. The branches are rendered as globular segments and topped with a crossbar. This menorah is reminiscent of the menorah images on the Hebrew University Torah Shrine plaque (Cat. 40) and the small bronze menorah discovered in the Ein Gedi synagogue. The menorah is flanked by two smaller objects that lend stability to the handle. On the left is a lulav bundle with an etrog and on the right is a shofar. This iconography is well known from representations on mosaics and stone carvings. No similar Jewish lamp is extant. A menorah lamp handle, however, was uncovered in the Beth Shean A synagogue. Clay lamps were also decorated with images of menorahs. It is likely that our rather costly lamp illuminated a Jewish public context, in all likelihood a synagogue. Similar lamps with cross-shaped handles are well known from church contexts.

SF

Rosenthal and Sivan 1978: 160, no. 662; Goodenough 1953: 3, fig. 941.

42 Fragment with Double Meander (Fig. 5.18)
Kefar Baram, fourth to fifth century C.E.
Limestone
54.4 × 85 × 34.7 cm
Jerusalem, Israel Antiquities Authority 50-599

E.L. Sukenik discovered this relief in the village of Kefar Baram in 1928. Interspersed between three strips of a double-meander pattern are a bovine animal, a quadruped, a goat, a vegetal motif, a defaced bust of a human figure, and a conch shell. The assortment of figures and motifs led Sukenik to believe that the relief represented the figures of the zodiac. R. Amiram has shown, however, that the figures did not represent the zodiac. She suggested that the motifs were purely ornamental. Similar meander reliefs have been excavated in the Hauran region of Syria—in particular, the town of Nawa (ancient Nave).

RT

Sukenik 1932: 57; Goodenough 1953: 1, 203; 3, figs. 513, 515; Amiram 1956; Chiat 1982: 29.

43 Lintel Fragment with a Menorah in a Wreath (Fig. 5.11b)
Golan Heights (?), fourth to sixth century C.E.
Basalt
51 × 51 × 17 cm
Jerusalem, Bible Lands Museum 1107

At the center of this essentially square lintel fragment is the relief image of a seven-branched menorah with segmented, rounded branches of differing lengths. It is enclosed within a segmented wreath that may have terminated in a small herculaean knot. The source of this piece is not known, though it certainly derives from the Golan Heights or from an adjacent area where basalt is common.

SF

Ilan 1987: 112; Muscarella 1981: 291.

44 Aedicula (Fig. 5.7)
Chorazin, fifth to sixth century C.E.
Basalt
85 × 50 × 143 cm
Jerusalem, Israel Antiquities Authority 66-768

Triangular gables carved with conches that originally surmounted aediculae were discovered in the Chorazin synagogue. Above the conch of the exhibited gable are two bands of repeated floral motifs. The upper edge of the gable is also decorated with floral motifs. These gables probably surmounted Torah Shrines on the southern wall of the synagogue. Aediculae similar to this one appear in the Beth Shean A mosaic and in the lintel from Belvoir (Cat. 65). Stone aediculae have been recovered from a number of synagogue excavations in Israel, the best preserved being the Torah Shrine gable from Nabratein.

SF

Kohl and Watzinger 1916: 41–58, 2; Yeivin 1985.

45 She-Wolf Feeding Young (Fig. 5.20)
Chorazin, fourth to fifth century C.E.
Basalt
33 × 42 cm
Jerusalem, Israel Antiquities Authority 93-1504

The fourth- to fifth-century Galilean-type synagogue of Chorazin was constructed of local basalt. Bas reliefs with images of Jewish symbols and general Greco-Roman iconographic themes appear on architectural members. These themes include, among others, the menorah, four viticulture scenes within a grapevine frame, Medusa (?), a lion devouring his prey, and a she-wolf nursing her young. The she-wolf image is enveloped in a stylized grapevine pattern.

SF

Kohl and Watzinger 1916: 50; Goodenough 1953: 1, 194–95; 3, fig. 492; Chiat 1982: 97–102.

46 Two Hanging Lamps (Fig. 1.12b)
Gush Ḥalav, 363–460 C.E.
Terracotta
5.3 × 10 cm diam.
Jerusalem, Israel Antiquities Authority 95-2414, 95-2413

Remains of hanging lamps were found in the "western corridor" of the Gush Ḥalav synagogue. This building has a large central nave separated from the side aisles by two rows of four columns. The Torah Shrine stood on a broad podium to the right of the main entrance, which was on the southern, Jerusalem-aligned wall. A mezzanine was constructed in the north, possibly providing extra seating. Adjoining rooms, located in the west and east, were probably used for storage. The excavators believe that the "western corridor" served as a storage space for lamps, roof tiles, and other maintenance materials. These open-bowl oil lamps resemble contemporaneous glass lamps. The stem of the bowl probably fit into a brace that hung from the ceiling.

RT

Meyers, Meyers, and Strange 1990: 129, 162–63, figs. 16–19.

47 Synagogue Coin Hoard (Fig. 5.8)
Merot
Coins: Bronze and gold, 80–73 B.C.E.–1193 C.E.
Jerusalem, Israel Antiquities Authority 17105, 17441

This coin hoard was discovered under the floor of a storeroom to the west of the main hall of the synagogue. In the northwest corner of the room the excavators discovered the remains of a stone through which a hole had been cut. Under the hole, writes Ilan, "there was a sort of sloping path hewn in the rock which led to a niche at the edge of the hollow. The dimensions of the niche, actually the treasury, are 35 × 37 cm. The distance between the edge of the hole and the top of the niche is 95 cm." The form of this construction is unique among synagogue treasuries that have been discovered. Within the treasury 485 coins were

uncovered; 245 were gold, the rest bronze. The coins date as early as 80–76 B.C.E. (a coin of Alexander Janneus); six date to the fourth century C.E. There is a continuous sequence from the time of Anastasius I (491–518) through 608–9, and a golden Abbasid dinar dating to 783 was uncovered. The latest coin, an Ayyubid coin, dates to 1193. This discovery substantiated the excavator's conclusion based upon excavation of the synagogue that it was in use from late antiquity until the late twelfth or early thirteenth century. This is the largest and most valuable synagogue treasury yet to be unearthed. "At the top level of the edge of the hollow" Ilan recovered "a number of gold coins scattered outside the treasury as well as small bronze scales."

RT

Ilan and Damati 1987: 122–30; 1995: 1, 272–75.

48 Mosaic with Pomegranates and Shofars (Plate XXVI)
Merot, c. sixth century C.E.
Tesserae
158.5 × 144 cm
Jerusalem, Israel Antiquities Authority 87-113/5

In front of the south facade of Merot's basilica-form synagogue was a courtyard. This mosaic panel was found in the southeast corner of the building, which occupied most of the courtyard area. This building has been identified by the excavators as a "study hall," though the evidence is inconclusive.

Before this mosaic was laid, the artist sketched a plan in red paint on the plaster base. This panel was found in the southeast corner of the study hall. The floor is framed by a border of lily-like flowers. Geometric patterns divide the floor into diamond shapes, each containing a motif. In the upper row a heart-shaped leaf is extant. In the row below this are pomegranates. Only one diamond shape survives in the row beneath this, and only the upper area of the interior motif, a pointed projection, survives. Two shofars are in the row beneath this motif. Directly beneath the pointed projection is a date cluster motif.

GMG

Ilan and Damati 1987: 81–83, 152; Ilan 1995: 280–83.

49 Mosaic Depiction of a Roman Soldier (Plate XLb)
Merot, sixth century C.E.
Stone tesserae
1.70 × 2.15 m
Jerusalem, Israel Antiquities Authority 84-319

This mosaic panel was uncovered along the northern edge of the eastern aisle of the synagogue, underneath the sixth-century stone pavement. Framed within a guilloche pattern is a young red-headed warrior surrounded by his weapons. The warrior is dressed in a white long-sleeved tunic with a red cloak draped over his shoulders. Shown in a seated position, he appears to be leaning against an ovoid shield. Flanking his head are a helmet on the left and a long sword within a scabbard on the right. The eyes of the figure have been eradicated, possibly by iconoclasts. Depth and shading were achieved by using red, pink, yellow, white, and black tesserae. The model for this image was a Roman soldier. Great attention to detail is noted in the fibula and in the insignia on the soldier's garment. The design on the insignia closely resembles the emblem of the Victores, a Roman military legion. Y. Yadin identified the Merot soldier as David with the weapons of Goliath. This identification is not supported by the extant evidence or by any iconographic parallels. Between the shield and the helmet is an Aramaic inscription:

יודן בר שמעון
מני

Yudan son of Shimon, mny.

The inscription is presented vertically, in the manner of Syrian and Palmyrine inscriptions. Scholars disagree with the translation of "mny." Naveh suggests that the word "mny" refers to the donation of one silver *maneh*, a unit of currency.

RT, SF

Ilan and Damati 1987: 51–56; Ilan and Damati 1989: 26–29; Ilan 1995: 261–67; Naveh 1989: 305.

50 Chancel Screen Post with Aramaic Inscription (Fig. 6.6b)
Dalton, fourth to seventh century C.E.
Limestone
65 × 18 cm
Jerusalem, Israel Antiquities Authority 52-704

This chancel screen post has an eighteen-line inscription on its front side. Naveh suggests that the post, which is poorly carved and otherwise effaced, contains the ends of phrases that were carved on the now-lost screen. He suggests a similar solution for a difficult inscription on a chancel screen post from Khirbet Susiya. Of particular interest on the Dalton chancel screen post is the term *takah raḥmana* (line 4), "cabinet of the Merciful (One)." "Merciful (One)" as a Divine appellation appears in the Belvoir and Ein Gedi inscriptions and in Rabbinic sources. In line 7 we find *qetedra*, a loan word from the Greek referring to a large chair. This term appears in no other synagogue inscription. *Kathedra* in Greek is the term for synagogue chairs in the New Testament (Matt. 23:2) and is a loan word in Rabbinic sources (*Pesiqta de-Rav Kahana*, ed. Mandelbaum 1:6). In both literatures we hear of a "Chair of Moses." Sukenik identified large synagogue chairs discovered at Delos, Chorazin, and Ḥammath Tiberias A as "Chairs of Moses."

SF

Naveh 1978: 144–46; Bacher 1897; Rahmani 1990.

51 Polycandelon (Fig. 2.14)
Kefar Ḥananyah, fifth to sixth century C.E.
Bronze
Diameter 51 cm
Mariemont, Musée Royal de Mariemont B.321

This is the only synagogue dedicatory inscription in Aramaic or Hebrew to mention a place:

דן כלילה פְּתגשאפֻֿלְ קתיפת לאתרה קדישה דכפר חנניה דכירין
לטב אמ סלה שלום
ן פטפ ט

This crown . . . to the holy place of Kefar Hananyah . . . . May they be remembered for good. Ame[n] sela, shalom. ptp t.

The term "crown" for round lamps is also known from Christian sources. The designation of the synagogue as a "holy place" occurs often in dedicatory inscriptions. Kefar Hananyah is a village on the border between the Upper and the Lower Galilee. The conclusion of the inscription, "ptp t," may have magical significance. This formula appears on an amulet from the Cairo Genizah as well. The lamp is decorated with two menorahs, each flanked by a lulav and shofar. The donation of lighting fixtures with dedicatory inscriptions to synagogues is evidenced in the literary sources as early as the second to early third century C.E. One early source instructs that a lamp that has been donated to a synagogue cannot be sold "until the names of the donors have been rubbed off of them" (Tosefta Megillah 2:16).

SF

Naveh 1978: 34–35; 1989: 303; Hüttenmeister and Reeg 1977: 1, 256–58; Ilan 1991: 153–54.

52 Sherds with Image of a Torah Shrine (Plate VI)
Nabratein, sixth to eighth century C.E.
Terracotta
10.4 × 7.7 cm
Jerusalem, Israel Antiquities Authority 95-2864

Twenty-seven fragments of the vessel were found in a house near the Nabratein synagogue. When reconstructed, the shards revealed the image of a Torah Shrine incised onto a shiny black surface. Two spirally fluted columns support a gable roof decorated with cross-hatched rhomboids. Between the columns are two cross beams, which are joined to the lintel. The zigzag lines are probably meant to represent decorative reliefs. Two horns, curving down from the acroteria, terminate in a long chain. A large circular ring, open on the left, hangs from the roof on a short chain. The excavators have hypothesized that the suspended chains represent hanging lamps The basic elements of this Shrine resemble those seen in the mosaics at Beth Shean and Beth Alpha and in the Hebrew University Torah Shrine plaque (Cat. 40).

RT

Meyers and Meyers 1981: 30–39; 1982: 176–85; Hachlili 1988: 270, Fig. 19; Magnes 1994: 199–206; Fine 1996.

53 Pilaster Capital with Dedicatory Inscription (Fig. 2.10a)
Tiberias, c. fifth to sixth century C.E.
Marble
34 × 24 cm
Jerusalem, Israel Antiquities Authority 69-5281.

Ἡ θεοῦ χάρις μετὰ Ἀβραμίου μαρμαρίου

The Gracious God [be] with Abraham the marble worker.

This pilaster capital, based upon the Corinthian order, derives from either a synagogue or a study house in Byzantine Tiberias. The trades of the donors were occasionally found in synagogue inscriptions. Jews are known to have engaged in the stone-cutting and construction trades in late antique Palestine. The phrase "The Gracious God" does not appear elsewhere in Jewish epigraphy. Abraham (or Abram) was a rare name for Jews during antiquity. The name is known from other Jewish inscriptions in the Land of Israel. It appears in an inscription from Beth Shearim, in a bilingual inscription from the area of Yavne in the Coastal plain, and in Diaspora contexts.

SF

Roth-Gerson 1987: 58–59, fig. 14.

54 Chancel Screen Fragment Inscribed with *Shalom* (Fig. 6.11)
Tiberias, fourth to seventh century C.E.
Marble
55 × 40 cm
Jerusalem, Israel Antiquities Authority 69-5296

This is the left side of a chancel screen. Inscribed upon it is the word "Shalom" followed by a leaf. "Shalom" is the final word of a longer, probably dedicatory, inscription. This is the final word of a number of synagogue dedicatory inscriptions, including inscriptions from Baram, Abelim, Ḥammath Gader, and Beth Shean B.

SF

Naveh 1978: 45–46.

55 Open-work Chancel Screen (Plate XXIXb)
Ḥammath Tiberias, fifth–sixth century C.E.
Marble
68.5 × 70 × 7.5 cm
Jerusalem, Israel Antiquities Authority 64-558

Many screens have been discovered in sites from the Lower Galilee. This piece is cut from a single piece of stone in a lattice pattern. This pattern is well known from secular and church screens during late antiquity. At the top of the screen two incised birds have been defaced, apparently by iconoclasts.

SF

Hachlili 1988: 187–88.

56 Chancel Post (Plate XXVIII)
Ḥammath Tiberias A, fifth–sixth century C.E.
Marble
61 × 19 cm
Jerusalem, Hebrew University, Institute of Archaeology 1550

This chancel post has the appearance of a small column. The stylized "capital" is decorated with acanthus leaves imitating the Corinthian order. A seven-branched menorah is incised beneath the capital. The menorah is rendered in a linear style with a tripod base. The branches of the menorah are topped with a horizontal bar. Flanking the menorah is a shofar on the left and a palm frond on the right. The linear design carved into the shaft is probably meant to imitate the grooves on a column drum.

RT

Slouschz 1921: 6, 24, pl. III; Eshkoli and Narkiss 1934–35: 179.

57 Menorah (facsimile) (Plate XXV)
Ḥammath Tiberias A, fifth to sixth century C.E.
Limestone
43 × 57.5 × 13 cm
Jerusalem, Israel Museum 1729.66

This seven-branched menorah was unearthed in Ḥammath Tiberias by Slouschz in 1921. The menorah was found buried in the floor of the synagogue. The branches are rendered in an alternating pomegranate and bud motif. Above each branch of the menorah is a small socket. These were probably used to hold glass lamps, as depicted in the mosaics of Ḥammath Tiberias B and Beth Shean B. Remains of other large seven-branched menorahs have been uncovered at Susiya and at Maon in Judea.

SF

Slouschz 1921: 32, pl. XIV; Goodenough 1953: 1, 214; 3, fig. 562.

58 Capital with Menorah (Plate XXXVII)
Ḥammath Tiberias A, fifth to sixth century C.E.
Marble
15 × 27 × 28 cm
Jerusalem, Hebrew University, Institute of Archaeology 1547

A number of Corinthian order capitals bearing images of menorahs have been discovered in the Land of Israel. These pieces directly parallel the placement of crosses on capitals during the Byzantine period. A capital with a menorah and another with a cross from Caesarea Maritima both derive from the same workshop.

RT

Slouschz 1921: 11, pl VII; Eshkoli and Narkiss 1934–35: 175–96, fig. 1; Hüttenmeister and Reeg 1977: 1, 159–63.

59 Menorah Panel (Plate XXXIX)
"Peace unto Israel" Panel (Plate LI)
Ḥuseifa, fifth to sixth century C.E.
Stone and glass tessarae
105 × 95 cm/109 × 97 cm
Jerusalem, Hebrew University, Institute of Archaeology/Israel Antiquities Authority 36-2150, 1447, 1448, 1450

Excavated in 1933 by Avi-Yonah, this synagogue was constructed on the highest level of the village of Ḥuseifa on Mount Carmel. The nearly square building had a nave with flanking side aisles. Evidence of a niche or an apse for a Torah Shrine has not been found. The floor was paved with a mosaic pavement. The space surrounding the nave was paved in a geometric pattern. Elements of the mosaic exhibited here include a panel containing a wreath (Plate LI), at the center of which is the Hebrew inscription "Peace upon Israel" (Ps. 125:5 and parallels) flanked by two menorah panels. These panels stood nearly opposite the main entrance of the synagogue on the west. The menorah on the left is flanked by an incense shovel, a shofar, an etrog, and a lulav. The menorah on the right is flanked by an incense shovel and a shofar on the right side. The left side is not extant. The synagogue was destroyed by fire, apparently under Christian auspices. Its destruction, along with the demise of other synagogues in the Land of Israel, is bemoaned in a *piyyut* discovered in the Cairo Genizah.

SF

Makhouly and Avi-Yonah 1933; Assaf 1948; Goodenough 1953: 1, 257–59; 3, figs. 649–54, 658; Naveh 1978: 65–66; Hachlili 1988: s.v. Ḥuseifa.

60 Fragment of Zodiac Wheel (Plate XLIII)
Ḥuseifa, fifth to sixth century C.E.
Stone and glass tesserae
105 × 95 cm
Jerusalem, Hebrew University, Institute of Archaeology 1449

Fragments of a dedicatory inscription in Aramaic, an inhabited scroll pattern, and portions of a zodiac wheel were discovered in the center of the nave. The zodiac wheel is reminiscent of the zodiac wheels of Ḥammath Tiberias B, Beth Alpha, Naaran, and Sepphoris. In these mosaics the zodiac wheel is divided into twelve sections. Each section depicts a symbol of the zodiac, and its name appears in Hebrew. At Sepphoris the labors of the months are also illustrated, together with the names of the months in Hebrew. Within the interior of the wheel is a chariot of four horses, called a quadriga. At Ḥammath Tiberias B, Beth Alpha, and Sepphoris the chariot is driven by the god Helios. Framing the wheel on four corners are figural representation of the four seasons. The Ḥuseifa fragment exhibited here preserves part of the sign of Aquarius, represented by an amphora and a personification of autumn. Autumn is presented as a female wearing a headdress and a necklace. Two pomegranates, often associated with autumn, together with other vegetation, appear in the background.

RT, SF

Makhouly and Avi-Yonah 1933; Assaf 1948; Goodenough 1953: 1, 257–59; 3, figs. 649–54, 658; Hachlili 1988: s.v. Ḥuseifa.

61 Lamp Handle in the Form of a Seven-Branched Menorah (Fig. 5.14)
Beth Shean A, sixth to seventh century C.E.
Bronze
Jerusalem, Israel Antiquities Authority 63-206

This seven-branched menorah with a crossbar connecting its branches served as a handle for a bronze oil lamp. It was uncovered together with other bronze pieces in a room on the northeastern side of this synagogue (designated by the excavator as room 4). A complete lamp with a similar handle appears in the Hebrew University Institute of Archaeology (Cat. 41). An important bronze incense burner was discovered in another room of the synagogue. A mosaic inscription written in Samaritan script in a small room on the eastern side of the synagogue (room 8) may suggest that this building belonged to a Samaritan community. The inscription in room 8 is different in execution from the rest of the Beth Shean A mosaic. An inscription attributes this mosaic to the same artisans responsible for the Jewish synagogue at Beth Alpha.

SF

Zori 1967; Chiat 1982: 128–32; Pummer 1989.

62 Carpet Mosaic Inscription (Fig. 6.3)
Beth Shean B, fifth to sixth century C.E.
Stone tesserae
173 × 63 cm
Jerusalem, Israel Antiquities Authority 72-141

This synagogue mosaic was discovered in a complex on the eastern side of the Roman–Byzantine city. It is relatively small, approximately 7 meters square. It consisted of but one room in a public complex containing the "house of Leontis" and a bath, both bearing dedicatory inscriptions. In this it is unique, since all other extant Palestinian buildings were free-standing halls. The walls of this small room were lined with benches, with perhaps the remains of a Torah niche on the southern, Jerusalem-aligned wall. The carpet mosaic is decorated with an inhabited scroll motif, with a menorah at its center. Inhabited scrolls are known from other synagogues and from churches in Palestine. From the lowest branches of the menorah are suspended on the left a lamp and on the right an incense censor. Above the menorah is the world *shalom*. There are three inscriptions within this building, all commemorating anonymous benefaction. Two of the inscriptions are in Aramaic and the third is in Greek. The longest inscription, in Aramaic, is in the inner border of the mosaic, on the northern side:

דכירין לטב כל בני חבורתה קדישתה
דהנון מתחזקין בתקונה דאתרה
[קדי]שה ובשלמה תהוי להון ברכתה אמן
[   ]ברוב שלום חסד בשלום[

Remembered for good all the members of the holy society
[ḥavurta qadisha] who support the repair of the holy place
and its completion. May they have blessing. Amen . . . in
abundant peace, covenant love in peace.

"Remembered for good" is the standard introductory formula
in Aramaic dedicatory inscriptions. "Holy place" is a common
term for synagogues in Palestinian epigraphy. The concluding
formula is reminiscent of liturgical formulae. The constitution
of the "holy society" that repaired and completed this building
is unclear. In literary sources, "holy society" refers to a high-
level Rabbinic academy. Ilan suggests that this building is the
"synagogue of the sages of Beit Shean."

SF

Naveh 1978: 77–79; Bahat 1981: 82–85; Roth-Gerson 1987: 41–42;
Ilan 1991: 117; Fine 1996.

63 Chancel Screen with two Chancel Posts (Fig. 5.9a)*
Reḥov, sixth century C.E.
Screen: 107.5 × 64 × 5.5 cm
Jerusalem, Israel Antiquities Authority 68-1001

The front of this screen is decorated with a relief carving of a
seven-branched menorah in a wreath. This menorah is very
similar to one portrayed on a screen from Beth Shean. On the
back of the screen are four lilies that issue from a common center to form a quatrefoil. The screen is quite fragmentary and
has been constructed from eleven segments. On both sides the
design is enclosed in a triple frame. This frame is repeated in a
double frame pattern on the faces of the rectangular chancel
posts. The posts terminate in round finials resembling column
bases. In a source from the Cairo Genizah a chancel screen is
referred to as a *geder* (partition) for the bema.

SF

Bahat 1973.

64 Model of the Beth Alpha Synagogue (Plate I)
Early sixth century C.E.
63.5 × 152.4 × 121.9 cm
New York, Yeshiva University Museum 89.84

In 1928, while digging an irrigation channel for a nearby settlement, the foundations and mosaic pavement of the Beth Alpha
synagogue were accidentally uncovered. The synagogue was
then excavated in 1929 under the direction of E.L. Sukenik.
This model, constructed under the direction of Rachel Wischnitzer in 1971 for the inaugural exhibition of Yeshiva University
Museum, is based on the plans published by Sukenik. It
depicts the second stage of the synagogue, c. sixth century C.E.
In this model the apse has been left empty. There is no attempt
to posit a reconstruction of the Torah ark or other elements,

*Object not included in the exhibition.

although a reconstruction was presented by the excavator.
Sukenik identified the balcony as a women's gallery. More
recent scholars have questioned this identification.

GMG

Sukenik 1932; S. Safrai 1963: 329–38; Brooten 1982: 117, 119.

65 Lintel with a Menorah and Two Aediculae (Fig. 2.9a)
Belvoir, fourth to seventh century C.E.
Basalt
105 × 55 cm
Jerusalem, Israel Antiquities Authority 66-76/3

This is one of several basalt stones with floral and geometric
patterns that were discovered in secondary use in the Crusader
fortress of Belvoir—Kokhav ha-Yarden in modern Hebrew. The
lintel is carved in bas relief, a large menorah at its center. On
the left of the menorah is a rectangular object, perhaps an
incense shovel. Flanking the menorah were two aediculae,
Torah Shrines, each with four columns supporting an arched
gable. Each aedicula was topped with a conch motif, reminiscent of the Torah Shrine picture in the Beth Shean A mosaic.
In the upper register, next to each of the aediculae, were two
tabula ansata. In the lower register, on the right, is an inscription in Aramaic:

[Remembered for good so-and so]
who donated this
lintel from
the Merciful [One] and from his [own] property
Amen, Amen, Selah

This piece is unusual in that it shows two aediculae flanking a
menorah, and not menorahs on either side of a Torah Shrine.
The dedication of a synagogue lintel is also mentioned in an
inscription from Tiberias. The name Merciful (One) for God
appears in an inscription from Ein Gedi and in Rabbinic
sources. The late antique settlement of Belvoir was located on a
natural terrace 700 meters southeast of the Crusader fortress.
Remains of a building that may have been a synagogue have
been identified there. While Gal dates this piece to the second
to third century, a fourth- to seventh-century date is more likely.

SF

Gal 1995: 167; Naveh 1978: 70–72.

66 Drawing of Gerasa Synagogue Mosaic (Fig. 5.16)
Jordan, fifth century C.E.
Artist: Nachman Avigad
Ink on paper
Jerusalem, Hebrew University, Institute of Archaeology

This drawing was prepared by Avigad for E.L. Sukenik's report
on the Beth Alpha synagogue excavation. The Gerasa synagogue mosaic contains images of numerous animals, including
a leopard, an antelope, and various birds. These were apparently part of an elaborate portrayal of Noah and the Ark. Names

of Noah's sons, Shem and Jafeth, label two human figures, of which only the heads remain. A dove with a twig in its mouth is shown on a branch above the human figures. Two other inscriptions, one in Greek and the other in Hebrew, appear in this mosaic. The Greek inscription surrounds the image of a menorah, flanked by a lulav and an etrog, a shofar, and an incense shovel:

> . . . to the most holy place [*hagio (tato) topo*)]. Amen, Selah. Peace to the community [*sunagogai*].

The Hebrew inscription from the same synagogue closely parallels the Greek text:

> Peace be upon all Israel (Ps. 125:5 and parallels), Amen Amen
> Selah . . . .

SF

Kraeling 1938: 473, no. 285; Sukenik 1932: pl. 26; Roth-Gerson 1987: 46–50.

67 Mosaic Panel with Gorgon Head (Plate XLI)
Yafia, fifth to sixth century C.E.
Stone/glass tesserae
105 × 74 cm
Jerusalem, Israel Antiquities Authority 69-88512

In 1921, two lintels, one carved with a menorah and rosettes, were discovered in reuse in the Arab village of Yafia, approximately 2 kilometers southwest of Nazareth. In 1950, Sukenik and Avigad excavated the remains of a synagogue located on a peak to the north of the village. The few surviving remains of this basilica-form synagogue include a segment of the south wall, a row of four column pedestals and the foundation stones of a fifth pedestal, and fragments of mosaic pavement, including one complete panel in the southwest end of the nave.

The synagogue mosaic at Yafia featured a mosaic with twelve circles, which has only partially survived. These circles probably contained symbols of the twelve tribes or of the zodiac. In this panel from the southwest corner of the nave, a gorgon head between double volutes is surmounted by an eagle. Sukenik identified the head as Helios. Goodenough suggested Medusa based on the head's curling tendrils of hair. The eagle, rendered in shades of yellow, is a golden eagle, a symbol of the sun.

GMG

Sukenik 1951: 6–24; Goodenough 1953: 1, 217; 3, fig. 993; 7, 225.

68 Capital with Three Menorahs (Fig. 5.22)
Caesarea, c. fifth century C.E.
Limestone
Jerusalem, Hebrew University, Institute of Archaeology

Found within the fourth-century synagogue of Caesarea was a Doric capital with a menorah incised on the face. This capital is stylistically different from the other capitals with the

menorah motif. A Corinthian capital with a menorah was discovered in Caesarea and another at Hammath Tiberias A (Cat. 58).

RT

Goodenough 1953: 1, 263; 3, fig. 997; Roth-Gerson 1987: 123.

69 Oil Lamp with Image of a Torah Shrine
Caesarea, fourth to sixth century C.E.
Terracotta
9.8 × 7.9 cm
Jerusalem, Israel Antiquities Authority 76-652

This oil lamp was discovered in a burial context in Caesarea and is of a form known as the Caesarea type. The body of the lamp is round, with a small handle to the rear and a wide nozzle. The outer edge of the upper side is decorated in a ribbed pattern. In the center is a gabled structure, a Torah Shrine, supported by two columns. At the center of the gable is a design reminiscent of a conch motif. Cross-hatching between the columns represents a partition, perhaps doors or a cloth curtain. The iconography of this shrine is well known from both Jewish and Samaritan synagogue mosaics and also appears in the Jewish burial catacombs of Beth Shearim. It is impossible to assign decisively this piece to either community. Both Jews and Samaritans were present in large numbers in Byzantine Caesarea.

SF

70 Plaque Listing Priestly Courses (*Mishmarot*) (facsimile) (Fig. 6.9)
Caesarea, fourth to seventh century C.E.
Fragment A: 15.5 × 12.4 cm; B: 14.5 × 14 cm
Jerusalem, Israel Antiquities Authority 66-1305

Inscriptions containing the twenty-four priestly courses as mentioned in 1 Chronicles 24 have been found in Ashkelon, Rehov, and Nazareth and in Beit al-Hatzer in Yemen. These verses were the subject of numerous synagogue liturgical poems as well, thus reflecting the close relationship between synagogue furnishings and liturgy.

RT

Avi-Yonah 1964: 124–28; Naveh 1978: 87–88; Levine 1989: 171–72, 174; Eshel 1991: 125–36.

71 Dedicatory Inscription with Menorah (Fig. 2.10b)
Binyamina, fourth to seventh century C.E.
Limestone
29 × 22 cm
Jerusalem, Israel Antiquities Authority 80-787

On the surface of this inscribed tablet is a large seven-branched menorah, perhaps flanked by a shofar and lulav. A Greek inscription frames the stele. It reads:

Εἷς Θεὸς βο(ή)θ(ε)ι Ἰούδα
πϱεσ(βυτέϱῳ).
Ἔτ(ους) αου’

One God, help Judah the elder. Year 471.

The phrase "One God" also appears in Christian and Samaritan contexts in the Land of Israel. The donor's name, Judah, suggests that this piece is Jewish, since Judah was not a name used by Samaritans. Di Segni suggests that this inscription was attached to the wall of a synagogue. It is not clear which epoch is referred to by the date on this inscription. Di Segni proposes tentatively that it may be "a unique piece of evidence of the use of a Pompeian era in the territory of Caesarea." The use of local epochs is attested in Greek synagogue inscriptions from Gaza.

RT

Di Segni 1993b: 133–36.

72 Samaritan Oil Lamp Depicting a Torah Shrine and Ritual Implements (Fig. 1.14)
Netanya, fifth to sixth century C.E.
Terracotta
9.2 × 6.5 × 3.0 cm
Jerusalem, Israel Antiquities Authority 82-1051

Immediately behind the nozzle of this lamp the upper side is decorated with a large gabled four-columned structure, apparently a Torah Shrine. A four-columned structure is used to represent a Torah Shrine in the recently discovered Samaritan synagogue mosaics from Khirbet Samara and El-Khirbe, in a Jewish synagogue mosaic in the Susiya synagogue, and in a Christian context in the Chapel of the Priest John on Mount Nebo. Beneath the gable is the word "Arise" in Samaritan script, apparently a reference to "Arise O Lord and scatter your enemies" (Num. 10:35). To the right of the shrine is a round object, perhaps a pitcher, a pomegranate, or a bird. Below, on the left, is a seven-branched menorah with enlarged burners. To the right of the menorah is a shofar and below an incense shovel. On the right side of the lamp are two pomegranates.

SF

V. Sussman 1988: 133, Hebrew; Magen 1993: 4, 1424–27.

73 Plate with Menorah and Torah Shrine (Fig. 5.15)
Naanah, fourth to seventh century C.E.
Bronze
50 cm diam.
Paris, Musée du Louvre AO 1265

This bronze plate was discovered in the late nineteenth century by French archaeologist C.J. Clermont-Ganneau. The lower part of the plate is missing. The center is ornamented with a floral motif. A vine-scroll pattern ending in alternating rosettes frames the border; within the open spaces are a menorah and a Torah Shrine. The branches of this highly stylized menorah are rendered as globular segments and topped with a crossbar and

possibly spikes. The tripod base seems to blend into the vegetal design. Flanking the Shrine are palm branches.

Clermont-Ganneau likened the plate to that used in the Christian Eucharist. Goodenough suggested that the plate was used to serve bread or fish. The vine-scroll design is similar to the inhabited scroll pattern found on mosaic floors.

RT

Clermont-Ganneau 1885: 78–79; Dussard 1912: 76, no. 97; Goodenough 1953: 1, 173; 3, 434; Dauphin 1978: 400–401.

74 Dedicatory Inscription (Fig. 6.8)
Ashkelon, fourth to seventh century C.E.
Marble
26 × 29 cm
Paris, Musée du Louvre AO 1274

This fragmentary Aramaic inscription was discovered by C.J. Clermont-Ganneau in 1878. This is the only extant synagogue dedicatory inscription on stone to be carved in bas relief rather than being incised. The text reads:

```
                               ]
          [ כל חד וחד ]
            [ו דשמיה ]
     [   ] [שתלמ]
                               ]
```

. . .
each and every one . . .
of heaven and . . .
. . . sh.t.l.m . . .

The phrase "each and every one" commonly appears in Rabbinic sources. Joseph Naveh suggests that "of heaven" in line 3 might have been preceded by the the word מריה (master). This is, in fact, the reading in an inscription from Horvat Ammudim that reads מרי שומיא, "Master of Heaven." The final line of this inscription has not been deciphered.

Clermont-Ganneau 1885: 71, pl. lb; Naveh 1978: 89–90.

75 Inscribed Pot Sherds (Fig. 2.8a)
Horvat Rimmon, fifth to sixth century C.E.
Terracotta
Jerusalem, Israel Antiquities Authority 80.880

Five sherds were found in a room of the Horvat Rimmon synagogue along with cooking pots, oil lamps, and parts of a chancel screen. The sherds were inscribed in Aramaic upon the surface of a vessel. The potter made cuts on the vessel and broke it along the incisions. The inscription was made before firing.

הראות אתבאות קולהון
[ ] ספתון סוסגר
[אתון מלאכיה קד]ישיה (ותקיפיה)
[משבע אנה] יתכון כמ[ה דיקד חספה]
[הדין כן] יקוד לבה דרן.. ברה/ברתה]
[דמר]י[ן בתר]י[) אנה (י)י[... ותהפכן]
[לבה והו](נה ו)כוליתה ו/י/תעבר]

[   ] מוד[ ]בהד[ן] ציביוני
[   ] (magic characters)

1 hr'wt 'tb'wt qwlhwn
2 sptwn swsgr [   ]
3 You ho[ly (and mighty)] angels
4 [I adjure] you, just as [this sherd]
5 [burns, so shall] burn the heart of R[. . . son/daughter of]
6 [Mar]ian after me, I . . . [. . . and you should turn]
7 [his/her heart and mi]nd and kidney, so [that he/she will do]
8 my desire in this [   ]
9 (magic characters)

The petitioner seeks the burning love from the subject of his or her desire. The sherds could have been designed as part of sympathetic magic, where an inanimate object acts as a surrogate for the desired person. Just as this sherd burns, so shall burn the heart of the beloved. The appearance of black marks may denote that the sherds were burned in accordance with the text. Naveh and Shaked's translation was reconstructed from Judeo-Arabic Genizah fragments containing similar phrases. The names of the angels (lines 1–2) are circled to emphasize their particular properties. The last line of the text is made up of what Naveh calls "magical characters." He suggests that they usually appear on amulets for decorative purposes, devoid of any real meaning.

RT

Naveh and Shaked 1985: 86–89, pl. 9.

76 Mosaic Pavement with Image of a Shrine (Plate IX)
Eastern Mediterranean, sixth century C.E.
Stone tesserae
141 × 108 cm
Jerusalem, Bible Lands Museum 1105

To the right of this fragmentary mosaic is a large shrine. A domed gable is supported by two columns with Corinthian capitals that stand on a raised podium, perhaps ascended by steps. Within the Shrine is the image of a free-standing screen decorated in cross-hatch pattern. Suspended from the gable is a red curtain tied at the center. Above the gable are two birds. To the left of the shrine is a tree flanked by tall flowers. It is likely that this piece derives from a church. Images of shrines with screens and curtains before them are known from Christian art in Palestine and elsewhere.

This piece, and others like it, have been ignored in the continuing debate as to whether images of shrines flanked by menorahs from synagogues in Hammath Tiberias B, Beth Alpha, Beth Shean A, Naaran, and Susiya represent Torah Shrines. Since the discovery of the Beth Alpha synagogue mosaic in 1929 scholars have debated whether these mosaics primarily reflect the furnishings of late antique synagogues or are symbolic representations of the Jerusalem Temple or of the supernal realm. The remains of Torah Shrines and seven-branched menorahs in Palestinian synagogues prove conclu-

sively that the images which appear in the synagogue mosaics reflect actual synagogue furnishings. While this was demonstrated by E.L. Sukenik, evidence discovered since his time, particularly the Nabratein Torah Shrine gable, has removed any doubt of this conclusion. The Bible Lands mosaic demonstrates that Christians decorated their churches with images of church furnishings, providing an important parallel to the representation of synagogue furnishings in Jewish (and probably Samaritan) mosaic depictions.

SF

Muscarella 1981: 308, fig. 284; Merhav 1987: fig. 156.

77 Mosaic Pavement from Samaritan Synagogue (Fig. 1.13)*
Shalabim, sixth century C.E.
Stone tesserae
Jerusalem, Israel Antiquities Authority 48-3001/1

Remains of a Samaritan synagogue were excavated by E.L. Sukenik outside the village of Shalabim. The structure was aligned toward Mount Gerizim, the Samaritan sacred place. Two mosaic floors were found within the building. In a large panel of the lower floor two menorahs flank a triangular element, possibly a representation of Mount Gerizim. Above this scene is a Greek inscription. Lifshitz suggests the following reading:

Restoration of the place of prayer.

The scene and the inscription are framed within a roundel set within a geometric pattern. Unlike menorahs from Jewish mosaics, the ones presented here are of disproportionate size. The branches of the menorahs are composed of alternate bands of light and dark tesserae. The triangular element is also composed of light and dark tesserae arranged as concentric stepped triangles. Two rhomboids appear to the left of the larger menorah. At the northern end of the synagogue is Exodus 15:18 in Samaritan script:

The Lord will reign forever and ever.

Based upon the material evidence, E. L. Sukenik proposed that the synagogue existed during the fourth century C.E. There might have been an earlier structure, as suggested by the Greek inscription mentioned above.

RT

Sukenik, 1949: 26; Goodenough 1953: 1, 262–63; 3, figs. 661, 663, 665; Lifshitz 1967: 71; Hüttenmeister and Reeg 1977: 635, 636; Pummer 1989: 140; Reich 1994: 228–33.

78 Column Fragment with Dedicatory Inscription (Fig. 2.9c)
Beth Guvrin, fourth to seventh century C.E.
Limestone
40 × 30 cm
Jerusalem, Israel Antiquities Authority I 4219

This seven-line Aramaic inscription set within an irregular ellipsoid circle was found carved on a limestone column fragment. The inscription reads:

*Object not included in the exhibition.

דכיר
לטב קוריס
שימעיי ניח נפש
בר אוכסנטיס
דזבן הדין עמודא
ליקרה דכנישתא
שלום

Remembered
for good master
Shimai, may his soul rest,
son of Auxentios,
who purchased this column
to the glory of the synagogue
Shalom

This inscription parallels Aramaic dedicatory inscriptions from the Ḥammath Gader synagogue and Greek inscriptions from synagogues in many important ways. The Greek loan word *Kurios*, meaning "master," appears in the Aramaic synagogue inscription from Ḥammath Gader and in Greek synagogue inscriptions from Ashkelon and Beth Shean. "May his soul rest" is otherwise unknown from synagogue inscriptions, although it is common in funerary contexts. Providing the motivation for the dedication is rare in synagogue inscriptions in Aramaic, although it is well attested in Greek inscriptions. A donation to the Ḥammath Gader synagogue was also made "for the glory of the synagogue." The Aramaic term *kenishta* (synagogue) is epigraphically attested elsewhere only in the Ḥammath Gader synagogue. It is well known in Rabbinic sources.

GMG, SF

Sukenik 1930: 76–79; Naveh 1978: 109–11.

79 Chancel Screen Fragment with Menorah (Plate XXIXa)
Gaza, fifth to sixth century C.E.
Marble
18 × 15 × 4.5 cm
Jerusalem, Hebrew University, Institute of Archaeology 2558

This piece was discovered by Sukenik outside its archaeological context. Fragments of an open-work chancel screen were uncovered in a Gaza synagogue in excavations conducted by A. Ovadiah. The fragment presented here is decorated with a seven-branched menorah flanked by a stylized shofar and lulav. Remnants of a lattice pattern are apparent at the base of the fragment. The design was possibly drilled onto the marble surface.

RT

Sukenik 1935: 62, pl. XVIIb; Goodenough 1953: 1, 223, 3, fig. 583; Roth-Gerson 1987: 104.

80 Amulet (Fig. 2.7a)
Nirim, fifth to sixth century C.E.
Bronze
Extant fragment 130 × 45 mm
Jerusalem, Israel Antiquities Authority 57.733/737

Nineteen amulets were discovered in the apse of the ancient synagogue of Maon, near Kibbutz Nirim in the northwestern Negev. Fragments of an outer wrapping of a woven material were found on some of the tightly rolled amulets. One still has the remains of the thread by which it was suspended. The amulets may have been suspended from the wall near the Torah Ark or perhaps from the Shrine itself. In this way the power of the amulet would be enhanced by the power of the Torah Ark and the scroll within it. The placement of amulets in proximity to Torah Shrines is mentioned in an amulet from the Cairo Genizah.

Written in both Hebrew and Aramaic, this is one of the three deciphered amulets out of a group of nineteen discovered in the apse of the ancient synagogue. The purpose of this amulet is apparently the cure of a headache that is tormenting Natrun, daughter of a woman called Sarah. The word *Kephalargia* in line 5 is a Greek word for "headache." Of interest are the number of angels—Barkiel, Uriel, Milḥamiel, Nagdiel, Nahsur, Joel, Bael—invoked to accomplish this task. The translation follows Naveh and Shaked.

אהיה [א]שר אהיה בשם ק[ ]ה ש(נ)רון ארסכיאל (נ)[
אל מש(נ)]ידה שמגרון סכסך דוקון דוקון ואן[
אל [ב](ר)קיאל אוריאל מלחמיאל אה אה אה [א]ה אה אה[
א דתתעקרון מן רישה דנתרון ברתה דשאר[ה] אמן א[מן
ד[מתקרייא קפלרגיא ועלא בכורכוריא ד(נ)יא ולא[
בש[מה ד[נ](ג)דיאל מלאכה דכביש בשושלן דלא ד[נ]חש וב(ש)[
ד[לא דפורזיל ובשמה דנחשור ובשמה דסור(י)א[ל] מלא[כה
]זיקין ומזקין וטלנין יערקון מנה יואל יואל [
נ](ת)רון ברתה דשארה בשם אוה (ה)לוסא אל באל רבן[
]תעקרו מן כורכוריא דניה ומן רישה[
                              [...

1 . . . I-am-who-I-am. In the name of . . . s(n)rwn, 'rsky'l . . .

2 . . .] el, ms(n)ydh, smgrwn, sksk, dwqwn, dwqwn and . . .

3 . . .] el Barkiel, Uriel, Milḥamiel, 'h, 'h, 'h, 'h, 'h, 'h, . . .

4 . . . that you should depart from the head of Natrun, the daughter of Sarah, Amen, Amen . . .

5 . . . called KEPHALARGIA and goes into the bones (?) of the chest and does not (?) . . .

6 . . . In the name of Nagdiel the angel who is bound by chains, which are not of bronze, and . . .

7 . . . not of iron, and in the name of Nahsur and in the name of Suriel the angel . . .

8 . . . blast-demons, tormentors and shadow-spirits should flee away from her. Joel, Joel . . .

9 . . . Na]trun, daughter of Sarah. In the name of 'wh, hlws', El, Bael . . .

10 . . . remove from the bones (?) of her chest and from her head . . .

11 . . .

GT

Naveh and Shaked 1985: 90–94.

81 Mosaic with Hebrew and Aramaic Inscription (Fig. 5.12)*
Ein Gedi, c. fourth to seventh century C.E.
Stone/glass tesserae
2.5 × 1.55 m
Jerusalem, Israel Antiquities Authority

This 118-word, 18-line mosaic inscription was part of the pavement of the Ein Gedi synagogue, the narthex to the west of the main assembly hall. Only the synagogue inscription from Reḥov, with 29 lines and 365 words, is longer. The Ein Gedi inscription is divided by frames into four sections:

אדם שת אנוש קינן מהללאל ירד
חנוך מתושלח למך נוח שם חם ויפית
— — — — — — — — — — —
טלה שור תאומים סרטן ארי בתולה
מאזניים עקרב קישת גדי ודלי דגים
ניסן אייר סיון תמוז אב אילול
תשרי מרחשון כסליו טבית שבט
ואדר אברהם יצחק ויעקב שלום
חנניה מישאיל ועזריה שלום על ישראל
— — — — — — — — — — —
דכירין לטב יוסה ועזרון וחזיקיו בנוה דחלפי
כל מן דיהיב פלגו בן גבר לחבריה הי אמר
לשן ביש על חבריה לעממיה הי גניב
צבותיה דחבריה הי מן דגלי רזה דקרתה
לעממיה דין דעינוה משוטטן בכל ארעה
וחמי סתירתה היא יתן אפוה בגברה
ההו ובזרעיה ויעקור יתיה מן תחות שומיה
וימרון כל עמה אמן ואמן סלה
— — — — — — — — — — —
רבי יוסה בר חלפי חזקיו בר חלפי דכירין לטב
דסגי סגי הנון עבדו לשמה דרחמנה שלום

Adam, Seth, Enosh, Kenan, Mahalalel, Jered
Enoch, Methuselah, Lemach, Noah, Shem, Ham, Japheth
Aries, Taurus, Gemini, Cancer, Leo, Virgo
Libra, Scorpio, Sagittarius, Capricorn and Aquarius, Pisces
Nisan, Iyar, Sivan, Tammuz, Av, Elul
Tishrei, Marheshvan, Kislev, Tevet, Shevat
and Adar Abraham Isaac and Jacob, Peace
Hananiah, Mishael and Azariah Peace unto Israel
Remembered for good, Yose and Ezron and Ḥiziqiyu the sons of Ḥalfi.
Anyone who causes a controversy between a man and his fellow, whoever
slanders his fellow to the gentiles, whoever steals
the property of his fellow, whoever who reveals the secret of the

town to the gentiles—He whose eyes range through the whole earth
and who sees hidden things, will set his face on that man and on his seed and will uproot him from under the heavens.
And all the people said: Amen, Amen Selah.
Rabbi Yose son of Ḥalfi, Ḥiziqiyu the son of Halfi, may they be remembered for good.
For they did a great deal in the name of the Merciful [One]. Shalom.

Lines 1–2 of this inscription cite the thirteen progenitors of humanity from 1 Chronicles 1–4, lines 4–5 list the signs of the zodiac, and lines 5–7 the months of the Jewish year. The list of zodiac signs parallels their appearance in zodiac wheels in numerous Palestinian synagogues. The pairing of the zodiac signs with the months is also found on the Sepphoris zodiac wheel, where the names as well as the symbols of the zodiac and the months appear. The listing of Abraham, Isaac, Jacob and Hananiah, Mishael, and Azariah in line 8 parallels a tradition in Midrash Psalms 1:15 that refers to both of these sets as the three pillars "upon whom the world rests." Levine suggests the first eight lines of this inscription attempt "to fix the basic order of the universe." He suggests that it is structured in a chiastic pattern (A-B-B-A), where A refers to biblical ancestors and B is time-related. The text also moves from the universal to the particularly Jewish, concluding with "Peace unto Israel" (Ps. 125:5 and parallels).

The remainder of the inscription deals with issues of local concern. It is structured with parallel benefaction formulae framing a listing of local violations and curses against transgressors. In line 9 is a dedicatory inscription recalling three sons of "Ḥalfi." Two of these sons are mentioned again in the parallel inscription in lines 17–18. This reflects the importance of this family within the life of the Ein Gedi synagogue. In line 15, Yose son of Ḥalfi is referred to as "Rabbi." The use of this title does not necessarily mean that he was a member of the Rabbinic community. The reading of line 18 is uncertain. J. Naveh reads "they made a large staircase or upper stair" where Levine reads "a great deal." Neither of these interpretations is entirely satisfactory, though it seems likely that this inscription does, as Naveh assumes, commemorate a specific donation.

The remainder of this section, lines 10–16, contains a list of four offenses against the community and an elaborate curse against violators. This is the only such curse in synagogue epigraphy. The curse is composed in a biblicized, perhaps liturgical, idiom. It is not clear what the "secret of the town" refers to, and scholars have suggested varying interpretations. Intriguingly, Lieberman relates it to the trade "secret" of the well-known local balsam industry.

SF

Levine 1981: 140–45; Lieberman 1971: 24–26; Naveh 1978: 31–32; Cohen 1981: 1–17.

*Object not included in the exhibition.

Late Additions to the Exhibition

Fragment of a Cup Bottom
Rome, c. fourth century C.E.
Gold glass
Diameter 10.1–10.2 cm
Vatican, Biblioteca Apostolica Vaticana Inv. 233

Babylonian Talmud, Tractate Avodah Zarah
Ubeda, Spain, 1290
New York, Library of the Jewish Theological Seminary of
    America MS R15

Palestinian Targum to Genesis 40:5
Cairo Genizah, ninth–tenth century to mid-eleventh century
    C.E.
New York, Library of the Jewish Theological Seminary of
    America ENA 2755.2

Liturgy for the Festival of Sukkot
Cairo Genizah, tenth to twelfth century C.E.
New York, Library of the Jewish Theological Seminary of
    America ENA 2028.15

Piyyut (Liturgical Poem) by Rabbi Yannai to Leviticus 12
Cairo Genizah, tenth to twelfth century C.E.
New York, Library of the Jewish Theological Seminary of
    America ENA 414.1–6

Vetus Testamentum Ex Versio Septuagintum Interpretum
Franaeker, 1709
New York, Library of the Jewish Theological Seminary of
    America RB397:2A

Midrash Tanhuma
Yemen, seventeenth to eighteenth century C.E.
New York, Library of the Jewish Theological Seminary of
    America MS R 1670

Mishnah, Tractate Pesaḥim, Qedushin, Order Taharot
Yemen, seventeenth century C.E.
New York, Library of the Jewish Theological Seminary of
    America MS R31

Jerusalem Talmud
Venice, 1523
New York, Mendel Gottesman Library of Yeshiva University
    Strauss 6527

Fragment of *Revelation* 5:5–8
Egypt, fourth century C.E.
Papyrus Oxyrhynchus 1230
Newton Center, Andover Newton Theological Seminary P24

Acts of the Apostles
Greek New Testament
Basel, 1531
New York, Burke Library of Union Theological Seminary
    CB37 1531b

Against Apion
Flavius Josephus, *Opera Omni*
Basel, 1544
New York, Burke Library of Union Theological Seminary
    F/EG A 1544

Against the Jews
John Chrysostom, *Homiliae LXXVII*
Lutece, Paris, 1609
New York, Burke Library of Union Theological Seminary
    F/GM3 CS 1H 1609

Notes

CHAPTER 1

1. King 1983: 276.
2. Ibid. 63–66, 74–84.
3. Ibid. 105.
4. Silberman 1993: 21.
5. Ibid. 23.
6. Meyers 1992b: 1–4.
7. Avigad 1983; King 1983: 104–5. See Slouschz 1921: 5–40; 1924: 49–52.
8. See Dothan 1983.
9. Silberman 1993: 25–26.
10. Ibid. 27.
11. Meyers, Kraabel, and Strange 1976.
12. For my principal essays on the subject of regionalism, see Meyers 1976: 93–101; 1979: 686–701; and 1985: 115–31. Groh 1995: 51–69, has convincingly shown how stratigraphic excavation of synagogues in their site context is the only way to proceed. His conclusions accord with mine.
13. See Meyers and Fine forthcoming; and Fine 1996.
14. After Levine's translation in Levine 1987: 17.
15. Guttman 1972: 72–76.
16. Meyers 1994: 25–42.
17. Meyers 1992a: 251–60. See also Griffiths 1995: 3–16; Grabbe 1995: 17–26; and Flesher 1995: 28–40.
18. Hachlili 1992: 261; Bruneau 1982: 465–504; White 1990.
19. Hachlili, 1992.
20. Ibid.
21. Ibid. and literature cited on Sardis.
22. In a most impressive review of recent literature Wharton 1994: 1–25, has placed the Dura frescoes in the much broader context of the discussion about their relation to the beginnings of Christian art and to orientalism in general.
23. Kraabel 1987: 49–60; see also Hachlili 1988: 272–84.
24. Hachlili 1992: 261.
25. See above, especially n. 30. This point is proved by Fine 1996. See also Rutgers in this volume.
26. Levine 1993: 1421–24.
27. Ibid. 1422. Cf. Groh 1995: 57–60, who begins his examination of the Roman period synagogues with a consideration of Migdal and Gamla. I find the evidence for identifying Migdal as a synagogue unconvincing, however.
28. Cf. Sperber 1974, with Safrai 1994: 172–73. Safrai seems to have a more optimistic view of the economic situation.
29. Meyers, Meyers, and Strange 1982: 35–54.
30. The death of the old view was proclaimed in Levine 1987. Both Levine 1993 and Meyers 1992a begin with that assumption.
31. On this text, see Fine 1996 and the bibliography cited there.
32. Foerster 1981a: 24–29. See, however, the remarks of Netzer 1991: 410–13, who does not endorse Foerster's view on

orientation. He concludes (p. 410) that "it is still too early, in our view, to determine whether the entrance from the east (actually from the southeast!) and the structure's general orientation toward Jerusalem constituted a consideration, major or otherwise, in the planning of the original building or the Zealot's conversion of it into a synagogue."

33. See above n. 32.

34. Levine 1993: 1422.

35. Levine 1993b: 1423.

36. Ibid.; Safrai 1963: 329–38. This issue is explored in an exhaustive manner by Fine 1993.

37. For the Bar Kokhba coins see Meshorer 1982: 2, pl.20: 1; pl. 21: 12–13b; pl. 22: 14–16b.

38. See also Kraabel 1984: 44–46, and above n. 24.

39. Magen 1993a: 1424–27. See also individual entries on these synagogue buildings.

40. Ibid. See also Magen 1992b: 228, and DiSegni 1993a: 231–39.

41. Magen 1992b: 225–28.

42. Ibid. 225.

43. Ibid. 225–26.

44. Ibid. 227, and his article in the same volume, "Mt. Gerizim and the Samaritans": 91–147. These articles and Magen's other articles on the Samaritans in this volume constitute the most up-to-date treatment of Samaritan archaeological remains. See Mishnah Megillah 3:3 and the discussion by Fine 1993: 47–56.

CHAPTER 2

1. This chapter is based on Fine 1996.

2. Tosefta Megillah 2:12, ed. Lieberman; Acts 6:9.

3. On other buildings that have been identified as Second Temple period synagogues, see Hachlili, ch. 5 in this volume.

4. Damascus Document 11:21–22; 4Q271 (photo CAM 43280).

5. Tosefta Megillah 3:23.

6. Ibid. 2:14, 16.

7. Mishnah Kelim 16:7, 28:4.

8. Ibid. 28:4, Tosefta Kelim, Baba Metzia 1:13.

9. Tosefta Baba Metzia 11:23.

10. Cf. Mishnah Nedarim 9:2.

11. According to the Vienna manuscript, as cited by Tosefta, ed. Lieberman.

12. See also Sifra, ed. Weiss, *Behukotai*, ch. 6.

13. Mishnah Rosh Ha-Shanah 3:7.

14. Mishnah Megillah 4:3, 6, 7.

15. Tosefta Berakhot 3:1, 3.

16. Tosefta Kippurim 4:18.

17. Exod. 20:21, *Ba-Hodesh* 11, ed. Horovitz and Rabin 243.

18. Pesiqte de-Rav Kahane: 89–90.

19. Babylonian Talmud, Berakhot 8a and 30b.

20. Following manuscript traditions.

21. Ginzberg 1928–29: 1: 152–53.

22. Deut. Rabba 3:1.

23. Pesiqte de-Rav Kahane.

24. Levine 1991: 54–56, presents the various interpretations of the synagogue appurtenances mentioned in this pericope.

25. Jerusalem Talmud, Yoma, 7:1 44b; Megillah 4:5, 75b; Sotah 8:6, 22a.

26. *Midrash Tanhuma*, ed. Buber, 124 and n. 32; and parallels.

27. T-S K 1.162; cited by Naveh 1989: 303.

28. Rahmani 1960.

29. Naveh and Shaked 1985: 91–92 and 16.

30. Ibid., nos. 11, 12, 13.

31. Naveh and Shaked 1985: 41, line 12; 57, line 23; Swartz 1990: 178; Schiffman and Swartz 1992: 58.

32. Naveh 1978: 34, 48, 54, 57, 60, 62, 70, 86, 122.

33. Schiffman and Swartz 1992: 2–9.

34. Sofrim, 14:6–11, ed. Higger.

35. Tosefta Megillah 2:14, 16; Jerusalem Talmud, Megillah 3:2, 74a.

36. B because this was the second synagogue to be discovered in Ḥammath Tiberias. On this building, see Dothan 1983: 53, 61.

37. Following Sokoloff 1990: 114. Cf. Naveh 1978: 48.

38. Following Sokoloff 1990: 170. Cf. Naveh 1978: 48–49.

39. Sokoloff 1990: 168.

40. Roth-Gerson 1987: 69.

41. Babylonian Talmud, Gittin 59a, Sanhedrin 36a. See Levine 1989: 33.

42. Levine 1989: 176–81.

43. Following Naveh 1978: 99.

44. Ibid. 34–35.

45. Bouras 1982: 480–82.

46. Cambridge University Library Or. 1080.6.19, T-S K 1.18; 1989: 303.

47. *Adversus Judaeos*, 6:7; *Patrologia Graeca*: 48, col. 913; 1:3, col. 847; 1.5, col. 850.

48. *Adversus Judaeos*, 6:7; *Patrologia Graeca*: 48, col. 913.

49. Kraabel 1979: 485.

50. Hanfmann 1967: 27–29.

51. Seager 1981: 182.

52. Hanfmann 1967: 29; Kraabel 1979: 486.

53. See Fine and Rutgers forthcoming.

54. Branham 1992; Wilken 1983: 128–60; Nibley 1959–60.

55. *Adversus Judaeos*, 6:7; *Patrologia Graeca*: 48, col. 914.

56. *Adversus Judaeos*, 8.5–6; 935; 8.7, 937–38; *Patrologia Graeca*: 48, 935–36; see Wilken 1983: 83–88.

57. Goodenough 1953: 9: 54.

58. Kraeling 1956: 19. See Smith 1957: 326–27.

59. Epstein 1983: 40–41; Oppenheimer 1983: 156–64, 276–93.

60. Medieval discussion of this concept is summarized by Gafni 1987: 155, nn. 4–6.

61. Here we follow a variant preserved in the *Iggeret Rav Sherira Gaon*, ed. Lewin: 73, Spanish recension.

62. On the origins of the name Shaf ve-Yativ, see Epstein 1983: 40–41.

63. Goitein 1971: 156.

CHAPTER 3

1. See Baron 1952: 170, 370–72.

2. See Kraabel 1979: 486.

3. The standard collection of ancient Jewish inscriptions is by Frey 1936–52. The most recent inscriptions are given by Louis Robert in his "Bulletin épigraphique," with reference to the year's volume in the *Revue des études grecques*, and by the annual *Supplementum Epigraphicum Graecum*. The inscriptions pertaining to donors and builders have been collected by Lifshitz 1967. For inscriptions originating from Egypt, see Horbury and Noy 1992. The inscriptions from Rome have been collected by Leon 1960: 263–346. A recent version, with much more extensive commentary, is Noy 1995. As to the papyri having references to Jews, the standard collection is by Tcherikover, Fuks, and Stern, 1957–64.

4. See Kant 1987: 674.

5. See the most recent student of the subject, McKay 1994.

6. Levinskaya 1990: 154–59, concludes that use of the word *proseuche* is an indication that a Jewish prayer house is meant. Gutmann 1981: 1–6, esp. 3, argues that the word *proseuche*, "prayer hall," so often found in inscriptions and papyri, refers not to a synagogue at all, at any rate not in the sense as understood by the Talmudic Rabbis.

7. See Noy 1992: 120.

8. See Oster 1993: 187–88.

9. See Feldman 1989: 265–305, esp. 274–82.

10. See Kraabel 1988: 66.

11. See Lifshitz 1967; Filson 1969: 41–46.

12. White 1990: 80.

13. E.g., Phil. 4:17.

14. Rivkin 1963: 350–51.

15. See Griffiths 1995: 3.

16. See Applebaum 1974: 465.

17. See Kraabel 1987: 52–53.

18. See Rajak and Noy 1993: 89–93, for a list of the occurrences of the word *archisynagogos* (including non-Jewish *archisynagogoi*) in inscriptions. For a survey of the meanings of the word *synagoge*, see Schrage 1971: 798–841.

19. Mark 5:22, 35, 36, 38; Luke 8:39, 13:14; Acts 13:15, 18:8, 17.

20. See Brooten 1982.

21. See Trebilco 1991: 111.

22. Brooten 1982: 41–55. See also Cohen 1980: 23–29.

23. Moreover, a recently published papyrus speaks of a certain Babatha, a Jewess from the province of Arabia, who in the second century owned considerable property. See Lewis 1989.

24. See Trebilco 1991: 111.

25. Burtchaell 1992: 245, n. 98.

26. See Rajak and Noy 1993: 87.

27. See Rajak 1992: 22–24.

28. Leon 1960: 183.

29. Burtchaell 1992: 236.

30. See Leon 1960: 184; Burtchaell 1992: 252.

31. Leon 1960: 190.

32. Ibid. 191–92.

33. See Kant 1987: 696–97.

34. McKay 1994, see esp. 247–51.

35. See Cohen 1989: 114.

36. See Tcherikover, Fuks, and Stern 1957–64, no. 138: 252–54.

37. See Reynolds and Tannenbaum 1987; Feldman 1989: 265–305.

38. See Feldman 1993: 288–415.

39. Reynolds and Tannenbaum 1987: 101.

40. See Kraabel 1979: 492.

41. Ibid. 493. See also White 1987: 139.

42. See Kant 1987: 700.

43. Cited by Filson 1969: 44.

44. Lifshitz 1967: 36, no. 34.

45. Tcherikover 1954: 84.

CHAPTER 4

1. On Sardis: Hanfmann 1983, esp. 148–61 and 168–90; on Stobi: Brenk 1991; Mano-Zissi 1973: 185–224; for a city plan of Plovdiv, Kesjakova 1989: 25, 39–40; Segal 1970: 103–82.

2. Frey 1936, no. 531.

3. Burket 1988: 27–47.

4. Busink 1970; Cohen 1984: 151–74.

5. Philo, *Embassy* 134, 346; *Against Flaccus* 41; Josephus, *Jewish Antiquities* 19.300; Gregory, *Letters* 9.195.

6. Biebel 1936, esp. 541–46.

7. Fernandez 1975: 241–44; Schlunk and Hauschild 1978: 143–47, who incorrectly claim that the building is a church.

8. Zevi 1972: 131–45; Squarciapino 1963: 194–203.

9. For a short discussion, see the remarks by Lattanzi 1986: 419–21 and pls. xlvii–xlviii; and Costamagana 1992: 313–17.

10. Kitzinger 1946, esp. his excellent analysis on 141–46; Hengel 1966; Poehlman 1981; Wiseman and Manno-Zissi 1972.

11. Danov 1985.

12. Goodenough 1953: 2: 75–76.

13. Plassart 1914; Bruneau 1982; White 1987.

14. Wiengand and Schrader 1904: 475–81.

15. Hanfmann 1983.

16. Mayence 1935: 199–204; Sukenik 1951; Brenk 1991.

17. Sauvaget 1941: 60–61. For other evidence, see Goodenough 1953: 2: 83.

18. Kraeling 1956.

19. See Kraabel 1979: 505–7.

20. Lifshitz 1967, nos. 9 and 13; and cf. no. 37.

21. Ibid. nos. 28 and 37; Tcherikover, Fuks, and Stern 1957–64: 3, no. 432.

22. Koranda 1988–89: 219.

23. Dunbabin 1978: 194, n. 33.

24. Lifshitz 1967, no. 57; Koranda 1990: 103–10.

25. Lifshitz 1967, nos. 20, 30, and 33; cf. no. 102.

26. *Supplementum Epigraphicum Graecum* 1984, no. 679. Wiseman and Mano-Zissi 1972: 410 n. 99, note that thirty-one large wooden trays were filled with fragments of wall paintings decorated with geometric patterns. To my knowledge these fragments have never been published.

27. Kraeling 1956: 132, 349, 354–55. And see Gutmann 1984.

28. Kraeling 1956: 40–54.

29. Lifshitz 1967, no. 102 (inscription); Tosefta Sukkah 4:6 and parallels.

30. Lifshitz 1967, no. 36.

31. Pensabene 1973: 109–10, no. 399.

32. Squarciapino 1970: 183–91.

33. Lifshitz 1967, no. 78 (Gerasa); Frey 1936, no. 694 (Stobi); Le Bohec 1981: 177–78, nos. 13–14 (Hamman Lif); Lifshitz 1967, nos. 28, 32, and 36 (Asia Minor); Lifshitz 1975: nos. 694b and 708c (Greece); Lifshitz 1967, no. 39; Fine 1996 and Fine, ch. 1 this volume.

34. Acts 17:2–3, 11.

35. Exod. 25:31–40, 37:17–24; Koranda 1988–89: 220.

36. Horbury and Noy 1992, nos. 9, 22, 24, 25, 27, and 117. Frey 1936, no. 531; Juvenal 3.296; Artemidorus, *Onirocritica* 3.53; Epipanius, *Panarion* 80.1; Tcherikover, Fuks, and Stern 1957–64, nos. 129 and 432; Lifshitz 1967, nos. 11 and 35; Frey 1936, nos. 683–84, 678a; Schlunk and Hauschild 1978. See also Josephus, *Antiquities* 14.258. A subject search under the headings *proseucha* and *synagoga* in the *Patrologia Latina*, which is now available on computer, shows that in writings of the Church Fathers who wrote in Latin, the word "*proseucha*" does not occur while the word "*synagoga*" is used fairly frequently (150 times); Gregory, *Letters* 1.34.

37. Josephus, *Antiquities* 16.164; Frey 1936, no. 752.

38. Philo, *Embassy* 156 and *On Dreams* 2.123–29 respectively.

39. *Didascalia* 13.

40. Luderitz 1983, no. 71.

41. *Patrologia Orientalis* 17: 91.

42. *Theodosian Code* 16.8.18 of 408 C.E.

43. Lifshitz 1967, nos. 10 and 66.

44. Kraeling 1956: 259.

45. Frey 1936, no. 683.

46. Bingen 1982: 11–16.

47. *Patrologia Graeca* 48, col. 852; Lieberman 1962: 121, n. 33.

48. E.g., MacMullen 1993: 54, relying on the unreliable and outdated article of Collon 1940.

49. See the classic study of Meiggs 1973, esp. 64–101. And see Pavolini 1981: 115–43.

50. *Theodosian Code* 16.8.22 of 415 C.E. repeated several times by imperial legislators during the fifth and sixth centuries.

51. Kraabel 1992: 29.

CHAPTER 5

1. Sources are assembled by Levine 1987.

2. Yadin 1981; Netzer 1991: 402–13.

3. Foerster 1981a.

4. Gutman 1981; Maoz 1981: 35–41.

5. Corbo 1976: 365–68; 1982: 165–72, x–xi.

6. Corbo 1982: 313–57; Strange and Shanks 1983: 25–31.

7. Another synagogue, now lost, was reportedly uncovered at Chorazin.

8. Theories of the origins of Second Temple period synagogue plans are discussed by Hachlili 1988: 86–87.

9. Netzer 1991: 402–13.

10. Netzer 1980: 116, n. 13; Maoz 1981a: 39.

11. Corbo 1982; Strange and Shanks 1983.

12. See Chiat 1981: 49–60.

13. Sukenik 1934: 2–7, surveys early exploration of late antique synagogues.

14. Kohl and Watzinger 1916: 4–41.

15. Vincent 1961: 163–73.

16. Sukenik 1932.

17. Kraeling 1956: 16.

18. Mayer and Reifenberg 1941: 314–26.

19. Avi-Yonah 1971.

20. This approach is summarized by Loffreda 1981: 52–56, esp. 55. For a negative response to this approach, see Foerster 1981a.

21. Avi-Yonah 1973: 38; rpt. in Avi-Yonah 1981b: 271–81.

22. See Meyers 1976, 1979; Levine 1987, 1993; Hachlili 1988.

23. See Avi-Yonah 1981b: 271–81; Meyers, Kraabel, and Strange 1976; Levine 1993: 1422–23.

24. Hachlili 1988: 396–400.

25. Ibid. 141–99.

26. Ibid. 143, 156–66.

27. Butler 1903: 103; 1907: 5, fig. 292. Hachlili 1988: 160; Dentzer-Feydy 1986: pls. 4, 16a.

28. E.g., the second-century C.E. temples of Habran and Braka. See Butler 1903: figs. 121, 123; 1907: 7, 29; Denzer-Feydy 1986: 297.

29. Hachlili 1988: 200–16.

30. Yeivin 1942: 69–76; Yeivin 1987: 30.

31. Safrai 1963; Brooten 1982: 103–23.

32. Meyers, Kraabel, and Strange 1976.

33. Yeivin 1989: 93–94, figs. 3–5.

34. On this synagogue, see Tsaferis 1982: 215–44.

35. The most recent study of this subject is Branham 1992.

36. Amit and Ilan 1990: 123–25.

37. Benziger 1902: 14.

38. Hachlili 1988: 115, 123–25.

39. Responses to Goodenough are collected by M. Smith 1967. See Fine 1996.

40. Exod. 20:4, 5; Deut. 5:8, 9. See Urbach 1959; Baumgarten 1970; Bildstein 1973.

41. *Targum Pseudo-Jonathan*, ed. Clarke. On this text see Bildstein 1974, Fine 1996.

42. Jerusalem Talmud, Avodah Zarah, 3:3, 42d, according to a Genizah fragment in the Antonin Library, St. Petersburg. See Epstein 1932: 20.

43. Goodenough 1953: 4: 71–97; Yarden 1971; Hachlili 1988: 234–85, Fine 1996.

44. Hachlili 1988: 272–80.

45. Narkiss 1935: 14–28; Hachlili 1988: 256–68.

46. Hachlili 1988: 280–85.

47. Ibid. 287–300.

48. If, in fact, this building was a synagogue. See Avi-Yonah 1981b.

49. Goodenough 1968: 1: 253ff.

50. Gutmann 1984: 115–22.

51. Avi-Yonah 1973: 128 and others.

52. For recent discussions of pattern book models, cartoons, drawings in "handbooks," and "schools" of mosaic workers, see Dauphin 1978: 401–23; Piccirillo 1991: 129; Hunt 1994: 121–23, n. 28.

53. Hachlili 1988: 321–28, 332–34, 346.

54. Josephus, *War*, 1, 648–55; *Antiquities*, 17, 151. Gutmann 1970: 10–11.

55. A term used by Avi-Yonah 1981a: 11–117, esp. 34–35; Hachlili 1988: 341, 343.

56. Hachlili 1988: 301–9; Netzer and Weiss 1994: 55–56.

57. Webster 1938: pl. 20; Hachlili 1977: 72–76, fig. 13.

58. Zori 1966: 123–34.

59. Avi-Yonah 1981b: pl. 52.

60. Avi-Yonah 1972: 118–22.

61. Netzer 1992: 36–45.

62. Alfoldi-Rosenbaum 1975: 150–51.

63. Avi-Yonah 1960: 46, pls. 10.1, 11.1.

64. Holum and Hohlfelder 1988: 178.

65. *Theodosian Code*, I tit. VIII.

66. Sussman 1974: 88–158; see also Sussman 1981: 146–53, Fine 1996.

CHAPTER 6

1. The characteristics of this literature are surveyed in brief by Heinemann and Petuchowski 1975.

2. See Levine 1987.

3. Elbogen 1993: 130–32.

4. See Urbach 1988: 9–49, and the bibliography cited there.

5. Urbach 1979: 286–314.

6. On the nature of the Rabbinic community during late antiquity, see Levine 1989 and the bibliography cited there.

7. *Against Apion*, 2.17, line 175; Acts 15:21; Jerusalem Talmud. Meg. 4:1, 75a.

8. Sources on Torah reading are collected by Elbogen 1993: 129–42.

9. Sources on readings from the Writings are collected by Elbogen 1993: 149–51.

10. In fact, this approach may have been adopted by Babylonian Jews from a Palestinian model.

11. On the history of this festival, see Yaari 1964.

12. Berakhot 4:1

13. For complete lists see Yoel 1968: 122–32.

14. Shinan 1987: 97–98, and the bibliography cited there.

15. *Differences in Religious Customs Between Babylonian and Palestinian Jewries*, ed. B.M. Levine 1942: 96.

16. On these traditions, see Ginzberg 1954: 1, 286–91, and sources cited there.

17. Sources on Torah reading are collected by Elbogen 1993: 129–42.

18. See ibid. Perhaps this practice was initiated as a polemic against the Samaritans, who recognized the sanctity of their version of the Pentateuch alone and denied all sanctity to the Prophets.

19. See Levine 1987: 16.

20. See *Aggadat Bereshit* ch. 32, and note the linguistic connection between the opening words of the *Aqedah* story, "Some time afterward, God put Abraham to the test," and this verse.

21. Synagogue inscriptions are discussed by Naveh 1978 and 1989; Roth-Gerson 1987. See also Foerster 1981b.

22. *Ki-Tavo* 4; Ilan and Damati 1987: 77.

23. On social groupings within ancient synagogues, see Levine 1992.

24. See Naveh 1978 and Roth-Gerson 1987.

25. See Naveh 1978: 72–73. It is not clear whether this text refers to Justin I (ruled 518–27 C.E.) or to Justin II (ruled 567–78 C.E.).

26. On the language mix in late antique Palestine, see Greenfield 1978.

27. On the Targumic literature, see Shinan 1992a and b, and the bibliography cited there. See also Fraade 1991.

28. On the functions of this functionary, see Shinan 1992b: 11–15.

29. Traditionally known as *Targum Jonathan ben Uzziel*. See Clarke 1984.

30. Heinemann 1974: 186–89.

31. Fragment Targum, ed. Klein.

32. Aramaic original in Heinemann 1981: 153ff.

33. On the *darshan*, see Hirshman 1991.

34. Genesis Rabba 55: 585–86.

35. Ginzberg 1928–29: 53–56.

36. See Bregman 1981: 34–41; Sarason 1982: 557–67; Shinan 1987: 100.

37. Berakhot 2:4, 4d; and parallels.

38. On prayer in Rabbinic literature, see Elbogen 1993: 187–218; Heinemann 1977; Fleischer 1989–90.

39. On the history of Jewish prayer from the Middle Ages on, see Elbogen 1993. See also Hoffman 1987. The history of the prayer book versions is summarized by Hoffman 1987: 46–59.

40. See Babylonian Talmud, Shabbat 12a–b; Elbogen 1993: 43–44.

41. Mishnah Berakhot 3:3.

42. Heinemann 1983: 77–79.

43. Ed. I. Davidson, S. Assaf, B.I. Joel, Jerusalem, 1985: 18.

44. *Siddur Rinat Yisrael*, 1977.

45. Schechter 1898: 657.

46. De Sola Pool 1909.

47. On this phenomenon, see Fine 1993: 135–50; and Fine 1996 forthcoming.

48. Foerster 1981b: 23–25. Translation of texts follows Fine, forthcoming.

49. Naveh 1978, nos. 32–34, 69, and 82.

50. Naveh 1978, nos. 20 and 104. Compare, for example, *Siddur Rinat Yisrael*, Ashkenazic version, ed. A. Tal, Jerusalem, 1976: 277.

51. Goldschmidt 1970: 257–58.

52. Margulies 1973: 134.

53. This text is cited and translated by Fine 1993: 107, and Fine 1996, forthcoming.

54. On the *piyyut* literature, see Elbogen 1993: 210–47; Fleischer 1975; Yahalom 1987.

55. See selected examples in Yahalom 1987.

56. Fleischer 1975: 201.

57. Ibid. 134–36.

58. Hebrew original in Mirsky 1977: 139–40.

59. Goldschmidt 1970: 120.

60. On this midrashic technique, see Heinemann 1970: 30.

61. These are discussed in detail by Hachlili in this volume.

62. Hebrew original appears in Goldschmidt 1977: 29–30. See also Yahalom 1987: 119–20.

63. Cf. also Mishnah Taanit 4:2.

64. On these poems, see Trifon 1989–90; Levine 1989: 171–72; 1991: 83, n. 245.

65. Hebrew original in Goldschmidt 1977: 146–47.

66. See Trifon 1989–90: 78, esp. n. 5; Levine 1991: 83, n. 244; Yahalom 1980: 55.

67. Sources are collected by Fine 1993: 125–27.

68. This text is discussed in detail by Sussman 1974: 88–158. See also Sussman 1981: 146–53.

69. Produce that is suspected of not having been tithed properly.

70. The translation generally follows Sussman 1981: 152.

71. Including Jerusalem Talmud, Demai 2; Shevi'it 6.

72. Zulay 1942: 3. Translated in Killebrew and Fine 1991: 51. See also Yahalom 1980: 55–56.

73. See Kutscher 1970: 3: 270–74, 277–82.

74. The first draft of this chapter was translated by Peretz A. Rodman.

Glossary

Acanthus a decorative motif of stylized leaves of the acanthus plant, a prickly herb found in the Mediterranean region.

Acroteria decorative elements on opposing ends of a tile roof.

Aedicula(e) a niche composed of columns or pillars supporting a pediment or lintel. Used in synagogues as a Torah Shrine.

Amoraim Rabbinic scholars in Palestine and Babylon during the Talmudic period (third–fifth centuries C.E.). Their scholarship served as the basis for the Palestinian Talmud and the Babylonian Talmud and for Amoraic and post-Amoraic Midrashic collections.

Apse a semicircular or polygonal termination of a building, appearing in synagogues from the late fifth or early sixth century C.E.

Architrave the horizontal beam spanning the interval between two columns or piers.

Babylonian Talmud ostensibly a commentary on thirty-seven Mishnaic tractates, the Babylonian Talmud, c. 550 C.E., is a carefully crafted literary document that contains the traditions of the latter Rabbinic (Amoraic) academies in Babylonia (modern Iraq). The Babylonian Talmud is the most important document for the history of late antique Babylonian Jewry.

Baraita a purportedly Tannaitic, early Rabbinic tradition not included in the Mishnah of Rabbi Judah the Prince (c. 200 C.E.).

Basilica a rectangular building, often with internal aisles, a central nave, and an apse opposite the entry.

B.C.E./C.E. Before the Common Era/Common Era; terms used by non-Christians in place of B.C. (Before Christ) and A.D. (Anno Domini).

Bema an elevated dais or platform in a church or synagogue.

Beit Midrash (pl. Batei Midrash) house of study; a meeting place in which Rabbinic Sages studied and fulfilled other religious functions.

Broadhouse a synagogue building whose Torah Shrine is situated on the long wall; examples include the synagogues of Dura Europos, Khirbet Shema, Eshtemoa, and Khirbet Susiya.

Capital the uppermost member of a column.

Chancel screen a lattice-work or solid screen erected around the bema in a synagogue or church. Like the apse, the chancel screen was taken over by the synagogue from church architecture during the late fifth or sixth century C.E.

Corbel an architectural member that projects from a wall to support weight.

Corinthian capital an inverted bell-shaped capital decorated with acanthus leaves, stems, and volutes.

Decapolis a loose federation of ten hellenized cities in northern Transjordan, northern Palestine, and southern Syria beginning during the second century B.C.E.

Diaspora   the collective term for all Jewish communities outside the Land of Israel.

Entablature   the upper part of an order that rests on columns, consisting of architrave, frieze, and cornice.

Etrog   a citron fruit that is used ritually with the *lulav* during the Jewish festival of Sukkot (Tabernacles) in observance of Leviticus 23:40.

Genizah   a depository for damaged, unusable books, documents, or ritual objects; often located in a synagogue. The most famous is the Cairo Genizah of the Ben Ezra Synagogue in medieval Fostat.

Haftarah   literally "completion." Prophetic reading that accompanies the weekly Torah reading in the synagogue.

Halakhah   literally "the way." Halakhah refers to Jewish Law in contrast to *Aggadah*, Jewish lore.

Ḥazzan   in antiquity a leader of a synagogue community who performed various educational and liturgical functions; today a cantorial specialist.

Jerusalem Talmud   a commentary on thirty-nine of the Mishnah's sixty-three tractates, containing the traditions of later Rabbinic (Amoraic), mainly Palestinian, Sages, c. 400 C.E. This Talmud is also known as the Palestinian Talmud or the Talmud of the Land of Israel.

Late antiquity   the period between the destruction of the Jerusalem Temple in 70 C.E. through the early Islamic period (c. eighth century C.E.). Later antiquity corresponds to the later Greco-Roman period and with the period of the Mishnah and the Talmud.

Lintel   a horizontal beam bridging an opening.

Lulav   branches of three trees—palm, myrtle, and willow—bound together and used ritually with the *etrog* during the Jewish festival of Sukkot (Tabernacles) in observance of Leviticus 23:40.

Meander   ornamental pattern of lines winding in and out.

Menorah   a seven-branched candelabrum described in Exodus 25:31–40 and 37:17–24 and elsewhere. The menorah, usually with seven branches, appears in Jewish art of the latter Second Temple and Talmudic periods and became symbolic not only of the Temple service but of Jews and Judaism as a whole.

Midrash   from the Hebrew *D.R.SH.*, "to seek or search." Midrash refers to Rabbinic exegesis of Scripture. Major Tannaitic Midrashic collections include the Mekhilta of Rabbi Ishmael on Exodus, the Sifra on Leviticus, and Sifre Deuteronomy. Amoraic (Classical) collections include Genesis Rabbah, Leviticus Rabbah, and the Pesikta de-Rav Kahana.

Miḥrab   the niche aligned with Mecca in a mosque.

Mikveh   a Jewish or Samaritan ritual bath used for purposes of ritual purification.

Mishmarot   priestly divisions that served in the Jerusalem Temple in rotation, based upon Chronicles 24.

Mishnah   redacted by Rabbi Judah the Prince, c. 200 C.E., the Mishnah conceptually organizes early Rabbinic (Tannaitic) traditions, the vast majority of which are of *halakhic* (legal) interest, into six orders and sixty-three tractates.

Narthex   vestibule leading to the nave of a synagogue or church.

Nave   central hall of a basilica separated from the side aisles by colonnades.

Ner Tamid   literally "eternal light"; the name used in recent centuries for a lamp that burns perpetually before a synagogue Torah Shrine.

Paytan(im)   the author(s) of synagogue liturgical poetry.

Pediment   a low-pitched triangular gable above a portico, door, window, and so on.

Piyyut(im)   Hebrew and Aramaic liturgical poetry composed from the late Rabbinic period and early Middle Ages. The most prominent late antique poets were Yannai (c. 550 C.E.) and Eleazar son of Qallir (c. 600 C.E.).

Polycandelon   a hanging lamp with multiple lights.

Proseuche   Greek "prayer place," a title used for synagogues, particularly in the western Diaspora during the Second Temple period.

Samaritans   a community centered in Samaria that was in confrontation with Jews throughout much of the Greco-Roman period. Samaritans and Jews shared numerous religious conceptions and visual symbols.

Shofar   a ram's horn prepared as a musical instrument, which was sounded on Rosh ha-Shanah in late antique synagogues.

Tabula ansata   the frame of an inscription, which has a triangular ear on the right and left sides.

Tannaim   Rabbinic scholars of the late first to early third centuries C.E. Their teachings are preserved in the Mishnah, Tosefta, and Tannaitic Midrashim and in Baraitot in Amoraic literature.

Targum   Aramaic translations and paraphrases of Hebrew Scriptures. The two complete Targums of the Pentateuch are *Targum Neofiti* and *Targum Pseudo-Jonathan*.

Tesserae   small pieces of marble, glass, or other materials from which mosaics are made.

Torah scroll   a manuscript scroll of the Pentateuch. The Torah, like other biblical books, was written on parchment according to carefully preserved scribal traditions.

Torah Shrine   a niche, closet, or chest for storing Torah scrolls. Today called a Holy Ark in Jewish communities of Ashkenazic (Central or Eastern European) origin.

Tosefta   literally "the addition," the Tosefta is a collection of early Rabbinic (Tannaitic) traditions. It is designed as a supplement to and commentary on the Mishnah.

Selected Bibliography

PRIMARY SOURCES

Hebrew Scriptures

Biblia Hebraica Stuttgartensia. 1967–77. ed. R. Kittel, P. Kahle, W. Rudolph, and K. Elliger. Stuttgart.

Tanakh: A New Translation of the Holy Scriptures. 1985. Philadelphia, New York, Jerusalem.

Rabbinic Sources

Aggadat Bereshit. 1903. ed. S. Buber, Cracow.

Babylonian Talmud. 1520–23. Venice. rpt. Jerusalem.

_____. 1884. Vilna.

Genesis Rabba. 1965. ed. J. Theodor and Ch. Albeck. Jerusalem.

Jerusalem Talmud. 1523. Venice. rpt. New York.

_____. 1932. ed. J.N. Epstein. Fragments of the Yerushalmi. *Tarbiz* 3.1:15–26. Hebrew.

Masseket Sofrim. 1937. ed. M. Higger. New York.

Mekhilta de-Rabbi Ishmael. 1970. ed. H.S. Horovitz and I.A. Rabin. Jerusalem.

Midrash on Psalms. 1947. ed. S. Buber. rpt. New York.

Midrash Rabba. 1975. Vilna. rpt. Jerusalem.

Midrash Tanhuma. 1563. Mantua. rpt. Jerusalem, 1970–71.

_____. 1913. ed. S. Buber. Vilna.

_____. 1833. rpt. Jerusalem. nd.

Mishnah. 1929. Codex Kaufmann A50. ed. G. Beer. Heidelberg, Jerusalem. facsimile.

_____. 1979. ed. Ch. Albeck. Tel Aviv.

Pesiqta de-Rav Kahane. 1962. ed. B. Mandelbaum. New York.

Sifra. 1947. ed. I.H. Weiss. New York.

Tosefta. 1970. ed. M.S. Zuckermandel. 2nd ed. Jerusalem.

_____. 1992. ed. S. Lieberman. 2nd ed. New York.

Targum

The Fragment-Targums of the Pentateuch. 1980. ed. M.L. Klein. Rome.

The Palestinian Targum to the Pentateuch (Neofiti 1). 1970. Jerusalem. facsimile.

Targum Pseudo-Jonathan on the Pentateuch: Text and Commentary. 1984. ed. E.G. Clarke. New York.

Liturgy

Assaf, 1946. An Early Lament on the Destruction of Communities in the Land of Israel. *Text and Studies in Jewish History*, 9–16. Jerusalem. Hebrew.

Goldschmidt, D. 1970. *Prayerbook for High Holy Days.* Jerusalem.

_____. 1977. *Order of Elegies for Tishah be-Av.* Jerusalem. Hebrew.

Mirsky, A. 1977. *The Liturgical Poetry of Jose b. Jose.* Jerusalem. Hebrew.

Rabinovitz, Z.M. 1985–87. *The Liturgical Poetry of Rabbi Yannai*. Jerusalem. Hebrew.

Schechter, Solomon. 1898. Geniza Specimens. Liturgy. *Jewish Quarterly Review* old series 10:654–59.

Siddur Rinat Yisrael. 1976. ed. S. Tal. Ashkenazic version. Jerusalem.

_____. 1977. ed. S. Tal. Jerusalem.

Siddur R. Saadja Gaon. 1985. ed. I. Davidson, S. Assaf, and I. Joel. Jerusalem.

Zulay, Menachem. 1942. From the Treasury of Poetry and Piyyut. *Ha-Aretz* April 1:3. Hebrew.

Second Temple Period Sources

Josephus Flavius. 1961–65. *The Complete Works*, tr. H. St. J. Thackery, R. Marcus, A. Wikgren, and L. Feldman. Cambridge, Mass., and London.

Philo of Alexandria. 1929–62. *The Complete Works*, tr. F.H. Colson, G.H. Whitaker, and R. Marcus. Cambridge, Mass., and London.

Rabin, Chaim. 1958. *Zadokite Documents*. Oxford.

Christian Sources

Chrysostom, John. 1862 *Adversus Judaeos. Patrologia Graeca*, ed. J.P. Migne. 48:839–942. Rome.

_____. 1979. *Discourses Against Judaising Christians*, tr. P.W. Harkins. Washington.

Gregory, P. Minard, ed. 1991. *Registre des lettres. Sources Chrétiennes*, 370–71. Paris.

New Testament. 1986. *Greek-English New Testament*. ed. P.W. Nestlie-Aland. Stuttgart.

Patrologia cursus completus. *Series Graeca*. 1857–66. ed. J.P. Migne. Paris.

Patrologia cursus completus. *Series Latina*. 1841–64. ed. J.P. Migne. Paris.

Patrologia Orientalis. 1904. Paris.

Greek and Latin Sources

Herbert, Kevin. 1972. *Greek and Latin Inscriptions in the Brooklyn Museum*. Brooklyn, N.Y.

Stern, M. *Greek and Latin Authors on Jews and Judaism*. Jerusalem.

The Theodosian Code, and Novels and Sirmondian Constitutions. 1952. ed. C. Pharr. Princeton.

Gaonic Sources

Differences in Religious Customs Between Babylonian and Palestinian Jewries. 1942. ed. B.M. Lewin. Jerusalem.

Iggeret Rav Sherira Gaon. 1921. ed. B.M. Lewin. Haifa.

Corpora of Epigraphic Sources

Fox, Sherwood. 1917. Greek Inscriptions in the Royal Ontario Museum. *American Journal of Philology* 38:411.

Frey, Jean-Baptiste, ed. 1936. *Corpus Inscriptionum Judaicarum. Europe. (CIJ)* Rome. prolegomenon by B. Lifshitz. rpt. New York, 1975.

Horbury, William, and David Noy, eds. 1992. *Jewish Inscriptions of Graeco-Roman Egypt*. Cambridge.

Kroll, J.H., ed. forthcoming. The Greek Inscriptions. *Ancient Synagogues in Sardis and the Jewish Community, Final Report V*. Cambridge, Mass.

Lewis, D.M, ed. 1964. The Jewish Inscriptions of Egypt. 1957–64. *Corpus Papyrorium Judaicarum*, ed. Victor A. Tcherikover, Alexander Fuks, and Menahem Stern. Jerusalem and Cambridge, Mass.

Lifshitz, Baruch, ed. 1967. *Donateurs et fondateurs dans les synagogues juives*. Paris.

_____. 1975. Prolegomenon. *Corpus Inscriptionum Judaicarum, Europe*. 1: 21–107, ed. J.B. Frey. Rome, 1936. rpt. New York.

Naveh, Joseph, ed. 1978. *On Stone and Mosaic: The Aramaic and Hebrew Inscriptions from Ancient Synagogues*. Jerusalem. Hebrew.

_____. 1989. The Aramaic and Hebrew Inscriptions from Ancient Synagogues. *Eretz-Israel* 20:302–10. Hebrew.

Naveh, Joseph, and Shaul Shaked. 1985. *Amulets and Magic Bowls: Aramaic Incantations from Late Antiquity*. Jerusalem and Leiden.

_____. 1993. *Magic Spells and Formulae: Aramaic Incantations of Late Antiquity*. Jerusalem.

Noy, David, ed. 1993. *Jewish Inscriptions of Western Europe*. Vol. 1. Cambridge and New York.

_____. 1995. *Jewish Inscriptions of Western Europe*. Vol. 2. Cambridge.

Pleket, H.W., and R.S. Stroud, eds. 1923. *Supplementum Epigraphicum Graecum*. Leiden.

Roth-Gerson Lea, ed. 1987. *Greek Inscriptions in the Synagogues in Eretz-Israel*. Jerusalem. Hebrew.

Tcherikover, Victor A., Alexander Fuks, Menahem Stern, eds. 1957–64. *Corpus Papyrorium Judaicarum*. Jerusalem and Cambridge, Mass.

SECONDARY SOURCES

Alfoldi-Rosenbaum, E. 1975. A Nilotic Scene on Justinianic Floor Mosaics in Cyrenaican Churches. *La Mosaique greco-romaine*, 150–52. Paris.

Amiram, Ruth. 1956. A Fragment of an Ornamented Relief from Kfar Baram. *Israel Exploration Journal* 6:239–45.

Amit, D., and Z. Ilan. 1990. The Ancient Synagogue at Maon in Judah. *Qadmoniot* 23:123–25. Hebrew.

Appelbaum, Shimon. 1974. The Organization of the Jewish Communities in the Diaspora. *The Jewish People in the First Century: Historical Geography, Political History, Social, Cultural, and Religious Life and Institutions*, ed. Shmuel Safrai and Menahem Stern. Compendia Rerum Iudaicarum ad Novum Testamentum, 1:464–503. Assen, Maastricht, and Philadelphia.

Avigad, Nachman. 1983. *Discovering Jerusalem*. Nashville.

Avi-Yonah, Michael. 1960. The Synagogue of Caesarea: Preliminary Report. *Louis M. Rabinowitz Fund for the Exploration of Ancient Synagogues Bulletin* 3:44–48.

_____. 1964. The Caesarea Inscription of the Twenty-Four Priestly Courses. *Eretz-Israel* 7:24–28. Hebrew.

_____. 1971. Synagogue Architecture in the Late Classical Period. *Jewish Art*, ed. C. Roth, 65–82. London.

_____. 1972. The Haditha Mosaic Pavement. *Israel Exploration Journal* 22:118–22.

_____. 1973. Ancient Synagogues. *Ariel* 32:29–43.

_____. 1981a. The Mosaic of Mopsuestia—Church or Synagogue? *Ancient Synagogues Revealed*, ed. L.I. Levine, 186–90. Jerusalem.

_____. 1981b. *Art in Ancient Palestine: Selected Studies*, ed. H. Katzenstein and Y. Tsafrir. Jerusalem.

Bacher, Wilhelm. 1897. Le Siège de Moïse—Qathedra d'Moshe. *Revue des Etudes Juives* 34:299–301.

Bahat, Dan. 1973. A Synagogue Chancel Screen from Tel Rehob. *Israel Exploration Journal* 23:181–83.

_____. 1981. A Synagogue at Beth-Shean. *Ancient Synagogues Revealed*, ed. L.I. Levine, 82–85. Jerusalem.

Baker, Avrom. 1981–82. The Illustrations of Signs of the Zodiac for the Tal and Geshem Prayers. *Journal of Jewish Music and Liturgy* 4:11–13.

Baron, Salo W. 1952. *A Social and Religious History of the Jews*. New York.

Baumgarten, Joseph M. 1970. Art in the Synagogue: Some Talmudic Views. *Judaism* 6:196–206.

Benziger, Immanuel. 1902. Art Among the Ancient Hebrews. *Jewish Encyclopaedia* 2:138–41. New York and London.

Biebel, Franklin M. 1936. The Mosaics of Hamman Lif. *Art Bulletin* 18:541–51.

Bildstein, Gerald J. 1973. The Tannaim and Plastic Art: Problems and Prospects. *Perspectives in Jewish Learning* 5:13–27.

_____. 1974. Prostration and Mosaics in Talmudic Law. *Bulletin of the Institute of Jewish Studies* 2:19–39.

Bingen, J. 1982. L'Asylie pour une synagogue CIL III Suppl. 6587 = CII 1449, ed. J. Quaaegebeur, 11–16. Studia Paulo Noster Oblata. II. Orientalia Antiqua. Orientalia Lovaniensia Analecta 13, Leuven.

Bonner, C. 1950. *Studies in Magical Amulets, Chiefly Graeco-Egyptian*. Ann Arbor.

Bouras, Laskarina. 1982. Byzantine Lighting Devices. XVI Internationaler Byzantinstenkongress Akten. *Jahrbuch der Österreichischen Byzantinistik* 32.3. 2.3:479–91.

Branham, Joan R. 1992. Sacred Space under Erasure in Ancient Synagogues and Churches. *Art Bulletin* 74.3:375–94.

_____. 1993. Sacred Space in Ancient Jewish and Early Medieval Christian Architecture. Ph.D dissertation. Emory University.

_____. 1995. Vicarious Sacrality: Temple Space in Ancient Synagogues. *Ancient Synagogues: Historical Analysis and Archaeological Discovery*, ed. D. Urman and P.V.M. Flesher, 2:319–46. Leiden.

Bregman, Mark. 1981. Circular Proems and Proems Beginning with the Formula 'Zo hi shene'emra beruah ha-qodesh.' Studies in Aggadah, Targum and Jewish Liturgy in Memory of Joseph Heinemann, ed. J. Petuchowski and E. Fleisher, 34–51. Cincinnati and Jerusalem.

Brenk, B. 1991. Die Umwandlung der Synagoge von Apamea in eine Kirche. Eine mentalitätsgeschichtliche Studie. *Tesserae, Festschrift für Josef Engemann, Jaahrbuch für Antike und Christentum*, Ergänzungsband 18:1–25.

Brettman, Estelle Shohet. 1985. *Vaults of Memory: Jewish and Christian Imagery in the Catacombs of Rome*. Boston, Mass.

Brooten, Bernadette J. 1982. *Women Leaders in Ancient Synagogues*, Chico, Calif.

Bruneau, P. 1982. Les Israélites de Délos et la juiverie délienne. *Bulletin de correspondance héllenique* 106:465–504.

Burkert, W. 1988. The Meaning and Function of the Temple in Classical Greece. *Temple in Society*, ed. M.V. Fox, 27–47. Winona Lake, Minn.

Burtchaell, James T. 1992. *From Synagogue to Church: Public Services and Offices in the Earliest Christian Communities*. Cambridge.

Busink, T.A. 1970. *Der Tempel von Jerusalem von Salomon bis Herodes: Eine archaologisch-historisch Studie unter Berücksichtigung des westsemitischen Tempelbaus*. Leiden.

Butler, H.C. 1903. *Architecture and Other Arts*. New York.

_____. 1907. *Ancient Architecture in Syria*. Leiden.

Chiat, Marilyn Joyce. 1981. First-Century Synagogue Architecture: Methodological Problems. *Ancient Synagogues: The State of Research*, ed. J. Gutmann, 49–60. Chico, Calif.

_____. 1982. *Handbook of Synagogue Architecture*. Chico, Calif.

Clermont-Ganneau, C.J. 1885. *Mission en Palestine et Phénicie*. Paris.

Cohen, Shaye J.D. 1980. Women in Synagogues of Antiquity. *Conservative Judaism* 34.2: 23–29.

_____. 1981. Epigraphical Rabbis. *Jewish Quarterly Review* 72:1–17.

_____. 1984. The Temple and the Synagogue. *The Temple in Antiquity*, ed. T.G. Madsen, 151–74. Provo, Utah.

_____. 1987. Pagan and Christian Evidence on the Ancient Synagogue. *The Synagogue in Late Antiquity*, ed. L.I. Levine, 159–81. New York and Philadelphia.

Collon, S. 1940. Remarques sur les quartiers juifs de la Rome antique. *Mélanges de l'école française de Rome* 57:72–94.

Corbo, V. 1976. La citta romana di Magdala. *Studia Hierosolymitana* 1:365–68.

_____. 1982. Resti della Sinagoga Primo Secolo a Cafarnao. *Studia Hierosolymitana* 3:313–57.

Costamagna, L. 1992. Seminari di archeologia cristiana. *Rivista di archeologia cristiana* 68:313–17.

Danov, C.M. 1985. Neues aus der Geschichte von Philippopolis und Altthrakien in der Spätantike. *Römische Geschichte, Altertumskunde und Epigrahik. Festschrift für Artur Betz zur Vollendung seines 80 Lebensjahres*, ed. E. Weber and G. Dobesch, 107–23. Vienna.

Dauphin, Claudine. 1978. Byzantine Pattern Books: A Reexamination of the Problem in the Light of the Inhabited Scroll. *Art History* 1:400–401.

Dentzer-Feydy, J. 1986. *Décor architectural et développement du hauran dans l'antiquité*. Paris.

De Sola Pool, David. 1909. *The Jewish Aramaic Prayer: The Kaddish*. Leipzig.

Di Segni, Leah. 1993a. The Greek Inscriptions in the Samaritan Synagogue at El-Khirbe, with Some Considerations on the Function of the Samaritan Synagogue in the Late Roman Period. *Early Christianity in Context: Monuments and*

Documents, ed. F. Manns and E. Alliata, Studium Biblicum Franciscanum, 38:231–39. Jerusalem.

_____. 1993b. A Jewish Inscription from the Vicinity of Caesarea Maritima. *Atiqot* 22:133–36.

Dothan, Moshe. 1983. *Hammath Tiberias: Early Synagogues and the Hellenistic and Roman Remains*. Jerusalem.

Dunbabin, K.M.D. 1978. *The Mosaics of Roman North Africa. Studies in Iconography and Patronage*. Oxford.

Dussaud, R. 1912. *Monuments palestiniens et judaiques*. Paris.

Elbogen, Ismar. 1993. *Jewish Liturgy: A Comprehensive History*, tr. R.P. Scheindlin. Philadelphia.

Epstein, Jacob N. 1983. *Studies in Talmudic Literature and Semitic Languages*, ed. E.Z. Melamed, tr. Z. Epstein. Jerusalem. Hebrew.

Eshel, Hanan. 1991. A Fragmentary Inscription of the Priestly Courses? *Tarbiz* 61.1:159–61. Hebrew.

Eshkoli, A.Z. and M. Narkiss. 1934–35. Catalogue of the Finds at Tiberias in 1920–1921. *Journal of the Palestine Exploration Society* 3:175–96.

Feldman, Louis H. 1989. Proselytes and Sympathizers in Light of the New Inscriptions from Aphrodisias. *Revue des études juives* 148.3–4:265–305.

_____. 1993. *Jew and Gentile in the Ancient World: Attitudes and Interactions from Alexander to Justinian*. Princeton.

Fernandez, R. Ramos. 1975. *La ciudad romana de Ilici, estudio arqueologico*. Alicante.

Filson, Floyd V. 1969. Ancient Greek Synagogue Inscriptions. *Biblical Archaeologist* 32:41–46.

Fine, Steven. 1989. On the Development of a Visual Symbol: The Date Palm in Roman Palestine and the Jews. *Journal for the Study of the Pseudepigrapha* 4:105–18.

_____. 1993. Synagogue and Sanctity: The Late Antique Palestinian Synagogue as a Holy Place. Ph.D dissertation. Hebrew University of Jerusalem.

_____. forthcoming. Chancel Screens in Late Antique Palestinian Synagogues: A Source from the Cairo Genizah. *Religious and Ethnic Communities in Later Roman Palestine*. ed. C. Lapin.

_____. forthcoming. Synagogue Inscriptions. *Oxford Encyclopedia of Near Eastern Archaeology*, ed. E.M. Meyers.

_____. 1996, forthcoming. *"This Holy Place": On the Sanctity of Synagogues During the Greco-Roman Period*.

Fine, Steven, and Miriam Della Pergola. 1995. The Ostia Synagogue and Its Torah Shrine. *The Jews of Ancient Rome*, ed. J. Goodnick Westenholz, 42–57. Jerusalem.

Fine, Steven, and Leonard Victor Rutgers. forthcoming. New Light on Judaism in Asia Minor During Late Antiquity: Two Recently Identified Inscribed Menorahs. *Jewish Studies Quarterly*.

Fleischer, Ezra. 1975. *Hebrew Liturgical Poetry in the Middle Ages*. Jerusalem. Hebrew.

_____. 1989–90. On the Beginnings of Obligatory Jewish Prayer. *Tarbiz* 59.3–4:397–441. Hebrew.

Flesher, Paul Virgil McCracken. 1995. Palestinian Synagogues Before 70 C.E. A Review of the Evidence. *Ancient Synagogues:*

Historical Analysis and Archaeological Discovery, ed. D. Urman and P.V.M. Flesher, 1:27–39. Leiden.

Foerster, Gideon. 1981a. The Synagogues at Masada and Herodium. *Ancient Synagogues Revealed*, ed. L.I. Levine, 24–29. Jerusalem.

_____. 1981b. Synagogue Inscriptions and Their Relation to Liturgical Versions. *Cathedra* 17:12–40. Hebrew.

Fraade, Steven D. 1991. *From Tradition to Commentary: Torah and its Interpretation in the Midrash Sifre to Deuteronomy*. Albany.

Gafni Isaiah. 1987. Synagogues in Talmudic Babylonia: Traditions and Reality. *Synagogues in Antiquity*, ed. A. Kasher, A. Oppenheimer, and U. Rappaport, 155–64. Jerusalem. Hebrew.

Gal, Zvi. 1995. Ancient Synagogues in the Eastern Lower Galilee. *Ancient Synagogues: Historical Analysis and Archaeological Discovery*, ed. D. Urman and P.V.M. Flesher, 1:167–73. Leiden.

Ginzberg, Louis. 1928–29. *Genizah Studies in Memory of Doctor Solomon Schechter*. New York. Hebrew.

_____. 1954. *Legends of the Jews*. Philadelphia.

Goitein, S.D. 1971. *A Mediterranean Society*. Berkeley, Los Angeles, and London.

Goodenough, Erwin R. 1953. *Jewish Symbols in the Greco-Roman Period*. New York.

Grabbe, Lester L. 1995. Synagogues in Pre-70 Palestine: A Reassessment. *Ancient Synagogues: Historical Analysis and Archaeological Discovery*, ed. D. Urman and P.V.M. Flesher, 1:17–26. Leiden.

Greenfield, Jonas. 1978. The Languages of Palestine, 200 B.C.E.–200 C.E. *Jewish Languages: Theme and Variation*, ed. H. Paper, 143–54. New York.

Griffiths, J. Gwyn. 1995. Egypt and the Rise of the Synagogue. *Ancient Synagogues: Historical Analysis and Archaeological Discovery*, ed. D. Urman and P.V.M. Flesher, 1:3–16. Leiden.

Groh, Dennis S. 1995. The Stratigraphic Chronology of the Galilean Synagogue from the Early Roman Period through the Early Byzantine Period. *Ancient Synagogues: Historical Analysis and Archaeological Discovery*, ed. D. Urman and P.V.M. Flesher, 51–69. Leiden.

Gutmann, Joseph. 1970. *Beauty in Holiness*. New York.

_____. 1972. The Origins of the Synagogue. *Archäologische Anzeiger* 87:72–76.

_____. 1981. Synagogue Origins: Theories and Fact. *Ancient Synagogues: The State of Research*, ed. J. Gutmann, Missoula.

_____. 1984. Early Synagogue and Jewish Catacomb Art and Its Relation to Christian Art. *Aufstieg und Niedergang der Römische Welt* 221.2:1313–42.

Gutman, S. 1981. The Synagogue at Gamla. *Ancient Synagogues Revealed*, ed. L.I. Levine, 30–34. Jerusalem.

Hachlili, Rachel. 1977. The Zodiac in Ancient Jewish Art: Representation and Significance. *Bulletin of the American Schools for Oriental Research* 228:62–77.

_____. 1988. *Ancient Jewish Art and Archaeology in the Land of Israel*. Leiden.

_____. 1992. Early Jewish Art and Architecture. *Anchor Bible Dictionary*, ed. D.N. Freedman, 1: 447–54. New York.

Hanfmann, George M. 1967. The Ninth Campaign at Sardis. *Bulletin of the American Schools for Oriental Research* 197:9–62.

_____, ed. 1983. *Sardis from Prehistoric to Roman Times. Results of the Archaeological Exploration of Sardis 1958–1975*. Cambridge, Mass.

Heinemann, Isaac. 1970. *The Ways of Aggadah*. Jerusalem. Hebrew.

Heinemann, Joseph. 1974. *The Aggadah and Its Development*. Jerusalem. Hebrew.

_____. 1977. *Prayer in the Talmud*, tr. R.S. Sarason. Berlin and New York.

_____. 1981. *Studies in Jewish Liturgy*, ed. A. Shinan. Jerusalem. Hebrew.

Heinemann, Joseph, and J.J. Petuchowski. 1975. *Literature of the Synagogue*. New York.

Hengel, Martin. 1966. Die Synagogeninschrift von Stobi. *Zeitschrift für die neutestamentliche Wissenschaft* 57:145–83.

Hirshman, Marc. 1991. The Preacher and His Public in Third-Century Palestine. *Journal of Jewish Studies* 42.1:108–14.

Holum, K.G., and R. L. Hohlfelder. 1988. *King Herod's Dream: Caesarea on the Sea*. New York and London.

Hunt, L.A. 1994. The Byzantine Mosaics of Jordan in Context: Remarks on Imagery, Donors and Mosaicists. *Palestine Exploration Quarterly* 126:106–26.

Hüttenmeister, Frowald G., and Gottfried Reeg. 1977. *Die antiken Synagogen in Israel*. Wiesbaden.

Ilan. Zvi. 1987. *Synagogues in the Galilee and Golan*. Jerusalem. Hebrew.

_____. 1991. *Ancient Synagogues in Israel*. Tel Aviv. Hebrew.

_____. 1995. The Synagogue and Study House at Meroth. *Ancient Synagogues: Historical Analysis and Archaeological Discovery*, ed. D. Urman and P.V.M. Flesher, 1:256–81. Leiden.

Ilan, Zvi, and Emmanuel Damati. 1987. *Meroth: The Ancient Jewish Village*. Tel Aviv. Hebrew.

_____. 1989. The Synagogue at Meroth. *Biblical Archaeological Review* 15.2:20–36.

Kant, Laurence H. 1987. Jewish Inscriptions in Greek and Latin. *Aufstieg und Niedergang der römischen Welt* 2.20.2:674.

Kee, Howard Clark. 1990. The Transformation of the Synagogue after 70 C.E.: Its Import for Early Christianity. *New Testament Studies* 36:1–24.

Kesjakova, E. 1989. Une Nouvelle Basilique à Philippopolis. *Actes du XIᵉ congrès international d'archéologie chrétienne, Lyon, Vienne, Grenoble, Genève, et Aoste (21–28 septembre 1986)*. Vol. 3, *Studi antichità cristiane* 41. Vatican City.

Killebrew, Ann, and Steven Fine. 1991. Qatzrin—Reconstructing Village Life in Talmudic Times. *Biblical Archaeology Review* 27.3:44–56.

King, Philip J. 1983. *American Archaeology in the Middle East: A History of the American School of Oriental Research*. Philadelphia.

Kitzinger, Ernst. 1946. A Survey of the Early Christian Town of Stobi. *Dumbarton Oaks Papers* 3:81–161.

Kohl, Heinrich, and Carl Watzinger. 1916. *Antike Synagogen in Galilaea*. Leipzig.

Koranda, Christian. 1988–89. Menora-Darstellungen auf spätantiken Mosaikpavimenten. *Kairos* 30–31:218–28.

_____. 1990. Pedaturangaben in frühchristlichen Mosaikinschriften. *Anzeiger der österreichischen Akademie der Wissenschaften Philosophisch-historische Klasse* 126:103–10.

Kraabel, Alf Thomas. 1979. The Diaspora Synagogue: Archaeological and Epigraphic Evidence since Sukenik. *Aufstieg und Niedergang der römischen Welt* 19.1:479–510.

_____. 1984. New Evidence of the Samaritan Diaspora Has Been Found in Delos. *Biblical Archaeologist* 47:44–46.

_____. 1987. Unity and Diversity Among Diaspora Synagogues. *The Synagogue in Late Antiquity*, ed. L.I. Levine, 49–60. New York and Philadelphia.

_____. 1988. The Synagogue at Sardis: Jews and Christians. *Sardis: Twenty-Five Years of Discovery*, ed. E. Guralnick. Chicago.

Kraeling, Carl H., ed. 1938. *Gerasa, City of the Decapolis*. New Haven, Conn.

_____. 1956. *The Synagogue. The Excavations at Dura-Europos, Final Report VIII Part 1*. New Haven, Conn., reprint New York, 1979.

Kutscher, Eduard Yecheskel. 1970. Aramaic. *Encyclopaedia Judaica* 3:270–82. Jerusalem.

Lattanzi, E. 1986. Neapolis. *Atti del venticinquesimo convegno di studi sulla Magna Grecia*. Taranto: Istituto per la storia e l'archeologia della Magna Grecia. 419–21.

Le Bohec, Y. 1981. Inscriptions juives et judaïsantes de l'Afrique romaine. *Antiquités africaines* 17:177–78.

Leon, Harry J. 1924. A Jewish Inscription at Columbia University. *American Journal of Archaeology* 28.3:251–52.

_____. 1960. *The Jews of Ancient Rome*. Philadelphia.

Levine, Lee I. 1981. The Inscription from the En Gedi Synagogue. *Ancient Synagogues Revealed*, ed. L.I. Levine, 140–45. Jerusalem.

_____. 1987. The Second Temple Synagogue: The Formative Years. *The Synagogue in Late Antiquity*, ed. L.I. Levine, 7–32. New York and Philadelphia.

_____. 1989. *The Rabbinic Class of Roman Palestine*, Jerusalem.

_____. 1991. From Community Center to Small Temple: The Furnishings and Interior Design of Ancient Synagogues. *Cathedra* 60:36–84. Hebrew.

_____. 1992. The Sages and the Synagogue in Late Antiquity: The Evidence of the Galilee. *The Galilee in Late Antiquity*, ed. L.I. Levine, 201–22. New York and Jerusalem.

_____. 1993. Synagogues. *New Encyclopedia of Archaeological Excavations in the Holy Land*, ed. E. Stern, 4:1421–24. New York and Jerusalem.

Levinskaya, Irina. 1990. A Jewish or Gentile Prayer House? The Meaning of Proseuche. *Tyndale Bulletin* 41:154–59.

Levy, S. 1960. The Ancient Synagogue of Ma'on (Nirim). *Louis M. Rabinowitz Fund for the Exploration of Ancient Synagogues Bulletin* 3:6–40.

Lewis, N. 1989. The Documents from the Bar Kochba Period in the Cave of Letter. Greek Papyri, Jerusalem.

Lieberman, Saul. 1962. *Hellenism in Jewish Palestine.* New York.

_____. 1971. A Preliminary Remark on the Inscription of En Gedi. *Tarbiz* 40:24–26. Hebrew.

Loffreda, S. 1981. The Late Chronology of the Synagogue of Capernaum. *Ancient Synagogues Revealed*, ed. L.I. Levine, 52–56. Jerusalem.

Lüderitz, G. 1983. Corpus jüdischer Zeugnisse aus der Cyrenaika. *Beihefte zum Tübinger Atlas des Vorderen Orients*, Reihe B., Nr. 53. Wiesbaden.

McKay, Heather A. 1994. *Sabbath and Synagogue: The Question of Sabbath Worship in Ancient Judaism.* Leiden.

MacMullen, R. 1993. The Unromanized in Rome. *Diasporas in Antiquity*, ed. S.J.D. Cohen and E.S. Frerichs. Atlanta.

Magen, Yitzhak. 1991. El Hirbah—A Samaritan Synagogue. *Hadashot Archaeologiot* 96:13–14. Hebrew.

_____. 1992. Samaritan Synagogues. *Qadmoniot* 25.3–4:66–90. Hebrew.

_____. 1993a. Samaritan Synagogues. *The New Encyclopedia of Excavations in the Holy Land*, 4, 1424–27. New York.

Magnes, Jodi. 1994. The Dating of the Black Ceramic Bowl with a Depiction of the Torah Shrine from Nabratein. *Levant* 26:199–206.

Makhouly, M., and M. Avi-Yonah. 1933. A Sixth Century Synagogue at Isfiya. *Quarterly of the Department of Antiquities in Palestine* 3:118–31.

Mann, Vivian, ed. 1989. *Gardens and Ghettos: The Art of Jewish Life in Italy.* Berkeley and Los Angeles.

Mano-Zissi, D. 1973. Stratigraphic Problems and the Urban Development of Stobi. *Studies in the Antiquities of Stobi*, ed. J. Wiseman, 1:185–224. Belgrade.

Maoz, Zvi. 1981. The Synagogue of Gamla and the Typology of Second-Temple Synagogues. *Ancient Synagogues Revealed*, ed. L.I. Levine, 35–41. Jerusalem.

Mayence, F. 1935. La Quatrième Campagne de fouille à Apamée (rapport sommaire). *L'Antiquité classique* 4:199–204.

Mayer, Leo Ary, and A. Reifenberg. 1937. Three Ancient Jewish Reliefs. *Palestine Exploration Quarterly* 136–39.

_____. 1941. Synagogue in Eshtemoa. *Bulletin of the Jewish Palestine Exploration Society* 9:41–44. Hebrew.

Meiggs, R. 1973. *Roman Ostia.* Oxford.

Merhav, R. 1987. *Treasures of the Bible Lands: The Elie Borowski Collection.* Tel Aviv.

Meshorer, Yaakov. 1982. *Ancient Jewish Coinage.* New York.

Meyers, Eric M. 1976. Gallilean Regionalism as a Factor in Historical Reconstruction. *Bulletin of the American Schools of Oriental Research* 221:93–101.

_____. 1979. The Cultural Setting of Gallilee: The Case of Early Judaism. *Aufstieg und Niedergang der römischen Welt*, ed. H. Temporini and W. Haase, 686–701. Berlin.

_____. 1985. Galilean Regionalism: A Reappraisal. *Approaches to Ancient Judaism*, ed. W. S. Green, 5:115–31. Atlanta.

_____. 1992a. Synagogue. *The Anchor Bible Dictionary*, ed. D.N. Freedman, 6:251–60. Garden City, N.Y.

_____. 1992b. Nahman Avigad. *Proceedings of the American Academy of Jewish Research* 58:1–4.

_____. 1994. Second Temple Studies in the Light of Recent Archaeology: Part I: The Persian and Hellenistic Periods. *Currents in Research: Biblical Studies* 2:25–42.

Meyers, Eric M., and Steven Fine. forthcoming. Synagogues. *Oxford Encyclopedia of Near Eastern Archaeology*, ed. E.M. Meyers.

Meyers, Eric M., A. Thomas Kraabel, and James F. Strange. 1976. *Ancient Synagogue Excavations at Khirbet Shema, Upper Galilee, Israel, 1970–1972.* Durham, N.C. Annual of the American Schools of Oriental Research 42.

Meyers, Eric M., and Carol L. Meyers. 1982. The Ark as Art: A Ceramic Rendering of the Torah Shrine from Nabratein. *Eretz Israel* 16:176-85.

_____. 1981. Finders of the Lost Ark. *Biblical Archaeology Review* 7.4:24–39.

Meyers, Eric M., Carol L. Meyers, and James F. Strange. 1990. *Excavations at the Ancient Synagogue of Gush Halav.* Winona Lake, Minn.

_____. 1982. Second Preliminary Report on the Excavations at En-Nabratein. *Bulletin of the American Schools of Oriental Research* 256:35–54.

Mildenberg, Leo. 1984. *Coinage of the Bar Kokhba War.* Aaran.

Muscarella, Oscar White, ed. 1981. *Ladders to Heaven: Art Treasures from the Lands of the Bible.* Toronto.

Narkiss, M., 1935. The Snuff Shovel as a Jewish Symbol. *Journal of the Palestine Oriental Society* 15:14–28.

Netzer, Ehud. 1980. The Triclinia of Herod as the Prototype of the Galilean Synagogue Plan. *Jerusalem in the Second Temple Period—Abraham Schalit Memorial Volume.* ed. A. Oppenheimer, A. Rappaport, and M. Stern, 108–18. Jerusalem. Hebrew.

_____. 1991. *Masada III, The Yigael Yadin Excavations 1963–1965, Final Reports, the Buildings: Stratigraphy and Architecture.* Jerusalem.

_____. 1992. New Mosaic Art from Sepphoris. *Biblical Archaeology Review* 18:36–45.

Netzer, Ehud, and Zeev Weiss. 1994. *Sepphoris.* Jerusalem. Hebrew.

Nibley, Hugh. 1959–60. Christian Envy of the Temple. *Jewish Quarterly Review* 50:97–122, 229–40.

Noy, David. 1992. A Jewish Place of Prayer in Roman Egypt. *Journal of Theological Studies* n. s., 43.1:118–22.

Oppenheimer, Aharon, in collaboration with B. Isaac and M. Lecker. *Babylonia Judaica in the Talmudic Period.* 1983. Wiesbaden.

Oster, Richard E. 1993. Supposed Anachronism in Luke—Acts, Use of Synagogue. *New Testament Studies* 39:187–88.

Pavolini, C. 1981. Ostia (Roman). Saggi lungo la via Severiana. *Notizie degli scavi di antichità* 35:115–43.

Pensabene, P. 1973. I Capitelli. *Scavi di Ostia* 7: 109–10.

Piccirillo, Michele. 1991. The Mosaics of Jordan. *The Art of*

Jordan, Treasures from an Ancient Land, ed. P. Bieinkowski, 109–32. Liverpool.

Plassart, A. 1914. La Synagogue juive de Délos. *Revue Biblique* 23:523–34.

Poehlman, W. 1981. The Polycharmos Inscription and Synagogue I at Stobi. *Studies in the Antiquities of Stobi*, ed. B. Aleksova and J. Wiseman, 2:235–46. Titov Veles.

Pummer, Reinhard. 1989. Samaritan Material Remains and Archaeology. *The Samaritans*, ed. A.D. Crown, 135–77. Tubingen.

Rahmani, L.Y. 1960. The Ancient Synagogue of Maon (Nirim): The Small Finds and Coins. *Louis M. Rabinowitz Fund for the Exploration of Ancient Synagogues Bulletin* 3:14–19.

———. 1964. Mirror-Plaques from a Fifth-Century A.D. Tomb. *Israel Exploration Journal* 14:50–55.

———. 1990. Stone Synagogue Chairs: Their Identification, Use and Significance. *Israel Exploration Journal* 40.2–3:192–214.

Rajak, Tessa. 1992. The Jewish Community and Its Boundaries. *The Jews among Pagans and Christians in the Roman Empire*, ed. Judith Lieu, John North, and Tessa Rajak, 22–24. London.

Rajak, Tessa, and David Noy. 1993. Archisynagogoi: Title and Social Status in the Greco-Jewish Synagogue. *Journal of Roman Studies* 83:89–92.

Reich, Ronny. 1994. The Plan of the Samaritan Synagogue at Sha'alvim. *Israel Exploration Journal* 44:228–33.

Renan, E. 1883. Les Mosaiques de Hamman-Lif. *Revue archéologiques* 3rd ser. 1:157–63.

Reynolds, Joyce, and Robert Tannenbaum. 1987. *Jews and God Fearers at Aphrodisias: Greek Inscriptions with Commentary.* Cambridge.

Rivkin, Ellis. 1963. Ben Sira and the Nonexistence of the Synagogue: A Study in Historical Method. *In the Time of Harvest: Essays in Honor of Abba Hillel Silver.* Solomon B. Freehof et al. ed. 320–54. New York.

Rosenthal, Renate, and Renée Sivan. 1978. *Ancient Lamps in the Schloessinger Collection.* Qedem Monographs of the Institute of Archaeology, Hebrew University of Jerusalem 8.

Rostovtzeff, M., et al, eds. 1936. *The Excavations at Dura-Europos, Preliminary Report of the Sixth Season of Work October 1932—March 1933.* New Haven, Conn.

Rutgers, Leonard V. 1995. *The Jews of Late Ancient Rome: An Archaeological and Historical Study on the Interaction of Jews and Non-Jews in the Roman-Diaspora.* Leiden.

Safrai, Shmuel. 1963. Was There a Woman's Gallery in the Synagogues of Antiquity? *Tarbiz* 22:329–38. Hebrew.

Safrai, Z. 1994. *The Economy of Roman Palestine.* London.

Sarason, Richard S. 1982. The Petiḥtot in Leviticus Rabba: Oral Homilies or Redactional Constructions? *Journal of Jewish Studies* 33:557–65.

Sauvaget, J. 1941. *Alep. Essai sur le développement d'une grande ville syrienne, des origines au milieu du XIXᵉ siècle.* Paris.

Schiffman, Lawrence H., and Michael D. Swartz. 1992. *Hebrew and Aramaic Incantation Texts from the Cairo Genizah.* Sheffield.

Schlunk, H., and T. Hauschild. 1978. Die Denkmäler der frühchristlichen und westgotischen Zeit. *Hispania Antique* 9:143–47.

Schrage, Wolfgang. 1971. Synagogue. *Theological Dictionary of the New Testament*, tr. G. W. Bromley, 798–841. Grand Rapids, Mich.

Schwartz, Frances M., and James H. Schwartz. 1979. Engraved Gems in the Collection of the American Numismatic Society: I. Ancient Magical Amulets. *American Numismatic Society Museum Notes* 24:149–82.

Seager, Andrew R. 1972. The Building History of the Sardis Synagogue. *American Journal of Archaeology* 76:425–35.

———. 1981. The Synagogue at Sardis. *Ancient Synagogues Revealed*, ed. L.I. Levine, 178–84. Jerusalem.

———. 1989. The Recent Historiography of Ancient Synagogue Architecture. *Ancient Synagogues in Israel*, ed. R. Hachlili, 82–92. London.

Segal, J.B. 1970. *Edessa "The Blessed City".* Oxford.

Sheffer, Avigail, and Hero Granger-Taylor. 1994. Textiles. *Masada IV: The Yigael Yadin Excavations 1963–1965. Final Reports.* Jerusalem.

Shilo, Yigal. 1968. Torah Scrolls and the Menorah Plaque from Sardis. *Israel Exploration Journal* 18:54–57.

Shinan, Avigdor. 1987. *The World of the Aggadic Literature.* Israel. Hebrew.

———. 1992a. The Aramaic Targum as a Mirror of Galilean Jewry. *The Galilee in Late Antiquity*, ed. L.I. Levine, 241–51. New York and Jerusalem.

———. 1992b. *The Embroidered Targum: The Aggadah in Targum Pseudo-Jonathan of the Pentateuch.* Jerusalem. Hebrew.

Silberman, Neil A. 1993. *A Prophet from Amongst You: The Life of Yigael Yadin: Soldier, Scholar, Mythmaker of Modern Israel.* New York.

Slouschz, Nahum. 1921. The Excavations at Hammath Tiberias (First and Second Campaigns). *Journal of the Jewish Palestine Exploration Society* 1:5–37. Hebrew.

———. 1924. Supplements to the Excavations of Hammath Tiberias. *Qovetz* 1.2:49–52. Hebrew.

Smith, Morton. 1957. Review of *The Synagogue*, by Carl H. Kraeling. New Haven, Conn., 1956. *Journal of Biblical Literature* 76:324–27.

———. 1967. Goodenough's Jewish Symbols in Retrospect. *Journal of Biblical Literature* 86:53–68.

Sokoloff, Michael. 1990. *A Dictionary of Jewish Palestinian Aramaic.* Ramat Gan.

Sperber, Daniel. 1974. *Roman Palestine 200–400: Money and Prices.* Ramat Gan.

Squarciapino, Maria Floriani. 1963. The Synagogue at Ostia. *Archaeology* 16:194–203.

———. 1964. *La sinagoga di Ostia.* Rome.

———. 1970. Plotius Fortunatus archisynagogus. *La rassegna mensile di Israel* 36:183–91.

Strange, James F., and Hershel Shanks. 1983. Synagogue Where Jesus Preached Found in Capernaum. *Biblical Archaeology Review* 9:25–31.

Sukenik, Eleazar L. 1930a. The Throne of Moses in Ancient Synagogues. *Tarbiz* 1:145–51. Hebrew.

_____. 1930b. A Synagogue Inscription from Beit Jibrin. *Journal of the Palestine Oriental Society* 10:76–79.

_____. 1932. *The Ancient Synagogue of Beth Alpha.* Jerusalem.

_____. 1934. *Ancient Synagogues in Palestine and Greece.* London.

_____. 1935. *The Ancient Synagogue of El-Hammeh.* Jerusalem.

_____. 1949. The Samaritan Synagogue at Salbit: Preliminary Report. *Louis M. Rabinowitz Fund for the Exploration of Ancient Synagogues Bulletin* 1:26–30.

_____. 1951. The Ancient Synagogue at Yafa, near Nazareth. *Louis M. Rabinowitz Fund for the Exploration of Ancient Synagogues Bulletin* 2:6–24.

Sussman, J. 1974. A Halakhic Inscription from the Beth Shean Valley. *Tarbiz* 43:88–158. Hebrew.

_____. 1981. The Inscription in the Synagogue at Rehob. *Ancient Synagogues Revealed*, ed. L.I. Levine, 146–53. Jerusalem.

Sussman, Varda. 1988. Samaritan Cult Symbols as Illustrated on Oil Lamps from the Byzantine Period. *Israel—People and Land. Eretz Israel Museum Yearbook*, n.s. 4.22:133–46. Hebrew.

Swartz, Michael D. 1990. Scribal Magic and Its Rhetoric; Formal Patterns in Medieval Hebrew and Aramaic Incantation Texts from the Cairo Genizah. *Harvard Theological Review* 83.2:163–80.

Tcherikover, Victor. 1954. The Sambathions. *Scripta Hierosolymitana* 1:78–98.

Torrey, Charles C. 1956. The Aramaic Texts. *The Synagogue. The Excavations of Dura Europos, Final Report VIII, Part 1*, ed. C.H. Kraeling, 261–76. New Haven, Conn.

Trebilco, Paul R. 1991. *Jewish Communities in Asia Minor.* Cambridge.

Trifon, Dalia. 1989–90. Did the Priestly Courses (*Mishmarot*) Transfer from Judaea to the Galilee After the Bar Kokhba Revolt? *Tarbiz* 59.1–2:77–93. Hebrew.

Tsaferis, Vassilios. 1982. The Ancient Synagogue at Maoz Hayyim. *Israel Exploration Journal* 32:215–44.

Urbach, Ephraim E. 1959. The Rabbinical Laws of Idolatry in the Second and Third Centuries in Light of Archaeological and Historical Facts. *Israel Exploration Journal* 9.3–4:149–65, 229–45.

_____. 1979. *The Sages—Their Concepts and Beliefs*, tr. I. Abrahams. Jerusalem.

_____. 1988. *The World of the Sages: Collected Essays.* Jerusalem.

Vincent, Louis Hugues. 1961. Un sanctuaire dans la région de Jéricho: La synagogue de Na'arah. *Revue Biblique* 68:161–77.

Webster, J.C. 1938. *The Labors of the Months in Antique and Medieval Art.* Evanston and Chicago.

Weitzmann, Kurt, ed. 1979. *Age of Spirituality.* New York and Princeton.

Westenholz, Joan Goodnick, ed. 1995. *The Jewish Presence in Ancient Rome.* Jerusalem.

Wharton, Annabelle. 1994. Good and Bad Images from the Synagogue of Dura Europos: Contexts, Subtexts, Interests. *Art Bulletin* 17:1–25.

White, L. Michael. 1987. The Delos Synagogue Revisited. Recent Fieldwork in the Graeco-Roman Diaspora. *Harvard Theological Review* 80:133–60.

_____. 1990. *Building God's House in the Roman World.* Baltimore and London.

Wiegand, T., and H. Schrader. 1904. *Priene. Ergebnisse der Ausgrabungen und Untersuchungen in den Jahren 1895–1898.* Berlin.

Wilken, Robert L. 1983. *John Chrysostom and the Jews: Rhetoric and Reality in the Late Fourth Century.* Berkeley and Los Angeles.

Wiseman, J., and D. Mano-Zissi. 1972. Excavations at Stobi 1971. *American Journal of Archaeology* 76:407–24.

Wischnitzer, Rachel. 1948. Paintings of the Synagogue at Dura-Europos: The Upper Register. *Gazette des beaux arts* 33:261–66.

Yaari, Abraham. 1964. *The History of the Festival of Simhat Torah.* Jerusalem. Hebrew.

_____. 1976. *Journeys of the Land of Israel: Jewish Pilgrims from the Middle Ages to the Beginning of the Return to Zion.* Jerusalem. Hebrew.

Yadin, Yigael. 1981. The Synagogue at Masada. *Ancient Synagogues Revealed*, ed. L.I. Levine, 19–23. Jerusalem.

Yahalom, Joseph. 1980. Synagogue Inscriptions in Palestine—A Stylistic Classification. *Immanuel.* 10:47–57.

_____. 1987. Piyyut as Poetry. *The Synagogue in Late Antiquity*, ed. L.I. Levine, 111–26. New York and Philadelphia.

Yarden, L. 1971. *The Tree of Light.* London.

Yeivin, Shmuel. 1942. Notes on the Excavation at Beth Shearim. *Bulletin of the Jewish Palestine Exploration Society* 9:69–76. Hebrew.

Yeivin, Ze'ev. 1985. Reconstruction of the Southern Interior Wall of the Khorazin Synagogue. *Eretz-Israel* 18:268–76. Hebrew.

_____. 1989. Khirbet Susiya, the Bima, and Synagogue Ornamentation. *Ancient Synagogues in Israel*, ed. R. Hachlili, 93–100. London and Oxford.

Yoel, I. 1968. A Bible Manuscript Written in 1260. *Kiryat Sefer* 38:122–32. Hebrew.

Zevi, F. 1972. La sinagoga di Ostia. *Rassegna Mensile di Israel.* 38:131–45.

Zori, N. 1966. The House of Kyrios Leontis at Beth Shean. *Israel Exploration Journal.* 16:123–34.

_____. 1967. The Ancient Synagogue at Beth-Shean. *Eretz-Israel.* 8:149–67. Hebrew.

Photographic Credits

Plates i, III, XXIII—photos: Dubi Tal and Moni Haramati, Albatross Aerial Photography; Maps 1 and 2, Fig. 2.17—Wilhelmina Reyinga-Amrhein; Figs. i, 5.4, 5.5—courtesy of Deutsches Orient Gesellschaft; Figs. iii, 6.1, 6.5—courtesy of the Library of the Jewish Theological Seminary; Plates ii, XII—Herbert Scher; Figs. 1.1, 2.1, 2.3a, 4.8a, 5.16—courtesy of the Hebrew University, Institute of Archeology; Figs. 1.2, 2.11, 5.3, 5.10, 5.21, 6.2, Plates XXX, XLII, XLIV—courtesy of the Israel Exploration Society; Figs. 1.3, 6.4, 6.7—courtesy of Magnes Press; Fig. 1.4—courtesy of the New York Times; Fig. 2.4—photo: Photographic Services, Yeshiva University, courtesy of Dr. David Jeselsohn; Plate I, Fig. 2.6—Photographic Services, Yeshiva University, courtesy of Mendel Gottesman Library; Plates II, VI, VII, Figs. 1.5, 1.9, 1.12a, 5.19—courtesy of Eric M. and Carol Meyers; Fig. 1.8—photo: Metropolitan Museum, property of the Yeshiva University Museum; Fig. 1.10a and b—drawings: Larry Belkin; Plate IV—courtesy of Crawford Greenewalt, Jr.; Fig. 1.11—drawing: John Thompson; Plates V, XIII, XXIV, XXVII, XXIXb, XXXIII, LI, Figs. 1.10c, 4.8b—courtesy of Steven Fine; Fig. 1.15—photo: Israel Museum, courtesy of the Israel Antiquities Authority; Plates VIII, XLVb—photos: Gabi Larom, courtesy of the Hebrew University of Jerusalem, Institute of Archaeology, Archeological Expedition at Sepphoris; Figs. 2.7, 2.8, drawing: Ada Yardeni; Figs. 2.13, 5.13, 5.17, 6.3, 6.9—courtesy of J. Naveh/Magnes Press; Plate IX, Fig. 5.11b—courtesy of the Bible Lands Museum, Jerusalem; Plates X, XIV, Figs. 2.15, 2.19b, 3.2–3.6, 3.13–3.15, 4.7, 4.19, 4.20—Archaeological Exploration of Sardis; Figs. 2.18, 4.5, 4.16—courtesy Soprintendenza Archeologica di Ostia; Fig. 4.1—drawing: Andrew A. Seager, courtesy of Archaeological Exploration of Sardis; Plate XI—courtesy of Miriam della Pergola; Plate XII—photo: courtesy of Andrew Seager; Plate XVb—courtesy of Biblical Archaeology Society; Plates XVI–XVII, Figs. 2.12, 4.8c and d—courtesy of Leonard V. Rutgers; Plate XVIII—courtesy of the Metropolitan Museum of Art; Fig. 2.14—courtesy of Musée Royal de Mariemont; Plate XIX—courtesy of Dr. David Jeselsohn, Zurich; Plate XX—courtesy of the Pontificia Commissione di Arceologica Sacra; Figs. 3.7, 3.10—photo: Pontificia Commissione di Arceologica Sacra, courtesy of International Catacomb Society; Fig. 2.16—photo: Taylan Sevil; Fig. 2.19a—courtesy of Staatliche Museum zu Berlin Preussischer Kunst, Museum für Spätantike und Bynzantisnische Kunst; Fig. 2.19c—photo: Susan Keniff, courtesy of Mr. and Mrs. Jonathan P. Rosen; Figs. 2.20, 4.2, 4.4, 4.6, 4.8–4.15, 4.17a—Yale University Art Gallery, Dura Collection; Plate XXIII—courtesy of the Israel Ministry of Tourism; Fig. 3.1—courtesy of Royal Ontario Museum; Fig. 3.8—courtesy of Museo Nazionale delle Terme; Fig. 3.9—courtesy of Simon Wiesenthal Center; Fig. 3.11—courtesy of Rare Book and Manuscript Library, Columbia University; Fig. 3.12—Museo Archeologica de Napoli; Plate XXV—courtesy of the Israel Museum; Fig. 4.3b—courtesy of the Brooklyn Museum, Museum Collection Fund; Fig. 4.17b—courtesy of the

Index

Sites are in capital letters; pages with illustrations are in boldface type.